The Gardener's Guide to
BULBS

The Gardener's Guide to
BULBS

Brian Mathew
Philip Swindells

MITCHELL BEAZLEY

CONTENTS

The Gardener's Guide to Bulbs

First published in 1994
by Mitchell Beazley
an imprint of Reed Consumer Books Limited
Michelin House, 81 Fulham Road
London SW3 6RB
and Auckland, Melbourne, Singapore and Toronto

A–Z Plant Directories by **Brian Mathew**
Essays by **Philip Swindells**

Editor: **Emily Wright**
Executive Art Editor: **Larraine Lacey**
Assistant Designer: **Barbara Zuniga**
Production Controller: **Sarah Rees**
Commissioned Photography: **Ian McKinnell and Clive Nichols**
Commissioned Artworks: **Fiona Bell-Currie**
Picture Research: **Emily Hedges and Caroline Hensman**

Executive Editor: **Anna Mumford**
Art Director: **Jacqui Small**

ISBN 1 85732 178 2

A CIP catalogue record for this book is available from the British Library

Typeset by Dorchester Typesetting Group Ltd

Produced by Mandarin Offset Ltd, Hong Kong

Printed in Hong Kong

Front jacket: Bulb Portrait by Ian McKinnell; Tulips by
The Dutch Bulb Company
Back jacket: Daffodil Life Cycle by Fiona Bell-Currie

FOREWORD

The aim of this book is to show how useful and rewarding bulbs are in design and planting terms, and how straight-forward their cultivation and care.

A comprehensive guide to the subject, *The Gardener's Guide to Bulbs* covers every aspect of gardening with bulbs. First comes information on where to grow bulbs, which is followed by a chapter on the use of colour. Next comes practicalities, an important section providing detailed advice on all practical aspects of bulb-growing, from purchase through to planting and propagation. Accurate step-by-step illustrations supplement the text and clarify specific tech-niques. As gardeners plan their gardens with year-round colour in mind, so the book progresses from season to season, making it easy to follow and to work from. Covering both out-door and indoor subjects, each seasonal section starts with design and planting ideas. From major naturalization projects to small-scale ideas for containers, this section concentrates on ways of using bulbs, either on their own or with other plants. This is followed by a full alphabetical plant directory for that season, which contains cultivation details.

ABOVE The vibrant heads of alliums can be dried for winter decoration.

RIGHT In a mixed border, alliums hold their own in a strong planting, the flower heads echoing the round shape of the formal, clipped box. Alliums are very versatile bulbs and will grow in the semi-shade, as seen here growing under laburnum trees.

INSET The contrast of colour and shape makes an unforgettable impression in this lavish, formal garden feature.

INTRODUCTION

What is a bulb?

Throughout this book, the term "bulb" is used in a general way to describe any plant with a swollen storage organ. However, this generalized group of plants consists of true bulbs, corms, tubers and rhizomes.

True bulbs, for example, daffodils, tulips and lilies, consist of a short basal stem covered with fleshy leaf scales wrapped around the growing point. The scales are attached to the base of the bulb, known as the basal plate, from which adventitious roots grow. Buds develop in the scale axils and these grow into daughter bulbs, which are used for propagation.

Corms, such as crocuses, colchicums and gladioli, also contain an embryo flower shoot and they are made up of solid modified stem tissue. The original storage organ dries up each year and a new one is formed on top of it.

Tubers, such as begonias, anemones and cyclamens, are formed of thickened stem tissue, but instead of flower shoots within, they have eyes or crowns on the upper surface that give rise to new growth.

Rhizomes are fleshy modified stems and most grow horizontally below ground, but occasionally, as with rhizomatous irises, the stems scramble near the surface of the soil.

LEFT This amaryllis bulb is ready to be planted: the firm, pale green shoots will soon burst into growth.

Life cycles

All bulbous plants have similar life cycles, that is to say, periods of growth and flowering, followed by an annual rest period, known as dormancy. During this period, the storage organ maintains the bulb until the growing season, when it puts forth new growth.

When planted in their dormant states, all bulbous plants quickly initiate roots and the stems inside begin to grow. As the soil warms up, the plants utilize their food reserves and push up shoots. By the time the plants are flowering, the storage organs are empty of food.

After flowering, the foliage continues to grow and, by a process known as photosynthesis, it accumulates new food reserves which are stored within the bulbous system to sustain the plants through the current and following growing seasons. The presence of the foliage is vital for the continued well-being of the plants; never remove unsightly foliage before it has had time to fuel the plant's energy reservoir.

After the foliage has died back, the embryo flowers complete their development within the bulbous system, and the system goes into dormancy, sustained by the food reserve inside it, until the next season.

BELOW Cross sections of, from left to right, a bulb, a corm, a tuber and a rhizome. Notice the different forms and compositions of each one.

Cross sections

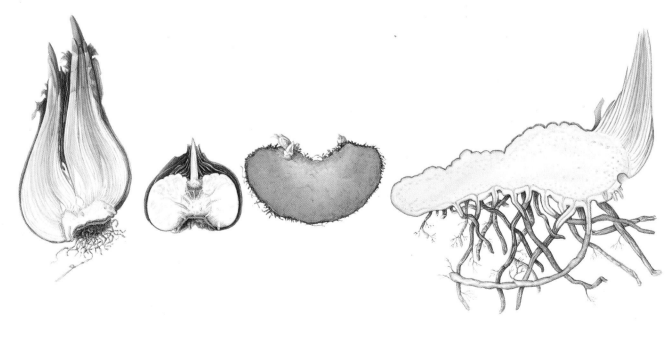

Life cycle of a daffodil

Most true bulbs are perennials, with a life of three to six years, during which time they self-propagate before dying down. A few bulbs, like some bedding tulips, are exhausted after a single season's growth, and these should be replaced annually by new plants grown from offsets or bulbils. Some bulbs, such as *Lilium lancifolium*, produce bulbils the size of pea seeds in their leaf axils, and these are nothing more than modified stems surrounded by fleshy leaves. When they fall from the parent plant, they sprout to form new individuals.

A dormant daffodil bulb consists of an embryo flower, a short stem and tightly packed leaves. The shoots of the bulb, along with its roots, start to grow during early autumn: the shoots usually remain just beneath the soil or at soil level until the days begin to lengthen during winter. At the same time, the roots become more active and extensive.

Once the soil has warmed up in the spring sunshine, the leafy shoots quickly extend, with the flower buds still hidden deep within the centre of the foliage. The bulb begins to split into parts and to produce dormant buds at its base. These buds develop into daughter bulbs later on in the cycle.

Flowering lasts for several weeks. Most flowers are insect pollinated, although many garden varieties have sterile flowers. After pollination, the flowers quickly die; sterile blossoms fade at the same rate as the fertile ones.

When flowering is over, remove the old flower stems to prevent seed formation which will drain the bulb's resources. The leaves remain green for weeks, building up energy reserves within the bulb. Remove once they are brown and faded. By the time the bulb goes into dormancy, it will have split into two or three parts, each of which, along with the daughter bulbs, will grow on as a new bulb next season.

Life cycle of a gladiolus

Corms are not permanent but are replaced every year by one corm or several new ones.

A dormant gladiolus corm is a hard starchy reserve. The corm has a fibrous protective tunic and a prominent base plate from which roots are eventually produced.

Once planted, the corm rapidly produces roots and spear-like shoots. There is no sign of a flower spike, although this is beginning to develop in the lower part of the foliage.

As the leaves develop and the root system expands, the central part of the foliage starts to swell. This is the embryo flower spike pushing upwards. As the leaves grow, the flat-tened, green flower head emerges above the foliage.

The leaves reach their full height and the flower spike continues to grow upwards. As it does so, the individual flower buds become separated along the extending stem, and the flower buds at the bottom of the spike begin to show signs of colour. The individual flowers open from the bottom of the spike upwards over two or three days, each flower lasting for several days. After flowering, remove the flower spike and leave the foliage to grow on in order to build up a new corm for next season. Gladiolus corms are replaced annually, a new corm being found on top of its exhausted parent once the leaves have died back completely.

Life cycle of a begonia

A tuber is a swollen stem that, when dormant, consists of a food reserve, a few old roots and a cluster of tiny dormant buds. These are grouped irregularly on the upper surface of the tuber, although they can occasionally appear at random around the edge.

Tubers are either totally or partially depleted during growth; in the case of popular varieties like cyclamens and begonias, the tubers wither during flowering but swell the next growing season and subsequently become larger than before.

A newly planted tuber sprouts quite vigorously. Each bud on the crown produces a congested mass of growth, although at this stage the shoots are generally thinned, and the strongest two or three left to grow on. If planted in soil, the shoots which have been removed will produce a tuber large enough to flower and survive the winter unaided in a single season.

The leaves of a begonia first appear in a cluster from the crown of the tuber but, as the season progresses, the tuber produces succulent stems which are liberally clothed in handsome serrated leaves. The leaves continue to push up vigorously, and the blossoms appear on short stems from the axils of the upper leaves. Several blooms are usually produced in a congested cluster, the dominant one being a fully double male flower. The smaller single flowers are female and of little decorative merit. If these are removed, the plant will not seed and the main double blossom will attain its full potential.

After flowering, when the foliage has gone into decline and the bases of the stems have turned brown, remove all the foliage and the tuber will go into dormancy and can be stored until spring.

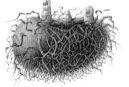

Life cycle of an iris

A rhizome is a continually extending fleshy rootstock which never becomes dormant. There is always some green foliage or a fleshy green shoot present, even in the depths of winter.

A newly planted iris begins to sprout during spring. As the shoots develop, it pushes out an extensive fleshy root system. A healthy young rhizome may have two or three fans of leaves growing from it, each with a potential to flower, although some newly planted shoots may only produce leaves during the first season.

The iris grows rapidly in spring and pushes up fleshy flower buds on strong stems. Several buds appear in a congested head but, as the flower stem continues to grow, these become more equally spaced out, although still tight and green in bud.

Once the flower stems have reached above the level of the leaves, the individual blossoms start to open, starting at the top of the spike and continuing towards the bottom. The majority are partially sterile, although occasionally seed pods are produced if cross pollination occurs. The seed in the rounded fruits are not worth using for propagation purposes, for they will not breed true. Instead, it is much better to concentrate on building up the iris for next year by removing the seed heads.

When the flowers have faded, remove the old stalks. Lift and divide the plant, if necessary, cutting the fans of leaves back to within a few inches of the iris.

Hardiness zones

The climatic conditions of an area are of prime importance when deciding what to plant, for some plants will only tolerate certain conditions. However, there will be isolated microclimates within the garden itself, caused by, for example, a sheltering wall or a hedge. These microclimates can be altered through the plantings themselves and by using mulches, and careful siting can modify the sun, shade, wind and humidity.

However, how well a plant grows in an area largely depends upon its native climate and how easily it can adapt to its new climatic environment. Certain plants, for example *Veltheimia*, of South African origin, can only be grown in areas of similar climatic conditions, and are known as tender. This means that they cannot survive an average winter temperature outside. If the plant can survive an average but not an exceptionally hard winter outside, it is said to be half-hardy, and those tolerating cold winters outdoors are known as hardy.

In the matter of plant hardiness, no one can be absolutely sure where one zone ends and the next begins because weather itself is a variable factor. The hardiness zone maps appearing here have been specially devised to enable you to measure the degree of cold a plant can tolerate. The maps have been divided into broad climatic areas or zones as a basis for judging the general viability of plants. There are 10 zones ranging from –50°F (–45°C) and below in zone 1 to 30°F–40°F (–1°C–4°C) in zone 10.

Every plant listed in the Plant Directories cites a hardiness zone, indicating that an individual species will survive and flower at the average minimum winter temperature of that zone and in the zones above it.

BELOW and RIGHT These specially devised maps are divided into ten broad climatic zones. The key gives the minimum temperature range for each zone.

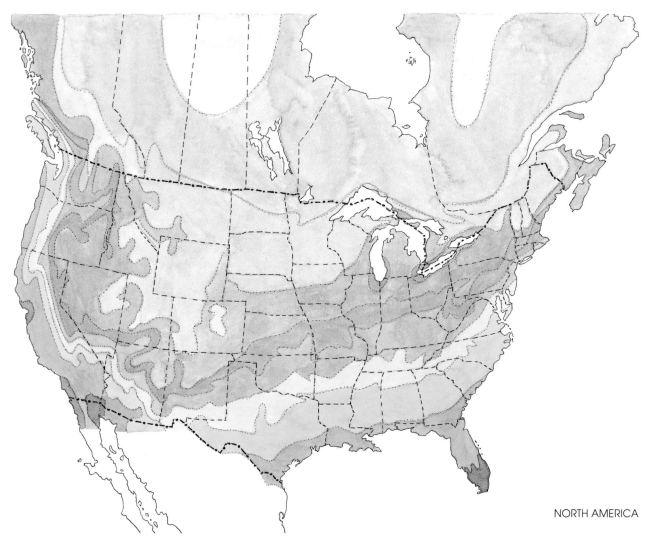

NORTH AMERICA

Temperature ranges

ZONE 1: Below −50°F (Below −45°C)
ZONE 2: −50 to −35°F (−45 to −37°C)
ZONE 3: −35 to −20°F (−37 to −29°C)
ZONE 4: −20 to −10°F (−29 to −23°C)
ZONE 5: −10 to −5°F (−23 to −21°C)
ZONE 6: −5 to 5°F (−21 to −15°C)
ZONE 7: 5 to 10°F (−15 to −12°C)
ZONE 8: 10 to 20°F (−12 to −7°C)
ZONE 9: 20 to 30°F (−7 to −1°C)
ZONE 10: 30 to 40°F (−1 to 4°C)

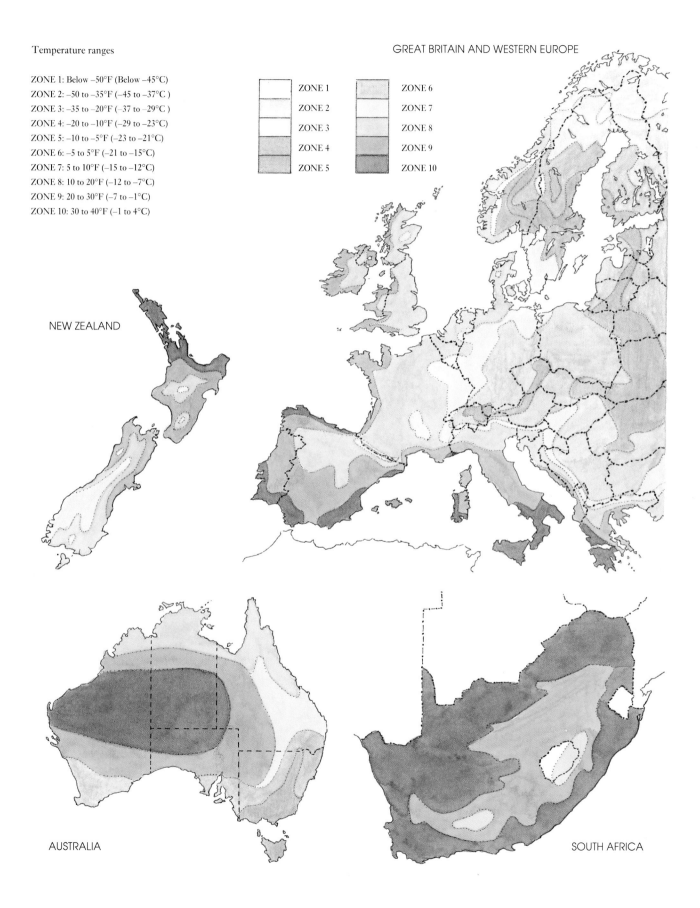

GREAT BRITAIN AND WESTERN EUROPE

ZONE 1
ZONE 2
ZONE 3
ZONE 4
ZONE 5

ZONE 6
ZONE 7
ZONE 8
ZONE 9
ZONE 10

NEW ZEALAND

AUSTRALIA

SOUTH AFRICA

USING BULBS

There is a bulb for almost every garden situation, including borders, bedding displays, rock gardens and raised beds. Many are excellent for naturalizing in grass or soil, while others are suitable for growing in containers and window boxes. Furthermore, some can be cultivated indoors, either forced into early winter flowering or as permanent pot plants.

Bulbs can be relied upon to provide a decorative display within a few months of being planted. Since they only flower for one season, spending the rest of the year in a dormant state below ground, they are particularly useful for creating short bursts of colour and, with careful selection, can supply year-round interest, adding variety to permanent plantings. Although most people associate bulbs with a springtime flowering carpet of daffodils and crocuses, there are many less familiar but equally attractive summer-flowering bulbs, as well as those for autumn and even winter.

There is a wide selection of bulbous plants to choose from. Some, like daffodils, with their bright, primary colours, are good for enlivening dull corners of the garden; but a more delicate spring planting might consist of bulbs like crocuses or snake's head fritillaries. For a strong summer display, use one of the tall, imposing bulbs like gladioli or lilies. For fragrance grow hyacinths, jonquils and lilies.

Most bulbs require well-drained soil in order to thrive, and sun or partial shade, depending on the individual bulb, although none will tolerate dense shade. Those that are natives of hot countries benefit from sun-baked conditions, that is to say, hot, sunny sites like sheltered borders where they will ripen, or "bake", in the sun, enabling them to perform better the following year. However, it is important to note that the majority will also tolerate summer rainfall. Native woodland bulbs prefer rich, organic soil, often dry conditions, and dappled shade, as provided by trees and shrubs.

BELOW Finding plants for shady locations can be a problem, but this combination of ferns, hellebores and trilliums is ideal, providing a colourful and interesting display.

RIGHT Bulbs make an invaluable contribution to the spring garden. Here tulips and daffodils light up a border with their intense colours and profuse flowering.

Mixed borders

Bulbs will grow happily among other plants provided they enjoy the same conditions and are tolerant of competition for nutrients. Herbaceous perennials are mostly strong, competitive growers and neighbouring bulbs must be able to withstand this. Early on in the season, when herbaceous plants are starting into growth, it is possible to grow small bulbs like crocuses and snowdrops, but later on, taller, robust bulbs such as narcissi, tulips, alliums and lilies are necessary. As permanent members of the border, the bulbs can be routinely lifted and divided. Most shrubs are less greedy than herbaceous perennials, and a wider range of bulbs can be introduced around them.

Bulbs add colour and form to a border. They can be grown as highlights in large, prominent clumps or mingled with other plants for a more harmonious, integrated planting. As underplanting, they link various taller-growing subjects and, planted in a small patch, they can be used as "fillers" to provide colour and interest in dull parts of a border. In informal situations, allow the bulbs to grow up through other plants, creating a cottage-garden type of border but, in formal borders, the bulbs should be planted in clumps rather than dotted around at random; a single well-placed clump will create much more impact than a few spots of colour.

LEFT Bulbs form an essential part of mixed borders. Here, alliums and Asiatic lilies combine with shrubs and herbaceous plants.

BELOW These 'Palestrina' tulips add bold splashes of bright colour to a spring bedding scheme of forget-me-nots and honesty.

BOTTOM Tall hybrid tulips are well-suited to formal borders, particularly when underplanted with forget-me-nots, as seen here.

Naturalizing bulbs

One of the most popular and familiar ways of growing bulbs like daffodils and crocuses is to naturalize them in drifts; that is to say, once planted, they are left to colonize, or "naturalize", at will. This is usually done in grass, but those bulbs preferring shady woodland conditions can be naturalized in soil under trees and shrubs.

When selecting a site for naturalizing in grass, remember that the grass cannot be cut for up to six weeks after flowering, during which time it will look rather wild and untidy. Although appropriate for informal gardens, this is a problem in formal gardens, where naturalizing is better restricted to small areas, for example, around a specimen tree or flanking a driveway. If naturalizing bulbs in established grass, the bulbs must be carefully selected as not all types can compete with turf, especially the more coarse vigorous-growing types. In such cases, it is better to plant the bulbs in well-cultivated soil and sow a type of fine grass over the top.

When naturalizing, the aim is to create an area that looks as natural as possible. Plant the bulbs at random in lawns or meadows, around trees and shrubs, or on grassy banks; for more of a feature, plant one or two irregularly shaped areas and mow a path in between. Either use a single type or, to recreate the look of an alpine meadow, grow a mixture of small bulbs. Depending on space, the naturalized area can be as large or small as you wish.

Naturalizing does not have to be confined to grass or soil, for it is possible to establish bulbs beneath a planting of ground cover. The looser-growing kinds such as scrambling ivies provide the most suitable foil because they are dense enough to hide the fading foliage and decaying flowers of the bulbs once they have flowered.

BELOW The dazzling colours of bright golden daffodils, midnight-blue muscari and butter-yellow iris have been kept in strictly separated blocks in this generous and formal naturalized waterside planting.

RIGHT The powdery blue of forget-me-nots is ideal for toning down any brightly coloured tulips. For the opposite effect, however, purple aubrieta accentuates the yellow of the tulips (FAR RIGHT).

Bedding displays

Bedding schemes are formal, seasonal displays in which the plants are arranged in colourful patterns. Bulbs are especially suitable for this type of planting, as their strong colours create an immediate and vivid impact. In fact, some very formal bulbs, like many of the hybrid tulips, really only look at home as part of a clearly defined bedding scheme. After flowering, the bulbs are rooted up and stored to make way for the next season's bedding plants. Of utmost importance for a good, even show is well-drained, fertile soil of a uniform quality, otherwise some bulbs will grow taller than others.

The best bulbs to use are those, like hyacinths, that have compact heads for uniform colour, or those with simple, bold flowers of a formal appearance, such as tulips. Either plant in big blocks of colour using one type of bulb for each block, or create a more intricate design consisting of smaller areas of different colours. Bulbs can also be used as highlight, or "dot", plants within the scheme. Scatter plants like cannas and galtonias among bedding plants to give the display height.

Rock gardens and raised beds

Rock gardens and raised beds are ideal for displaying some of the smaller, more delicate-looking bulbs.

A wide variety of bulbs can be grown in the rock garden because this type of habitat provides many microclimates. Some areas, such as those in the shadow of a rock, will be cool and shady, while other areas, for example, those facing the sun at the base of a rocky outcrop, will be warm and sheltered. Along with raised beds, rockeries also provide the free-draining conditions that bulbs enjoy so much.

Scale is an important factor when planting rock gardens and raised beds; make sure the smaller bulbs are not dwarfed by their larger neighbours or their impact will be lost. Dwarf bulbs can be planted on their own in pockets for a highlight display or, providing they are tolerant of other plants, they can be integrated with creeping or cushioning plants; these will provide long-term interest after the seasonal display of the bulbs. Where there are established plants, small bulbs can be pushed through the foliage into the soil.

Containers, window boxes and hanging baskets

Bulbs make excellent subjects for all types of containers. For year-round colour, treat the bulbs like annuals and plant a series of seasonal displays, one after the other. After flowering, the bulbs can be lifted and replanted in the garden. Alternatively, for permanent displays, mix the bulbs with other plants that flower at different times.

Bulbs tolerant of warm summer soil temperatures are best suited to container cultivation. All the African species grow well, including tigridias, acidantheras, sparaxis and ixias. Spring bulbs like crocuses and dwarf irises, which benefit from quick drainage, are also very good for containers.

Either plant one species per container and group the pots together, or plant a single pot of mixed bulbs and use it as a focal point at the bottom of some steps or beside a doorway, for example. If using tall bulbs as a focal point, underplant them with low-growing bulbs to create a balanced display.

Window boxes are less versatile than containers as their position is fixed and they must be filled with small, short-growing bulbs that will not grow too tall and block the view. Since the boxes are most likely to be seasonal, long-term cultivation is of little concern, and a variety of bulbs can be packed together for the greatest impact each season. This is also true of hanging baskets.

Shape is the most important consideration when planting a hanging basket. Remember that it will be viewed from below and sideways rather than from above, and the planting should be as spherical as possible. Since very few bulbs have trailing or hanging stems (the pendulous begonia being an exception), use foliage plants such as ivy as a basic framework. Build up layers of bulbs, poking the small ones through the sides of the basket, keeping the taller ones for the top.

Cut flowers

Bulbs grown especially for cut flowers should be planted separately, ideally in an inconspicuous spot like a corner of the vegetable garden. This means that they can be grown in practical rows rather than aesthetic groupings, and any amount of flowers can be cut without ruining the overall display. Furthermore, grown in neat rows, flower stems are easier to manage and can be staked if necessary.

However, if there is not enough room to do this, grow the bulbs in a border but, to compensate for those to be cut, plant more than normal so as not to impair the display.

ABOVE A potted cyclamen is combined to excellent effect with cut amaryllis for a vivid display.

TOP RIGHT Densely planted Iris reticulata *look most effective in this traditional basket.*

ABOVE Dwarf tulip, ranunculus and trailing ivy are here combined in a wooden container.

RIGHT The elegance of amaryllis flowers and foliage can be appreciated in this simple planting.

COLOUR

There is more to gardening than simply growing healthy plants. This, in itself, takes patience and a certain amount of knowledge, but successfully combining plants to create living, growing pictures – in other words, creating a garden – is an art. First and foremost think of practical matters like soil conditions and aspect, and then decide on the style of your garden before choosing any plants.

A garden that has been planned and planted with care is very rewarding. It is both public and private; it is part of the outside environment and can be enjoyed and appreciated by anyone who passes by, yet it is also an integral part of the house and reflects its owner's taste and personality. With so many different functions to fulfil, it can be hard to know where to begin, but having already taken into account the practical considerations, planting on the basis of colour is a good starting point.

As far as colour is concerned, nothing surpasses bulbs, so great is the range of colours available. Mixed with other plants or used on their own, they can be planted in blocks of contrasting colours for a formal, striking effect, or used in soft, subtle plantings to create a more relaxed and informal atmosphere. Furthermore, using different bulbs, it is possible to achieve year-round colour in the garden as there are flowering bulbs for each season. Although finding the right colour for the right place can be difficult, it is worth spending time on; a well-planned feature, for example, a small flower bed by the front door, will make an immediate impact. With a little care and attention, you will find it is possible to create a variety of attractive colour schemes throughout the garden to develop an integrated whole.

BELOW The vibrant combination of orange crocosmias and scarlet dahlias makes this border very colourful and eyecatching.

RIGHT Plenty of silver-grey foliage here helps to tone down the hot pink of the gladioli and the bright scarlet of the tulips.

USING COLOUR

Although personal taste should be the most important guideline when planning and planting for colour, it helps to understand how colours work together and the effects they produce in different styles of plantings. The same colour principles can be applied to any garden situation, be it an extensive border or a group of containers on a patio.

Colour theory

There are many complex theories on the subject of colour but, generally speaking, it is possible to divide colours into warm, cool and neutral. At the red end of the spectrum, colours seem warm, at the blue end, they appear cool. Greens fall somewhere in-between; they are restful, neutral colours, because the eye relaxes into an unstrained state when it perceives them. Strong, primary colours, as seen, for example, in red tulips, blue hyacinth and yellow daffodils, can be difficult to place in the garden unless used in brightly coloured bedding displays, but many of the cultivars are muted and more subtle, making them easier to use and allowing for a greater range of colour combinations.

Colour and perspective

As well as being decorative, colour is also functional, as it can be used to give a sense of perspective in the garden. Warm colours are strong and appear to advance towards the eye, thereby making the garden appear smaller. A sunny herbaceous border, glowing with the vibrant, flame-like colours of bulbs like *Crocosmia*, especially 'Lucifer', will have this effect. Cool colours and lighter tones, however, recede, giving the impression of space; a spring-time bed of palest cream tulips, such as 'Purissima', over a froth of light blue forget-me-nots will make the garden appear larger than it really is.

Pale and cool colours, as seen in these naturalized white and blue anemones and blue scillas, make an area of the garden seem relaxing and spacious.

The plentiful green foliage of these erythroniums provides a restful-looking background to the elegant flowers, with their intriguing reflexed petals.

The strongly contrasting, rather hot shades of crocosmia and lily create a busy feel that would make a border seem smaller than it really is.

Colour and mood

The choice of warm or cool colours in a planting will create different moods. Warm colours are intense and invigorating, while cool colours give a restful and harmonious feel.

When planting for colour, think about the function of different areas of the garden and plan accordingly. For example, an informal, meandering path edged with pale, cool colours will encourage unhurried lingering, while a functional, formal path lined with glowing, warm colours will give the impression of action. Work on producing colour effects in specific areas and plan the garden so that it changes constantly, with the focus moving from one area to another as one seasonal picture takes over from the last. The effect will be much more striking and all the lovelier for being short-lived.

Colour and climate

The quality of light has a significant effect on colour. Light varies not only with the seasons, but also in different latitudes. This will affect your choice of plants, as some colours work better than others in certain climates.

In temperate areas, the soft, blue-saturated light can make strong colours appear garish and hard, while pastel tints glow and are revealed in all their subtlety. Choose soft pinks, such as in *Nerine* 'Orion', or lemony yellows like *Hyacinthus* 'City of Haarlem', and the palest blues, as in *Allium caeruleum*. In hot climates with fierce overhead sun, the light is often hard and white, making pastels look dirty and washed-out, and only bright colours like red, yellow or pink will give a really satisfactory effect. Try the clear red form of *Ranunculus asiaticus*, the strong, orange-yellows of *Narcissus* 'Ambergate' or, for dramatic effect, the deep purple of *Fritillaria camschatcensis*.

Colour and light

Changes in light during the day, although more subtle, have similar effects on colour. Early morning and later afternoon light is soft and golden, while midday light is strong and bright. An area intended for sitting-out in the evening can be made truly magical by placing white or blue- and violet-tinted plants around the edge to define it, for, in twilight, these colours glow with a light of their own. For a garden to be enjoyed in the evening, avoid dark colours as these will disappear into the night as the light fades. White and yellow lilies in pots create just the right effect. Try *Lilium regale*, which is superbly fragrant and easy to grow.

Foliage

Almost all gardens start off with plant cover, whether grass, shrubs or trees. Take into account the colouring of background plants when devising new plant combinations. From severe, dark green backdrops of yew or holly to soft, delicate grey-leaved plants, such as helichrysum, santolina and lavender, there seems an almost infinite variety of foliage plants to choose from. A formally clipped hedge of yew, for instance, with a mid-spring planting of upright, creamy white tulips at its base, to be followed in summer by a mass of white lilies is simple and dramatic, but dark-coloured tulips and lilies would be lost against such a dark background. Planted against a pale silvery-green backdrop, however, these plants will show up clearly.

There are seasonal considerations, too. Foliage colours are usually brightest in spring and summer, with the fresh, young foliage predominating. In the autumn, changes in foliage colour are often striking, and can radically alter your perception of other surrounding plants, so choose your colour scheme with discretion to complement the bold

These creamy white tulips glow above a bed of purple pansies, particularly in the soft light of dusk, when they will stand out even more.

A strong and vibrant effect is achieved for springtime with glowing blue-mauve hyacinths and gold wallflowers, planted in a formal bedding scheme.

This silvery-grey foliage calms the bright pink of the alliums, and makes them easier to place in a border with other colours.

reds, oranges, browns and yellows of autumn leaves. In the winter months, when the garden is relatively bare, evergreens provide an elegant backdrop that shows up even the smallest flowers to their best advantage.

The decorative effect of bulb foliage is frequently underestimated. Cyclamen leaves are frequently marbled and blotched with silver, and make long-lasting ground cover that can act as a foil for other plants. The leaves of the arum make a valuable contribution to the garden in winter and spring, and are almost more decorative than the flower spikes. The linear, sword-like leaves of irises are also decorative, and can be used to give form and texture to a bed of flowers.

Planting in practice

The choice and success of colour associations depend on many factors, some of which are out of the gardener's control. The architecture of the house and any garden structures, for example, will play a major role in the overall effect of the garden, as will the framework of the garden and existing background plantings. Any features visible outside the area, such as a neighbouring tree, will also have to be considered in the design. When you are selecting a colour scheme, try to ensure that your choice blends well with the materials of the house or any other visible structures such as walls and fences.

Most gardeners will admit to learning from their mistakes, so do not be afraid to try out different ideas. The following examples give some idea of the effects that you can produce, by combining bulbs with strong colours to create vibrant impact planting; by concentrating on soft neutrals and gentle tints for subtle planting; and by basing your garden on a single colour for elegance and unity.

CONTRASTING COLOURS

Contrasting colours are used for impact planting, that is to say, to create bold and colourful displays. Some of the best colour combinations are red and green; yellow, orange and blue; and pink and purple, although there are countless others to experiment with.

The most successful plantings are those that make strong points of focus using solid, densely planted blocks of colour. It is not just a question of throwing the strongest, brightest colours together, for the effect is lost if the picture becomes confusing, with too many conflicting, bright colours or muddled shapes. The key to success is to keep it simple, and select only a few colours.

Positioning impact planting is important, too. Such plantings should make a statement and be used to highlight an area. A splash of bright colour will draw the eye towards it, thereby making the garden seem smaller, as well as drawing attention away from any less sightly areas. It will create a lively atmosphere and will brighten up dark areas. Indeed, a garden without areas of contrasting colours can be bland and unexciting. Do not forget to take into account the light: bright colours that may clash unpleasantly in full sun will be tempered into a pleasing contrast in shade.

For a spring display, use a golden yellow daffodil such as the double-flowered 'Tahiti', with its warm orange inner petals, and underplant it with a simple dark blue muscari, such as *Muscari armeniacum* or *M. neglectum*. A similar effect can be created with blue *Hyacinthus* 'Delft Blue' and yellow wall-flowers. Muscari can also make a tremendous impact in a raised bed or rock garden with purple aubrieta.

For a large border, plant red tulips such as 'Toronto' with purple *Lunaria annua* and blue forget-me-nots or, for more colour, combine the orange-red tulip 'Prinses Irene' and golden yellow 'Stresa' tulip with forget-me-nots and *Hosta fortunei* 'Albopicta'. In summer there are equally good contrasting colour combinations for borders, such as *Agapanthus* 'Blue Imp', the white *Galtonia candicans* and *Hemerocallis fulva* 'Kwanso Flore Plena', which has tawny orange flowers. In the pink and purple range, try the dark purple *Iris* 'Wild Echo' and the dark pink *Gladiolus communis* × *byzantinus*.

Planting for impact is just as successful with naturalized bulbs. In spring, grow a patch of bluebells under a bright yellow or orange azalea, and, as the seasons progress, autumn and winter cyclamen can be naturalized in large areas with contrasting ivy foliage or variegated *Vinca* (periwinkle).

Whatever the season, there are endless plant combinations using contrasting colours. Decide on the colours you wish to use in each area of the garden and select the bulbs accordingly, paying attention to form as well as colour.

ABOVE For a bold colour statement, plant hyacinths 'Queen of the Pinks' and 'Blue Peter Stuyvesant' close together to create a dense and effective display.

LEFT This glorious bed of tall yellow irises is made all the more memorable by the low border of contrasting purple–blue polyanthus flowers.

INSET These blocks of bright-coloured tulips balance each other well, and the underplanting of forget-me-nots adds some variety in texture as well as colour.

HARMONIZING COLOURS

Refined and elegant, spacious and restful – a subtle planting of harmonizing colours can be all these things, but it should not be bland. The essence of this style is to avoid strong contrasts of colour, form and texture that would create a single focal point, and concentrate on creating a uniform picture. The colours used should be restrained and matching, so that the eye moves easily over the planting.

Harmonizing colours are often used in informal gardens, where a tumbling disorder of flowers and foliage creates a timeless feel. A subtle planting will make you want to take your time in the garden, so use it to its full advantage for private sitting-out areas.

Foliage is always important in harmonizing colours. Rely on grey foliage to provide a soft, misty backdrop that will have the effect of toning down adjacent colours and be perfect for linking plants. Do not use very dark foliage, however, particularly if the flower colour is overwhelmingly pale. Large leaves will look stark and hard; instead, choose small-leaved plants.

Pale and soft shades are preferable to bright colours, and one main colour should be combined with related colours. Employ different subtle shades to

The icy charm of this white planting is created by the combination of pure white tulips and the boldly variegated leaves of the hostas.

build up a multi-layered effect; restrict yourself to two or three main colours, and use them in varying shades, drawing them together with some neutral foliage. In spring, for example, try the pale blue *Hyacinthoides hispanica*, beneath a spring-flowering shrub such as a pink-tinged magnolia. Continue the pink and blue theme in another part of the garden with a border of *Fritillaria meleagris*, combined with blue forget-me-nots. Hellebores, with their soft pink, white and green flowers, can be mixed with creamy coloured daffodils and snowdrops.

In a summer border, plant delicate blue Spanish irises rising out of the silvery grey foliage of *Dianthus*, continuing towards the back of the bed with *Allium christophii* and, perhaps, *Rosa* 'La Ville de Bruxelles'. For autumn colour, the colchicums are invaluable; *Colchicum agrippinum* harmonizes with any of the silver-leaved herbs, and with the pink flowers of *Sedum populifolium*.

The choice of harmonizing colour combinations is without bounds. However, resist the temptation to use too many different types. A variety of colours used indiscriminately will only cancel each other out and look messy.

ONE-COLOUR PLANTING

Whether vibrant or subtle, single-colour effects are always both impressive and memorable. The variation in shades of a single colour is almost infinite and, with the careful use of tints and shades, a remarkable range of colour contrasts can be achieved.

Single-colour gardens can be based on any colour, from white through to red. Using one colour, the emphasis falls on the texture and form of the plants as well as the colour, and neighbouring plants should contrast with each other in one or more of these aspects to avoid a dull and lifeless planting. In large gardens, it is easiest to restrict yourself to small areas of one colour based on seasonal planting rather than try and co-ordinate large expanses into a single colour. Foliage plays an important role, providing a background which will support the colour of plants around it; aim at using leaves with a good variety of different shapes and densities as well as colours.

When deciding which colour to select, choose one that will work well in the climate. In areas of cold winters and late springs, for example, warm-looking schemes are very successful. Plant a patch of yellow winter aconites in front of a gold-variegated shrub such as

For a timeless border planting, select shades of purple-pink and misty whites. Here, Gladiolus 'The Bride' *and* Allium caeruleum *are used.*

A mixed border in warm shades of plum and rose, with berberis and lilies, including the ever-reliable Lilium regale.

ABOVE Fiery shades of orange-scarlet are packed together in this composition of Asiatic lily hybrids and alstroemerias to create a single-coloured border.

Elaeagnus pungens 'Maculata' or one of the smaller mahonias, such as the yellow-flowered *Mahonia aquifolium*. Think bold for spring; red or blue will work well, but take care with the shades you use. In the case of red, avoid mixing bluish-crimsons with the orange-scarlets; red anemones blend in well with red tulips. When using blues, do not mix the harsh, bright blues with the purple-blues; indigo blue hyacinth look very good mixed with dark blue pansies.

Some wonderful white spring displays can be achieved with white 'Mount Tacoma' tulips, *Hyacinthoides hispanica* and the white-edged *Hosta crispula*, but white really comes into its own in summer as it looks so cool and refined. However, it is most effective used in temperate climates where the light is softer. Plant a mixture of *Crinum × powellii* 'Album', *Zantedeschia aethiopica* 'Crowborough' and any of the white lilies against a dark hedge of yew, with a cluster of softer *Ornithogalum thyrsoides* in front, intermingled with one of the grey-leaved herbs. The yellow-green

perennial *Alchemilla mollis* is indispensable in both white, yellow and orange one-colour plantings.

In autumn, cool pinks work well. Plant *Colchicum speciosum* in front of *Sedum spectabile*, with a few clumps of cherry-coloured *Schizostylis coccinea* 'Major' behind, against a backdrop of *Fuchsia* 'Mrs Popple'.

A single-colour planting can be restricted to a small flower bed or a large border, but the overall effect will be a sense of harmony and space that a vibrant planting of contrasting colours could never achieve.

PRACTICALITIES

Bulbs can be used in so many situations and for so much of the year that it is easy to take their excellent performance for granted. By their very design, they are intended to grow and flower from year to year. The bulbs, corms, tubers and rhizomes themselves are storage bodies that contain food made during the growing season which is used to produce growth in subsequent years.

Choosing, planting, aftercare and propagation are all of great importance in bulb cultivation, both indoors and outdoors. However, even the most lavish attention cannot make up for a poor quality bulb, or one planted the wrong way up or at the wrong depth. This section provides invaluable help for making the best choices in the garden centre and from mail order catalogues, as well as giving clear advice on site preparation, use of tools, soil improvers and fertilizers.

Of great importance to the bulb's survival in following years is how it is treated as it approaches the dormant season. Even the healthiest bulb will start to decline if left in waterlogged conditions winter after winter, and the correct storage of lifted bulbs over the dormant season is critical to their survival.

Indoor bulbs are another question altogether. Tremendous demands are made on the bulbs because of root restriction, low light levels, often low humidity and high daytime temperatures. Added to this, indoor bulbs are often required to flower out of season. Pests and diseases can be more frequent in such conditions, as the bulbs have to contend with considerable stress while growing and are therefore more vulnerable. Following the general and more specific advice given in this section will ensure the best performance from your indoor bulbs. Furthermore, with proper feeding and maintenance, there is no reason why most of these indoor bulbs should not be planted outside for flowering at the normal time in future seasons.

Pest and disease control is important for all bulbs. Bulbs are vulnerable during the growing season, especially when the foliage and flowers may attract unwanted attention. Even in the dormant season, however, both stored bulbs and those growing in the ground are subject to attacks from a range of pests including microscopic viruses and visible insect pests. Preventative action is preferable to dealing with established infestations, but even then, prompt action, which may involve destroying plants, will solve most problems.

Propagating bulbs is easier than most people imagine and it is the only means of producing a large quantity of plants free of cost. Techniques vary from simple seed sowing to the more specialized methods of vegetative propagation. This section provides all the instructions necessary for a healthy continuity of supply for all commonly grown bulbs.

BELOW Forced bulbs can be grown in trays, then selected for potting up into more attractive containers when ready to flower. This allows you to create displays of well-matched plants, all of similar size and maturity.

RIGHT Growing narcissi in gravel rather than compost gives attractive results. Unfortunately, the bulbs will suffer because of the lack of nutrients, and are unlikely to produce flowers the following year.

FIRST PRINCIPLES

Selecting and purchasing bulbs

Bulbs are usually sold in a "dry" state, that is to say, when they are dormant. Spring-flowering bulbs are purchased during late summer and autumn, while summer- and autumn-flowering bulbs are available in spring and late summer respectively. While some are packaged in nets or plastic bags, others are sold loose.

As a general rule, bulbs should be bought the moment the bulb-selling season gets under way, for the longer they are kept in shops and garden centres, the greater the likelihood that these vulnerable living organisms will be damaged. Although bulb storage is so highly sophisticated that many varieties of bulbs can be kept in a satisfactory dormant state all year round, no matter how good the storage conditions, problems can still arise in bulbs purchased from a chain store, where the temperature is usually so high that the bulbs start to deteriorate within about 10 days. Without protection, small fritillaries and softer bulbs like snowdrops are the first to spoil; they should never be purchased in pre-packed nets unless

The gladiolus corms on the left are in good condition, plump and firm, with their tunics clean and intact. Those on the right, however, have lost their tunics, and the marked skins show they are bruised.

The iris bulbs in the lower part of this picture are plump and healthy-looking, with clean skins. Those on the upper right, however, are wizened because they have been stored at too high a temperature.

These begonia tubers are clean, firm and in good condition. The pink shoots just visible on the upper sides indicate that growth is starting, and the tubers should be planted without delay.

The begonia tuber on the left is plump and firm and should give an excellent display of flowers. The one on the right, however, is shrivelled and unlikely to produce any growth at all.

bought soon after they arrive on the shelves. Only tough tubers like anemones and winter aconites and bulbs like alliums are likely to survive a protracted period of suspended display in a warm supermarket before being planted out. Bulbs may also begin to produce roots once they come out of storage and will start into premature growth if not planted out straight away.

Good-quality bulbs are available from specialist mail order firms, plant nurseries and garden centres. Most mail order firms have an extensive range of bulbs on offer, and they carefully package their bulbs before sending them to ensure they arrive in prime condition. If buying bulbs from a garden centre or nursery, make sure there is a dry atmosphere and cool temperature, the ideal environment for bulbs. A cursory glance at the display will quickly indicate whether the retailer does indeed know how to store bulbs: lilies, fritillaries and other soft bulbs vulnerable to rapid drying out should be covered with sawdust, wood shavings or peat. If such bulbs are exposed to the drying air, do not buy them.

Once purchased, the bulbs should be planted out within a few days. If this is not possible, they can be stored for 4-6 weeks. Remove them from the bag and spread them out on a seed tray, covering soft bulbs like lilies and fritillaries with peat or wood shavings. Put the tray in a cool, dry place such as a garden shed where the average temperature is approximately 45°F (7°C), until you are ready to plant them.

What to look for

The most important consideration when purchasing bulbs, corms, tubers and rhizomes is to select those that are firm and healthy-looking rather than ones that are soft and shrivelled. The entire structure must be solid, especially the area within the ring that forms the roots of bulbs and corms. To test this, invert the bulb or corm and press the finger or thumb firmly in the centre; if it is not solid, do not buy it. Narcissi in particular should be tested as a soft basal plate may indicate an attack of narcissus fly. If you were to cut open an afflicted bulb, you would find a fat, white grub nestling in the centre among the badly damaged embryo foliage. Also test the area around the neck of bulbs and corms for any signs of softness. Tubers and rhizomes should be firm but not hard, and wizened and dried ones should be avoided as the food reserve is desiccated and they are unlikely to break into growth.

Bulbs, corms, tubers and rhizomes must also have clean, blemish-free skins, although some hyacinth naturally have dark purple smears and stains on their surfaces. The skins of bulbous plants must also be intact, without cuts or bruises; always closely inspect tulip bulbs because their skins tend to split after being exposed to dry conditions. Any tulips that have lost most of their outer covering and resemble small potatoes should be avoided because they have no protection against fungal diseases.

With the exception of narcissi bulbs, which are often sold by the number of noses they have (the greater the number, the more flowers), most bulbs are sold according to their circumference, as measured around the fattest part of the bulb. This is universally noted in centimetres. There is a standard bulb size for each variety and charts stating this information are available.

It is important to choose the correct size of bulb, which does not necessarily relate to the size of the fully grown plant. Several large-growing narcissi, for example, are produced from relatively small bulbs. When purchasing hyacinths, any bulbs larger than 7in (18cm) in circumference should be saved for indoor pot cultivation, otherwise the resulting plants will blow over in strong winds because of their tall stems and the extra weight of the flowers. Smaller hyacinth bulbs produce equally good-quality flower spikes which are more weather resistant.

All bulbs are prone to storage mould and any showing signs of this should be avoided. Dwarf iris must also be carefully inspected for small black spots or blotches, symptoms of ink spot disease, which can easily devastate these marvellous plants. Only buy pure, creamy white *I. reticulata* bulbs, and check the brown coats of other types for any dark patches.

Unprepared and prepared bulbs

Besides choosing bulbs of good size, quality and health, it is also necessary to distinguish between the identical-looking unprepared and prepared bulbs.

Unprepared bulbs are those that have been harvested in the normal manner, being transported from the bulb fields to storage, and on to the shop. They form the majority of those sold to home gardeners and, apart from being graded and cleaned by suppliers, they are entirely in their natural state, although they may have spent some time in cool storage while awaiting shipment.

Prepared bulbs are for forcing into early flower for indoor displays. They are more expensive than unprepared bulbs, having received special treatment prior to selling. During the dormant period, they are lifted and subjected to a higher temperature than they would normally experience, and it is this that promotes premature bud formation. Prepared bulbs are available very early on in the season, and they should be planted immediately to take full advantage of their treatment. After flowering, they are discarded or replanted outdoors and left to grow on.

Planting bulbs outdoors

1 *A graduated bulb trowel takes the guess-work out of planting bulbs. Its long narrow blade has measurements marked on it so that the correct planting depth can be found.*

2 *Before planting a bulb, ensure it is the right way up with the growing point upwards. This may sound obvious, but with some corms and tubers it can be hard to tell.*

3 *Make sure that the base of the bulb is firmly in contact with the ground before you cover it with soil. If there is an air pocket beneath it, the roots will fail to develop.*

GROWING BULBS OUTDOORS
Preparing the ground

In order to thrive, bulbs, corms, tubers and rhizomes should be grown in well-prepared fine, crumbly soil. For the best results, thoroughly dig the area a minimum of seven days before planting; this will give the soil time to dry out and weather. Next, work the soil into a fine tilth using a hoe or a rake; if growing native woodland species such as lilies and trilliums, add a 2-3in (5-7.5cm) layer of organic matter such as leaf mould or pulverized bark. At this stage, it is also possible to enrich poor quality soil with a general garden fertilizer dug in according to the recommended amount. For bulbs that do not require very free-draining conditions, manure can be used to enrich the soil prior to planting. A selection of lilies, daffodils and fritillaries benefit from manure-enriched soil. Only use well-rotted mature that is rich brown, crumbly and odourless. Dig in the manure to below the level at which the bulb will be planted.

Good drainage is essential for all bulbs, and even those enjoying moist conditions will not tolerate waterlogged soil. Heavy soil can be improved by additions of sharp sand or grit; dig the sand or grit into the prepared soil at a rate of up to 25 per cent for very heavy soils and approximately 15 per cent for medium soils. Peat can be added to light, sandy soils to increase moisture retention if the soil is too free-draining. For bulbs like lilies which enjoy acid conditions, a proprietary acidifier can be incorporated into alkaline soil as instructed on the packet. To reduce acidity, however, hydrated lime can be dug into the soil at a rate of 2oz per square yard (50g per 0.8 square metres).

Planting

Once the soil has been prepared, the bulbs can be planted. A graduated bulb planter is very useful for determining the correct depths. Looking rather like a trowel, it has measurements marked along its length which ensure a correct planting depth. When laid horizontally across the surface of the soil, it can also be used to space the bulbs. Alternatively, a garden trowel can be used instead.

If planting individual bulbs, the hole should be the correct depth (see page 41) and approximately one-and-a-half times the circumference of the bulb. Once a hole of the correct dimensions has been dug, insert the bulb or corm with its pointed end upwards; also insert tubers with any eyes or buds uppermost, pressing them a little way into the soil. Cover the bulbous stock with soil, firm the surface, and water to encourage growth.

If you are planting a large quantity of bulbs it is both easier and quicker to dig an area to the overall depth required, and plant the bulbs together. Once you have dug the area, smooth the soil and, using a garden fork, lightly prick the surface. Space the bulbs as required; generally speaking, they should be spaced approximately 4-5in (10-13cm) apart, although some, like crocuses, must be almost touching, and others, such as galtonias, need to be up to 9in (23cm) apart. Do not space them too regularly, however, as this will look unnatural.

Gently scatter the soil over the bulbs, making sure that you do not knock them over in the process. When all the soil is in place, rake the surface level lightly and water the patch thoroughly.

Planting depths

The majority of bulbs, corms, tubers and rhizomes should be covered by their own depth in soil, although there are many variations to this rule. Bluebells, for example, should be planted at a depth of at least twice their own, and tuberous begonias require a shallow planting, just beneath the surface of the ground.

Some bulbs, notably daffodils, the majority of large-flowered narcissi and the larger species tulips and their cultivars, benefit from double-depth planting, which also means they are less likely to be damaged by weeding or hoeing. The only disadvantage of deep planting is that it produces a proliferation of foliage that will need thinning and

spraying with a systemic fungicide to ward off grey mould, which is of frequent occurrence among congested tulip clumps. However, deep planting is not recommended for *Narcissus* 'Sir Winston Churchill', as the bulbs tend to deteriorate over two or three years, or for *Narcissus cyclamineus* cultivars and the more delicate kinds like 'Hawera', which are too small for this method of planting.

The following seasonal charts indicate the planting depths of the given bulbs in relation to their heights. Generally speaking, spring-flowering bulbs must be planted in autumn, summer-flowering bulbs in spring, autumn-flowering bulbs in summer, and winter-flowering bulbs in autumn. See individual Plant Directory entries for specific details.

Spring-flowering bulbs

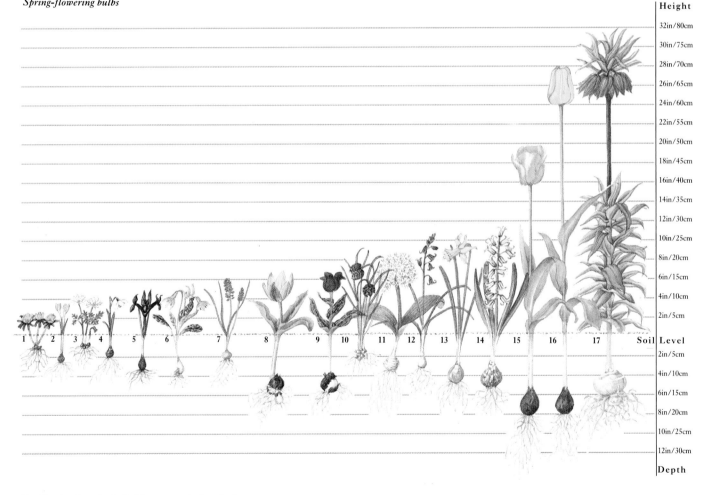

Small spring-flowering bulbs like anemones and galanthus need a shallow planting, whereas the taller tulips and fritillaries need a deeper planting to anchor them to the ground.

1 *Eranthis hyemalis*
2 *Crocus chrysanthus*
3 *Anemone blanda*
4 *Galanthus nivalis*
5 *Iris reticulata*
6 *Erythronium dens–canis*

7 *Muscari armeniacum*
8 *Tulipa kaufmanniana*
9 *Tulipa greigii*
10 *Fritillaria meleagris*
11 *Allium karataviense*
12 *Hyacinthoides hispanica*

13 *Narcissus* 'February Gold'
14 *Hyacinthus orientalis*
15 *Tulipa* 'Lady Diana'
16 *Tulipa* 'Golden Harvest'
17 *Fritillaria imperialis*

Summer-flowering bulbs

Height

58in/14
56in/14
54in/1
52in/1
50in/12
48in/12
46in/1
44in/1
42in/1(
40in/1(
38in/95
36in/9(
34in/85
32in/8(
30in/75
28in/7(
26in/6
24in/60
22in/5
20in/5(
18in/45
16in/4(
14in/35
12in/3(
10in/25
8in/20c
6in/15c
4in/10c
2in/5cm

Soil Level

2in/5cm
4in/10c
6in/15c
8in/20c
10in/25
12in/30

Depth

Lilies, crocosmias and cannas grow
into tall, vigorous plants and so must
be planted deeper than smaller plants
like irises and begonias.

1 *Begonia* × *tuberhybrida*
2 *Ornithogalum thyrsoides*
3 *Gladiolus nanus*
4 *Iris* 'White Excelsior'

5 *Allium aflatuense*
6 *Gladiolus* 'Peter Pears'
7 *Camassia leichtlinii*
8 *Lilium regale*

9 *Crocosmia masoniorum*
10 *Canna* × *generalis*

Autumn-flowering bulbs

Height

36in/90cm
34in/85cm
32in/80cm
30in/75cm
28in/70cm
26in/65cm
24in/60cm
22in/55cm
20in/50cm
18in/45cm
16in/40cm
14in/35cm
12in/30cm
10in/25cm
8in/20cm
6in/15cm
4in/10cm
2in/5cm

Soil Level

2in/5cm
4in/10cm
6in/15cm
8in/20cm
10in/25cm
12in/30cm

Depth

Colchicums, eucomis and amaryllis require deep planting, but the large autumn-flowering crinum grows best if planted with its neck just protruding from the soil.

1 *Cyclamen hederifolium*
2 *Crocus speciosus*
3 *Sternbergia lutea*
4 *Colchicum speciosum*
5 *Schizostylis coccinea*

6 *Eucomis comosa*
7 *Nerine bowdenii*
8 *Amaryllis belladonna*
9 *Crinum × powellii*

Winter-flowering bulbs

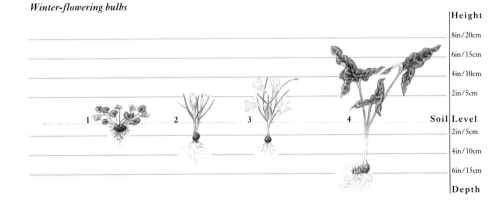

Height

8in/20cm
6in/15cm
4in/10cm
2in/5cm

Soil Level

2in/5cm
4in/10cm
6in/15cm

Depth

With the exception of the arum, which needs a deep planting, the taller the bulbs are, the deeper they should be planted.

1 *Cyclamen coum*
2 *Crocus laevigatus*
3 *Narcissus bulbocodium romieuxii*
4 *Arum italicum*

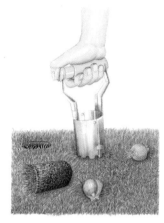

Using a bulb planter

LEFT A specially designed, hand-held bulb planter provides an easy method of planting bulbs in the garden. It can be used for planting large quantities of bulbs for naturalizing in grass as well as for planting individual bulbs in the soil of flowerbeds. When pushed into the ground to the required depth, the planter removes a plug of soil, leaving a hole in which the bulb is placed. Once the bulb is inserted in the hole, the soil plug is replaced and the bulbs left to grow.

Naturalizing bulbs

Bulbs for naturalizing can be planted in a number of ways. Either scatter them over the designated area and plant them where they fall, or purchase a special hand bulb planter which removes a plug of soil so the bulb can be inserted and the turf replaced. Although a tedious, back-breaking job, it is the only technique that can safely be used around established trees and shrubs. Where large quantities of bulbs are being naturalized, it is easier to lift the turf in several strips, plant the bulbs and replace the turf or, better still, to plant the bulbs in well-cultivated soil and grass over the top. This last method is particularly recommended for all bulbs requiring a fine grass that does not interfere with the growth of the bulb. Some bulbs such as winter aconites and snowdrops are best transplanted "in the green" with their foliage intact, rather than planted as dry tubers or bulbs. They are lifted and transplanted immediately their flowers have faded but before the leaves start to deteriorate, and must be watered well.

Cut flowers

If growing bulbs specifically for cut flowers, they will require staking. To avoid damaging the root systems, insert the stakes or canes as soon as the shoots emerge, but do not tie in the stems until the plant is approximately 6in (15cm) tall. To do this, using garden twine, loosely tie the top and bottom of the stem to the stake or cane. Alternatively, use horizontal metal hoops attached to metal stalks which are less obtrusive and just as effective, allowing the plants to grow more naturally.

Seasonal maintenance
Fertilizing

Feeding bulbs depends upon individual types and the purpose for which they are being grown. Those used in annual bedding displays do not require feeding as it is better to discard them once flowering is over and replace them with new plants. This also applies to large-flowering gladioli, which are rarely good a second year round. Most of the smaller summer bulbs like sparaxis and tigridia can be lifted and stored through the winter and then fed at planting time with a slow-acting fertilizer like bonemeal. Be careful not to over-feed them, however, because this can lead to soft growth and a greater vulnerability to diseases.

Naturalizing bulbs in grass

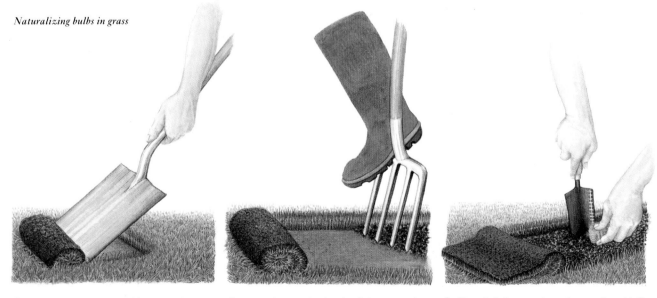

1 *Using a sharp spade, cut through the turf to a depth of 1–2in (2.5–5cm), then peel it back to reveal the soil underneath.*

2 *Loosen the exposed soil with a fork to aerate the soil and improve drainage so that the bulbs will be able to root easily.*

3 *Plant the bulbs at random using a graduated bulb trowel. Replace the turf, firm it down gently and then water it thoroughly.*

Permanent spring-flowering bulbs like daffodils benefit greatly from feeding in order to build up their resources during flowering and before leaf loss, to form the next season's flower head. Either apply a single dose of slow-release fertilizer at flowering time or, for a stronger feed, use a standard liquid or foliar tomato fertilizer containing potash, nitrates and phosphates as soon as the buds emerge, and continue feeding every two weeks. Being quick-acting, the liquid feed will supply more nutrients before the bulbs go into dormancy than a slow-acting fertilizer, as well as promoting better quality flowers. Select a liquid feed with a low nitrogen content of six parts nitrogen to 12 parts phosphorus and 12 parts potassium, or it will cause the bulb to become soft and vulnerable to rotting, especially on heavy clay, and do not use it on naturalized bulbs as it tends to feed the surrounding grass as well as the bulbs, making the grass too vigorous and competitive for the bulbs.

Dead-heading

Wherever possible, dead-head all bulbs, corms, tubers and rhizomes after flowering to divert all the plants' energy into the remaining flowers and, after flowering, into the development of next year's flower spike. Once the flower has faded and started to go brown, nip the flower off at the neck. After flowering, annuals can be lifted and discarded any time, but perennials should be kept growing by watering until the tips of the foliage turn yellow, after which they are either left to die back naturally or they are lifted and stored.

Mulching

Those that remain in the ground over winter are usually hardy enough to withstand the conditions, but, in very cold areas, some will need the protection of a heavy mulch in order to survive. Cover the ground around the bulbs with a layer of straw or bracken at the first signs of frost.

Winter storage

Of all the bulbs, corms, tubers and rhizomes requiring winter storage, most are summer-flowering subjects, like gladioli, which cannot withstand winter in the open ground and must be lifted and stored in a cool, dry place. Do not lift the bulbs when the foliage is still green because the ends of the leaves may be open to rapid fungal infection. Instead, wait until the first sharp frosts have blackened the foliage and sealed the leaf tissue.

Once the leaves have been well-frosted, using a sharp knife, remove any remaining foliage as close to the top of the bulb as possible. Spread the bulbs out on a tray or a wire rack to enable the air to circulate and dry them; corms with a hollow stem must be inverted so that any lingering moisture can drain away. When thoroughly dry, rub off any remaining soil and dust the bulbs with flowers of sulphur as a protection against storage moulds.

The subjects are then ready to be stored in a netting bag in a cool, dry place. To check against infection, they must be regularly inspected and any showing signs of softness or disease immediately removed.

Storing bulbs

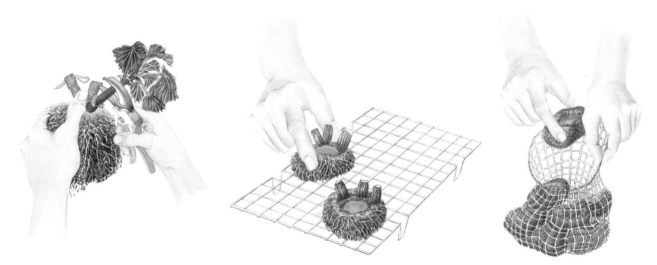

1 *Lift the bulbs from the ground and remove all the frost-blackened foliage to within 1–2in (2.5–5cm) of the top of the bulb.*

2 *Dry the bulbs by spacing them out on a wire rack in a cool, dry atmosphere. Rub off any soil and dust the bulbs with flowers of sulphur.*

3 *When thoroughly dry, the bulbs can be stored in a netting or paper bag. Store different varieties separately, and label them clearly.*

CONTAINERS, WINDOW BOXES AND HANGING BASKETS
Growing mediums

Indoor bulbs and those grown in containers, window boxes and hanging baskets will need planting up in compost. Contrary to popular opinion, bulb fibre is not necessarily the best growing medium for bulbs. Of variable formula, it incorporates sphagnum moss or coarse moss peat, or both, with added charcoal and oyster shell. The mixture has virtually no nutrients, and so the bulbs have to depend upon their stored energy resources to grow and flower, which usually exhausts them. It is much better to use a good-quality brand name potting compost.

There are two main types of potting compost, soilless and soil-based, both of which have added nitrogen, phosphorus and potassium, the amount varying according to the manufacturer. Soilless compost consists of peat, pulverized composted bark or another organic material, and some have additions of sharp or silver sand for extra drainage. Being almost entirely organic, it is not recommended for long-term planting as it is unstable in structure and will deteriorate after a season, but it can be used for short-lived bulbous or tuberous plants such as begonias and members of the arum family like arisaema and zantedeschia, which only grow for one season before the compost is discarded. Native woodland bulbs like achimenes (hot water plant), can also be planted in soilless mediums since they enjoy the organic content. Additions of up to 25 per cent by volume of perlite will act as a moisture reserve, keeping the medium moist but not waterlogged.

The soil-based composts are generally made up according to the John Innes scientific formulation. These are available in four types: seed compost, John Innes No. 1, John Innes No. 2 and John Innes No. 3. The seed compost consists of two parts loam, one of fibrous peat, one of coarse sand and ground chalk, with added nutrients. It is ideal for raising bulb seed with an added 25 per cent sharp grit to improve drainage. John Innes No. 1 consists of the same ingredients in different proportions, again with added nutrients, and is used for young plants and for short, seasonal displays, whereas John Innes No. 2 is longer lasting and suitable for bulbs that are repotted annually. To ensure the compost does not dry out too quickly, add about one-third by volume of added sedge peat. The much stronger John Innes No. 3 is only suitable for permanent bulb plantings of two years and over, such as amaryllis, that remain in their pots all year round. However, all of the John Innes composts are slightly alkaline and so are inappropriate for plants like *Lilium canadense*, which are not lime-tolerant.

These soil-based mixtures are equally useful for hardy bulbs grown as pot plants, particularly the small varieties of scilla and fritillaria often cultivated in alpine houses. They should be started off in J. I. No. 1, with an added 25 per cent by volume of sharp grit and, in subsequent years, repotted in No. 2.

Planting containers

Most bulbs will grow well in containers under the right conditions. A decent quantity of compost is the first essential ingredient, but equally important are sufficient root space and free drainage, and the success of hanging baskets depends upon steady watering.

There is a wide range of possible containers for bulbs, including imaginative vessels like chimney pots and sinks. Shallow containers, less than 6in (15cm) deep, with a large surface area are the least useful because they dry out rapidly; deep containers, from 6in (15cm) to 24in (60cm) deep, are much better, even if the roots of the bulb are unlikely to penetrate the lower depths, which can be filled with drainage material such as pieces of broken flower pot or small stones. Lilies look best in clay or wooden tubs; large Trumpet lilies require a pot at least 9in (23cm) in diameter, although the same pot will hold three to five of the smaller Asiatic lilies.

Before mixing compost or selecting bulbs, decide where the container is to be located. For most bulbous plants, an open, sunny position is required, but if this cannot be provided, select shade-tolerant bulbs. It is a good idea to position containers before planting them up as they can be very difficult to move when full.

Place a $\frac{1}{2}$in (1cm) layer of coarse gravel in the bottom of a container with drainage holes and a $1\frac{1}{2}$in (3.5cm) layer in those without; lilies benefit from a 1-2in (2.5-5cm) layer of organic matter, such as well-rotted leaves, covering the grit. Fill the container with John Innes No. 2 for permanent plantings; and use soilless compost, with up to 25 per cent by volume added perlite for temporary plantings; the few that tolerate damp conditions will require a growing medium mixed with up to 20 per cent by volume of organic material such as composted bark. If the bulbs are to accompany an established feature like a miniature conifer, they will have to tolerate the compost already in the container, most likely to be John Innes No. 3. Plant the bulbs in the compost at the correct depths (see Plant Directories), spacing them as required for each individual type. For stem-rooted lilies leave a gap of about 2in (5cm) between the surface and the rim of the pot so that more soil or well-rotted compost can be added as the stems develop roots above the bulb in summer.

If planting narcissi in a deep container, plant one layer of soil and bulbs and then another immediately above it, the base of the top layer of bulbs being level with the noses of those beneath. This method can also be applied to daffodils grown in pots indoors, but it is not a good method to use for long-term cultivation.

If planted in autumn, water the bulbs and keep the pot in a cool, frost-free place indoors over spring, preferably plunged in sand. As the shoots develop, increase the amount of light and water they receive, and finally move the pots outside to a sheltered spot when there is no longer any danger of frost. If the bulbs are to be kept for the next year, the stems can be cut off to the level of the compost and the bulbs repotted or top-dressed with new soil. They may require repotting every other year if they increase and become too congested.

Planting window boxes

As with containers, window boxes must be 6-9in (15-23cm) deep and free-draining. Many manufactured window boxes are excellent, but do not use any small ones that will restrict root development. It is also important to choose a relatively lightweight window box that can be fixed to the wall.

Place a 1in (2.5cm) layer of coarse gravel in the bottom of the window box and fill it up with J. I. No. 1 or soilless compost. As with containers, up to 25 per cent added perlite can be incorporated for moisture conservation. The compost layer should be a minimum of 4in (10cm) deep; a 6in (15cm) layer

is ideal. Plant the bulbs at the required depths and water them as necessary. A time-saving and easier alternative, however, involves planting up a series of seasonal displays in plastic inner troughs. Insert the current season's display in the empty window box and keep the others in a sheltered corner of the garden. As each season comes to an end, take the next trough and replace the previous one.

Planting hanging baskets

Hanging baskets must be replanted each season for a continuous show of colour. Both plastic and metal baskets are available and, although the plastic ones are less prone to drying out, the wire ones are much more attractive.

Line the basket with a 1½in (3.5cm) layer of moist sphagnum moss; this is an ideal medium because, while helping to prevent rapid moisture loss, unlike plastic, it does not restrict drainage to the extent of causing waterlogging. Compress it with the finger tips and fill the basket almost to the top with compost. From the point of view of weight, soilless compost is best since it is lighter, although J. I. No. 1 can also be used, and added perlite will help retain moisture. Using your hand, hollow out the planting holes and insert the bulbs, packing the remaining space with more growing medium. Place the newly planted basket in a container of water and leave it to soak until the compost is thoroughly wet, after which the basket can be fixed in its permanent position. Subsequent watering can be done with a watering can with a fine rose attachment.

Planting containers

1 *Drainage is important for container-grown bulbs. Always put a good layer of gravel into the container before adding the compost.*

2 *Place the bulbs on the compost so they are correctly spaced and at the right depth. Do not disturb them as you add the remaining compost.*

3 *Water in, then top up the compost if necessary. Feed and water regularly, particularly if your containers are made of wood or unglazed pottery.*

Seasonal maintenance

Containers and window boxes should be regularly watered (so the compost is always damp to the touch) and weeded, and a standard spraying programme against pests and diseases followed. As the flower buds show colour, start feeding the plants every two weeks using a liquid tomato feed, and dead-head them as soon as the flowers die to promote good growth. The same applies to hanging baskets, but they will need a stricter watering regime due to the rapid moisture loss. Rather than constantly sprinkling the basket, thoroughly soak it until surplus water runs out of the drainage holes.

Most container and window box displays will not survive the winter outside. Either discard the bulbs or store them indoors until warmer weather. Even early spring plantings may still need protection from lingering frosts, however; hyacinths are particularly vulnerable to cold weather. Lay a mulch of straw or bracken over the soil until the weather improves and put straw around the pot to insulate it completely.

GROWING INDOOR BULBS

Indoor bulbs enjoy temperatures of 50-60°F (10-16°C) and light, sunny positions, although some do not like direct sunlight, and none will tolerate draughty positions. Growing indoor bulbs is not that different from growing bulbs outdoors, except that the majority of indoor bulbs will lose their leaves and go into dormancy for part of the year, during which they should not be watered. Spring-flowering bulbs go into dormancy in late summer; summer-flowering bulbs become dormant in winter, and autumn- and winter-flowering bulbs are dormant in spring.

Planting

Some tender bulbs, such as some begonias, are bought as growing plants, but others, like hippeastrums, are purchased in their dry state and will need potting up. Plant the bulbs in a container of J. I. No. 2, with 25 per cent extra sharp grit to improve drainage; *Achimenes* and *Begonia* require a free-draining, moist, soilless compost. Either use one large bulb or several small ones, but allow a gap of approximately 1in (2.5cm) around the edge of the pot. Most bulbs barely need covering, and some prefer to have their tips poking above the surface of the compost.

Water the bulbs lightly and then, unless the compost dries out completely, do not water again until the bulbs start to grow, when regular watering should start.

Hippeastrums are very popular indoor plants. Purchase the bulb in autumn or early winter and pot it in John Innes No. 3, with approximately half the bulb above the soil surface. The pot should only be a finger's width larger than the diameter of the bulb. Once potted, the bulb should be well-watered and placed in a warm, bright position. A healthy vigorous hippeastrum should be capable of producing at least four long, bright green, strap-like leaves and a spike of magnificent, colourful, trumpet-like flowers; it is generally accepted that a plant with four healthy leaves throughout the year will produce good flowers the following season.

Seasonal maintenance

Once the flower buds appear, start feeding the bulbs once every two weeks with a liquid tomato fertilizer to promote good quality blossoms and stable growth, and this will also

Planting indoor bulbs

1 *Amaryllis bulbs are available in autumn and winter, often in kit form with a pot and compost.*

2 *If using your own pot, choose one slightly larger than the bulb and put grit in the bottom.*

3 *Place the amaryllis bulb in the pot with about half of it projecting above the top of the compost and ensure that*

the compost is well firmed. Water thoroughly but carefully around the sides of the bulb.

Dead-heading

Removing the spent flower heads not only greatly improves the appearance of your indoor bulbs but also has the effect of lengthening the flowering period because the plant will not use energy in forming seeds.

reduce the likelihood of diseases during the dormant period. Regularly water the bulbs, so the compost is always moist, until the foliage dies down and dead-head the plants once the flowers start to fade and go limp. With almost perpetually summer-flowering plants like begonias, faded blossoms must be regularly removed in order to promote the development of new flower buds. With double-flowered tuberous begonias, it is also necessary to remove the single female flowers, easily recognized by the tiny winged seed capsule behind the bud; they do not contribute to the floral display and reduce the impact of the double male flowers, significantly impairing their development. Some plants, for example begonias and achimenes, are also subject to mildew attacks during cool, humid weather and will need spraying regularly with a proprietary systemic fungicide as directed on the container. Incorporate a systemic insecticide to combat greenfly if they are a problem.

After flowering, most indoor bulbs gradually go into dormancy but some species may continue to grow. Watch the plant carefully; if it starts to turn yellow and goes into decline, reduce feeding and watering until the bulb goes into

dormancy, but if it continues to grow, carry on feeding and watering it. Indoor bulbs like *Lachenalia* and *Veltheimia* benefit from a dormant period induced by a reduced watering regime, commencing when the foliage starts to fade until the compost is bone dry. Provided that sufficient foliage has been allowed to remain for several months after flowering, the next season's flower display is guaranteed. If there is not enough space to store dormant indoor plants in their pots, the rootstocks can be disentangled and placed in an airtight tin layered with peat. Begonias should be removed from their pots and the tubers dusted with flowers of sulphur to combat fungal infections and storage moulds. They can then be placed in a cupboard or store at a minimum winter temperature of 40°F (4.5°C), but do not forget to check the tubers periodically for signs of decay and remove any suspicious individuals straight away.

Hippeastrums can be kept growing through summer provided their roots are not exposed. Leave them unwatered and in a cool, dark position until the following winter, when they will start into growth. To do this, place the pot on its side and leave it to dry out over summer. In winter, stand the pot upright and scrape away the surface compost until the roots are exposed. Top-dress the container with fresh growing medium, water thoroughly and place it in a warm, light place.

Many indoor bulbs spend the entire year in the same pots, save for certain exceptions like achimenes and gloriosa, which are better repotted the next season in fresh compost.

Forced bulbs

Specially prepared bulbs can be forced into early flowering for indoor displays. Hyacinths are the most widely cultivated prepared bulbs, and 'Pink Pearl', 'Delft Blue' and the pure white 'Carnegie' can all be recommended to provide bowls of colour and scent in early winter.

Forced bulbs

1 *Plant hyacinth bulbs for forcing with their shoulders just above the compost level.*

2 *Always place gravel or broken crocks at the bottom of the container to help drainage.*

Planting

For the finest results, the prepared hyacinths should ideally be 9in (23cm) in circumference; if planting only one bowl, restrict the choice to just one variety. As a precaution against skin irritation, wear gardening gloves when handling the bulbs.

If you wish, the bulbs can be planted in individual pots and, after the cool period, replanted in attractive containers, with those of similar-sized flower shoots for the same pots. However, the bulbs can be planted straight into ornamental containers if you wish. Plant the prepared bulbs in late autumn or early winter, with the tip just poking above the top of the soil, in John Innes No. 1 or a multi-purpose, soilless compost based on peat or peat and sand with added nutrients, or one based on a peat alternative such as coir or composted bark. If the bowls have little or no drainage holes, place a 1in (2.5cm) layer of gravel in the bottom of the container prior to planting to help drainage.

Forced bulbs need a cool period to develop a robust root system that will sustain forcing. Once planted, water the bulbs thoroughly and place the pots in a cool, frost-free place such as a garage, shed or outhouse for a minimum of 10 weeks.

After this period, bring the pots into the daylight, but not into bright sunshine. Once exposed to the heat and light, the yellow shoots will turn green after a few days. If you wish, top-dress the compost with fresh, green sphagnum moss to protect the pot against rapid moisture loss. Forced bulbs respond to a rise in temperature, but only if the light intensity is raised in proportion to the temperature.

Regularly water the bulbs so the compost is always moist but not waterlogged; in relatively cool conditions this should be done approximately once a week.

Narcissi, tulips and crocuses can be treated in a similar way to hyacinths. Forced crocuses will flower earlier on in the season than narcissi or tulips and are excellent for early colour. Tulips need a longer cool period than hyacinths, about 12-14 weeks, and narcissi require much cooler conditions. They are best planted in pots which are buried in the ground outside rather than the comparative warmth of a cupboard before being brought inside for flowering. Once potted, stand the bulbs in a cold frame or a trench in a vacant part of the garden, and completely cover them with an insulating layer of peat or composted bark and straw. To deter slugs, scatter the ground around the bulbs with slug pellets.

After 10 weeks, dig up the pots and bring them inside for flowering, after which they can be planted out in the open ground or discarded; even quite tiny, exhausted bulbs will produce a decent show within a couple of seasons if transferred to the garden.

Seasonal maintenance

Forced bulbs flower for two or three weeks under average house conditions. If necessary, support tall stems with small, split green canes and string or specially manufactured wire supports, although this will detract from the look of the bulbs. For the best results, start feeding the plants with a standard tomato liquid feed when the emerging flower buds develop a coloured flush, and this will toughen the bulbs so they are not soft and vulnerable to rotting when dormant.

After flowering, either discard the bulbs or plant them outside, in which case the foliage must be kept active and green for as long as possible for the bulbs to build up food reserves for the following season's flower display.

PEST AND DISEASE CONTROL

Effective control of pests and diseases during the growing period is crucial. In most cases, prevention is the key note, although it is not always possible because some pests like earwigs, which plague gladioli and other summer-flowering plants, can only be dealt with at the first sign of attack.

Aphids

Aphids and other pests can be controlled by using a systemic insecticide. The sap of the foliage absorbs the insecticide, effectively inoculating the plant against sucking insects. However, this is a short-lived measure and repeat sprayings every three weeks or so are necessary. While a systemic insecticide will not guarantee total protection against virus diseases transmitted by aphids, it is nonetheless a highly effective form of control, particularly benefiting lilies.

Earwigs

These seemingly harmless insects are in fact rather destructive, causing twisted or distorted, often chewed blossoms, together with a stippled chewing of the foliage, and tiny, irregular holes in the main veins of the leaves. These pests are only active at night, hiding in debris during the day and, while an insecticidal dust has some effect if applied around the plants, the most effective method of control is to capture them. Invert a plant pot filled with dried grass on a cane close to the damaged plants so that the earwigs will hide in the dried grass during the day and can then be collected and disposed of at night.

Snails and slugs

Slugs and snails are also a threat, attacking emergent shoots and leaves of succulent plants like lilies and gladioli, particularly during the spring. In some cases, most notably

Pests and diseases

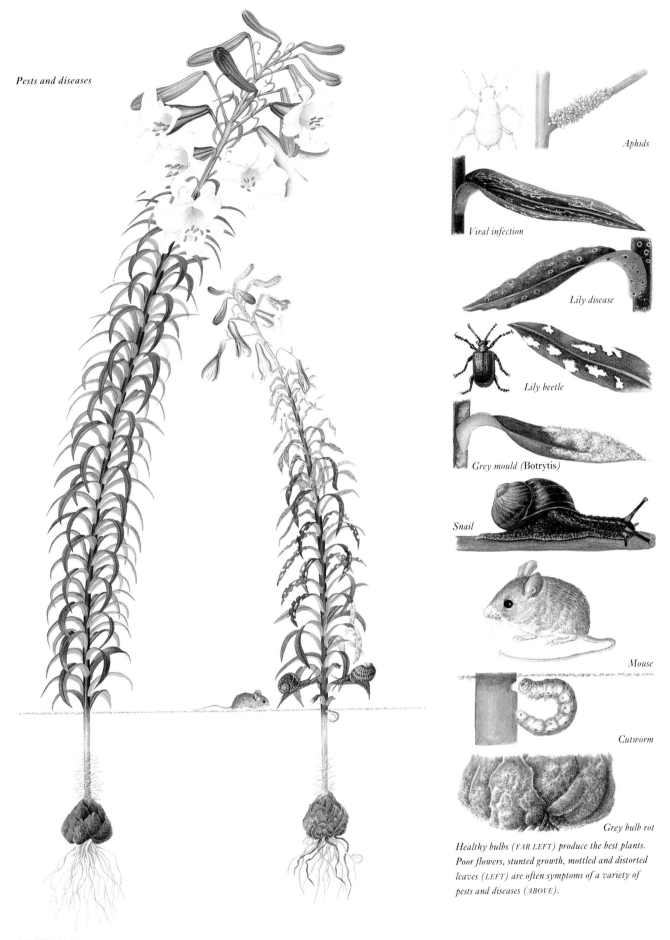

Aphids

Viral infection

Lily disease

Lily beetle

Grey mould (Botrytis)

Snail

Mouse

Cutworm

Grey bulb rot

Healthy bulbs (FAR LEFT) produce the best plants. Poor flowers, stunted growth, mottled and distorted leaves (LEFT) are often symptoms of a variety of pests and diseases (ABOVE).

among lilies, this can have a devastating effect, damaging the growing points and distorting growth. The shoots of summer-flowering *Sparaxis* and *Tigridia* can also be attacked if precautions are not taken, while the flowers of early flowering *Scilla* and *Puschkinia* can be fenestrated by their activities. Use slug pellets freely among the groups of plants worst affected; rather than scattering them around the plants, place a handful under a small piece of flat stone which is raised up above the soil level. This keeps the pellets dry while also preventing birds from picking them up, and encourages the slugs and snails to congregate under the stone and devour the pellets.

A more environmentally friendly method of control involves sinking a small plastic carton filled with beer into the ground to soil level. The slugs and snails are attracted to the liquid and, while trying to drink, fall in and drown. Alternatively, place the eaten halves of a grapefruit upside down on the soil surface beside vulnerable plants at night; the slugs will crawl underneath the fruit and can be removed the following day. Replace the grapefruit every three to four days once the interior has dried up.

Small animals

Small animals, including mice and squirrels, may sometimes feed on bulbous plants. Many chew the foliage and flowers, while others dig up and eat the bulbs. To deter or trap these pests, use physical barriers and traps.

Viral infection

Of all the bulbous plants, lilies are the most susceptible to viral infection and, once affected, will die. Typical symptoms include distorted foliage, absence or twisting of blossoms and, when the vigorous young shoots are stopped in their tracks, ugly spreading rosettes of contorted foliage. In such cases, there is no cure and the plants will have to be disposed of.

Bulb Diseases

Disease	Symptoms	Plants affected	Control
Basal rot *A fungus living in the soil that enjoys warm conditions*	*Soft, rotting bulbs with a coating of mould around the base; yellow, wilted leaves*	Narcissus	*Dig up and burn diseased plants*
Grey mould (Botrytis) *A widespread disease*	*Rotting bulbs and stunted plant growth; grey, fluffy mould on the leaves and flowers, with discoloration and dying patches*	Anemone Lily Snowdrop Tulip	*Remove diseased flowers, buds and leaves and spray plants with a systemic fungicide*
Hyacinth black slime *A disease living in soil*	*Dry, black decaying bulbs; yellow foliage rotting at the base*	Crocus Fritillary Hyacinth Scilla	*Dig up and burn diseased plants*
Ink spot disease *A disease caused by fungus*	*Black spots on the bulbs; yellow foliage with dark streaks*	Iris	*Dig up and burn diseased plants*
Lily disease	*Reddish-brown spots on withered foliage*	Lily	*Dig up and burn diseased plants*
Powdery mildew *A fungus thriving in drought conditions*	*A white, powdery growth on the foliage*	Begonia Cyclamen	*Spray diseased plants with a systemic fungicide*
Root rot *A disease living in the soil*	*Black and decaying roots*	Hyacinth	*Dig up and burn diseased plants*
Tulip fire (Botrytis) *A fungus thriving in warm soil conditions*	*Rotting bulbs and stunted plant growth; dark grey fungal blotches on the foliage*	Tulip	*Dig up and burn diseased plants*
Tulip grey bulb rot *A persistent fungus living in the soil which infects bulbs shortly after planting or in early spring*	*A dry rot consisting of white, mouldy patches; stunted plant growth*	Colchicum Crocus Hyacinth Lily Narcissus Tulip	*Dig up and burn diseased plants*
Viral infection *A variety of viruses*	*Streaked and mottled foliage with pale marks; distorted leaves and wilting*	Gladiolus Lily Tulip	*Dig up and burn diseased plants*

Bulb Pests

Pest	Symptoms	Plants affected	Control
Aphids *Small, green or yellowish insects which suck the sap of the foliage and excrete a sticky deposit*	*A sticky, sooty deposit on the foliage*	Begonia Lily Most other bulbs	*Spray affected plants with a systemic insecticide*
Cutworms	*Nibbled roots and chewed soft tissue of bulbs*	Most bulbs	*Dust the soil with soil insecticide prior to bulb planting*
Gladiolus thrips *Brownish-black insects with long bodies*	*A silvery white, black-flecked discoloration on the flowers and foliage*	Gladiolus	*Spray affected areas with a contact insecticide*
Mice and other small mammals	*Disturbed often nibbled bulbs*	Crocus Gladiolus Tulip Most other bulbs	*Deter the pests with barriers and traps*
Narcissus flies *Adult flies similar in appearance to bumblebees*	*Soft bulbs sometimes infested with white maggots; a few grass-like leaves if any*	Hyacinth Narcissus	*Dig up and burn affected plants*
Lily beetles *Bright red insects*	*Chewed leaves and flowers from early spring to mid-autumn*	Fritillary Lily	*Treat affected plants with an insecticidal dust or remove the beetles by hand*
Snails and slugs	*Chewed foliage, flowers and bulbs*	Gladiolus Lily Most other bulbs	*Deter the pests with slug pellets and traps*
Stem and bulb eelworms *Microscopic creatures which burrow into the plant tissue*	*Brown and soft bulbs and weak growth; twisted and streaked leaves and undeveloped flowers*	Hyacinth Iris Narcissus Snowdrop Tulip	*Dig up and burn affected plants*

By diagnosing and controlling pests and diseases in their early stages, you can save yourself a great deal of trouble and expense. Swift and appropriate action may even involve digging up and destroying the affected plants, but this will prevent the problem from spreading any further.

Fungal diseases

Fungal diseases like mildew are easier to treat, the majority being dealt with by a systemic fungicide. The more stubborn diseases can be tackled with a copper-based fungicide applied every three weeks but, in extreme cases, it is easier to buy healthy new bulbs and discard the badly infected ones. Mildew and leaf-spot diseases of various kinds can also be tackled with a systemic fungicide applied every three weeks, provided spraying commences early in the growing season, as soon as fresh young foliage appears; the combination of a compatible systemic fungicide and insecticide will considerably reduce the amount of sprayings needed.

PROPAGATION

There are a number of methods of propagating bulbs, corms, tubers and rhizomes, some of which are specific to individual genera. For specific details, see individual plant entries.

Division

During the growing season, many bulbs, such as narcissi, increase by forming offsets from the main plant. If the plants are lifted, the offsets can be detached and planted up as new plants, a process known as division.

Ideally, the bulbs should be lifted and divided during the dormant period, but this is frequently impractical as most gardeners have little idea of the number and position of the bulbs once they have died back. Bulbs can also be divided just as they are seen peeping through the soil in spring, provided they are handled very carefully and, at this time, they will split much more easily than when dormant. Snowdrops are different: they are divided when still in leaf.

To divide bulbs, take a garden fork and lift the clump carefully, gently shaking off the soil. Separate the offsets with your hands, grading them into flowering and non-flowering sizes; the flowering offsets will be bigger than the non-flowering ones. Do not force the offsets apart; resistance is a sure indication that the bulbs are not ready to be split. Pot the offsets or replant them, leaving them to grow on undisturbed.

Narcissi regularly produce "daughter" bulbs as part of the main structure, and these growing points (known as "noses") slowly separate from the main bulb. Provided the nose is attached to a tiny portion of the base plate, it will grow into a new plant. Never force the daughter bulbs apart or the base plate might be damaged; wait for them to divide naturally before collecting and replanting them.

Some tubers, for example begonias, can be propagated by dividing the main storage organ. Take a sharp knife and cut through the tuber, making sure that each piece has a dormant bud attached to it. Do not make the portions too small; a few large slices are ideal and a mature begonia usually provides three or four sections. Once the tubers have been divided, dress all the cut surfaces with flowers of sulphur to reduce the possibility of infection. Pot each portion and allow them to grow on before planting them out.

Division

1 *Bulbs that spread by self-seeding or offsets will eventually form overcrowded clumps. When this happens, the clumps should be lifted carefully with a garden fork.*

2 *Gently tease the congested clumps apart with your hands, taking care not to break the root fibres. Select the largest, healthiest bulbs from the clump and discard the rest.*

3 *Replant the bulbs you have selected, either singly or in small groups. Improve the soil by adding compost or digging in some fertilizer, and water the bulbs thoroughly.*

Bulbils

1 *Some lilies form bulbils in their leaf axils, and these can be easily detached when ripe, usually when the foliage starts to die back.*

2 *Dust the bulbils with flowers of sulphur to prevent the spread of fungal diseases, to which some lilies are particularly prone.*

3 *Seal the bulbils in a polythene bag with damp moss, and store in a cool place. They will soon grow, ready for planting the following spring.*

Bulbils

Some bulbs, notably some lilies, produce small bulbils in the axils of their leaves which can be used for propagation purposes, although they will take a whole summer season to develop. Flowering will depend upon variety, but most should perform in their third or fourth year.

Do not pick the bulbils until they are ripe as they are easily damaged and will not root properly. Ideally, the foliage of the adult plant should be showing signs of decline and fading before the bulbils are gathered. Detach the bulbils, dust them with flowers of sulphur and place them in a polythene bag, with a little damp green sphagnum moss. Store the bag in a cool place like the hydrator in the bottom of the fridge and, the following spring, plant them, just covered, in seed trays filled with soilless compost. They can remain here, being fed regularly from early summer until autumn, until the following spring, when they are planted out.

Alternatively, remove a section of the stem with the bulbils and remove any leaves. Place the stem horizontally in a tray of soilless compost, with the compost just covering the stem, and put the tray in a cold frame. In most cases, the bulbils will root and start to grow. Any sprouting vigorously before the onset of winter may be knocked back by its severity, even given the protection of a cold frame, but little control can be exercised over their rate of growth. Once the bulbils have sprouted and are growing strongly, carefully remove them from the old stem. Plant them in a seed tray of soilless planting medium and leave them to grow. Plant them outdoors the following spring.

Spawn

Many cormous plants such as gladioli, crocuses and crocosmia produce masses of tiny cormlets known as "spawn" around their bases at the onset of the dormant period. The cormlets can be detached and grown on for propagation purposes.

Gather the spawn and plant them in a tray of John Innes No. 1 compost, and place the tray in a cold frame. Keep it moist through the winter, and commence watering to encourage growth in early spring. Once large enough to handle, the plants can be planted in nursery rows outside and, after approximately three years, the spawn will have grown into flowering-size plants.

Spawn

ABOVE The masses of tiny spawn that grow around the base of gladioli and other cormous plants will gradually form congested clumps of foliage.

They can be detached from the adult plant and placed in compost to produce flowering-size corms in as little as three years.

Seed

This method of propagation produces large number of plants, but the bulbs may take from three to five years to produce flowering-size plants. Seed propagation works best when there are good strains of bulbs available, for example, Bellingham hybrid lilies. As a general rule, small-flowered varieties which have small bulbs and seed freely are the best to increase this way. These include the species of *Scilla* and *Chionodoxa* as well as mixed *Anemone blanda*. It is pointless with named cultivars as the seed gathered from these is often the result of a cross with another plant which, even if of the same type, will not necessarily produce identical progeny.

Either buy the seed or collect it from the plants; freshly gathered seed always germinates much more freely, especially if sown immediately after gathering. This particularly applies to bulbs like *Narcissus* and *Galanthus*, which belong to the *Amaryllidaceae* family, and whose members tend to yield seed of short viability. The *Liliaceae* family, which embraces many of the most popular bulb groups like lilies and fritillaries, and the *Iridaceae* family, which includes crocuses and irises, produce seed that, while better sown directly after harvesting, will tolerate being stored in a paper bag for up to six months.

For lime-tolerant seed, use a seed compost with up to 25 per cent by volume extra sharp grit for improved drainage; for lime-haters like some lilies, use ericaceous compost with the same amount of grit. Fill a seed tray with the compost, smooth the surface and firm it down, before sowing the seed. Barely cover it with compost, and gently water the tray using a watering can with a fine rose. Place trays of tender seed in a frost-free greenhouse or on a sunny window ledge and, for those that take a long time to germinate, a liberal topdressing of fine grit can be applied to help prevent an invasion of moss. Trays of hardy seed should be placed in a cold frame. Stubborn seed can sometimes be stimulated into growth by freezing; place the tray in the deep freeze for three weeks or so, before moving it to a warm, light place, where it will almost certainly start to grow.

When the seedlings are large enough to be handled, usually within two to three weeks of first appearing, they can be potted up in John Innes No.1 and watered in. Once well-established, the seedlings can either be potted up individually or planted out in a nursery bed for growing on.

Fine seed, like that of double-flowered begonias, requires a rich, organic soilless compost containing a mixture of peat or bark and sand, as this is warmer than soil-based composts. Fill a seed tray with the compost, smooth the surface and firm it down. To help sow such fine seed evenly, drop a pinch of dry silver sand in the open packet and shake it so that the sand and seed mix together, making it easier to distribute the seed more evenly. If sown in this way, the seed will not require covering with compost.

Place the tray in a warm place like an airing cupboard; begonias need a minimum temperature of 60°F (16°C). Close,

Sowing seed

1 *Although it takes longer than other methods, growing bulbs from seed is an easy and cheap way of producing large numbers of bulbs. Use a well-drained compost, and sow the seed thinly.*

2 *The seed should be covered with a scattering of compost. After sowing, water carefully, using a fine rose to avoid disturbing the seed or washing it all to one side of the pot.*

3 *Prick the seedlings out as soon as they are large enough to handle easily. They should be planted about 1–2in (2.5–5cm) apart so that they have enough room to develop their root systems.*

humid conditions can lead to damping off disease, which affects a wide range of seedlings, causing the stems to blacken at soil level, before the plant collapses and dies. The best precautionary measure is to apply a copper fungicide like Cheshunt compound; a systemic fungicide is of little use since it must be absorbed by green foliage whereas seedlings are often affected before their leaves have fully developed. Gently water the compound on to the compost immediately after sowing and re-apply every 10 days, until the plants have been pricked out.

Prick out the seedlings into a tray of soilless compost. If they have germinated in small clumps, prick out groups of seedlings until they grow a little more and are easier to separate out. Leave them to grow for two or three years, repotting them into individual pots as necessary. If they are to be planted outside, however, they must first be hardened off. If you have a cold frame, put the plants in the frame and close the lid. After four or five days, raise the lid a little more each few days until the plants are weaned from the warmth of the indoor or greenhouse environment in which they were raised. Alternatively, if you do not have a cold frame, move the seedlings outside for a day at a time, bringing them back indoors for the night. After approximately 10 days, they should be able to tolerate night conditions and can safely be left outside to grow.

With some bulbs, for example bluebells, seed raising by hand is unpredictable. Although bluebells will self-propagate into naturalized patches if left alone, you can encourage them. Instead of letting the seed fall naturally to the ground, gently shake the seed heads to dislodge the ripe seed and leave it to grow. In the case of naturalized crocus and scillas, cut back the old growth when the seed has ripened and the plant will self-seed.

Stem propagation

Stem propagation is a way of increasing a variety of tubers, including begonias. It is one of the most successful methods of quickly producing a large number of plants that will flower the same season, without impairing the quality of the blossoms, and is especially suitable for providing a large quantity of bedding plants.

Space the tubers out in boxes of soilless potting compost, scarcely covering them. Lay brown paper over the top to protect any emerging roots from bright sunlight, and water them regularly. Once they have started to penetrate the compost and immediately tiny green shoots start to appear, remove the paper. When the shoots reach a height of approximately 2in (5cm), carefully remove them at a leaf joint. Allow one shoot to remain on each tuber so that the tuber can be left to grow on, and dip the cuttings into a hormone rooting powder or liquid. Plant them in a tray filled with 50 per cent by volume peat and perlite, or peat and sand, and stand the tray in a warm but lightly shaded place. Within two weeks, the shoots will have rooted.

As soon as rooting takes place, the cuttings must be potted individually in soilless compost and provided with plenty of light and a steady temperature, a minimum of 60°F (16°C). The parent tubers can also be potted and grown on; they usually make slightly larger plants more quickly but by planting out time, all the plants will be of similar size.

If you wish to produce more cuttings than you have shoots for, do not remove the shoots from the tubers until they are 4-5in (10-12cm) long. Then, remove the shoots and cut them into short lengths approximately 1½in (3.5cm) long.

Remove any large leaves and dust the cut surfaces with flowers of sulphur. Dip the ends of each section in rooting powder or liquid and plant them as for single stem cuttings.

Stem propagation

1 *Begonias can be forced into growth for stem propagation. All they need is a little warmth, moist compost and protection from light until the first shoots show through.*

2 *Cut off all but one shoot from each tuber once the shoots are about 2in (5cm) long. Make sure the knife you use is sharp and clean to avoid damaging the shoots or introducing infection.*

3 *Hormone-rooting compound will help the cuttings establish quickly. Plant the cuttings and firm them in; protect them from draughts and full sun until they are established.*

Scooping

Scooping is a propagation technique used to produce large numbers of hyacinth bulbs. Use a sharp, clean

knife or a spoon to avoid bruising the flesh or spreading diseases and scoop out the middle of the bulb.

Scouring

Alternatively, make a V-shaped cut about ¹/₄ in (0.5cm) deep, using a sharp, clean knife, in the base plate of

the bulb. Place the bulb in moist sand or compost. The spawn will form around the cut areas.

Scooping and scouring

Hyacinths can be increased by processes known as scooping and scouring. Using a sharp knife, scoop out about a quarter of the central fleshy stem of the hyacinth bulb while it is dormant and discard it, leaving the circular hard ring and basal plate intact. Plant the scooped bulb in a large pot of soilless compost or J. I. No. 2, with the cut end uppermost.

Once the flowers have died back and the foliage has faded, lift the bulb; a mass of young bulbs, known as "spawn", will be growing around the damaged area. Tip the bulbs and their progeny out of the pots, and grow the young bulbs in a nursery bed for two or three years, until they reach flowering size, when they can be planted out.

Alternatively, make two incisions in the shape of a cross through the basal plate of the bulb, removing a sliver of flesh each time. Replant the scoured bulb, with the basal plate downwards, and it will produce up to a dozen young bulbs around the cuts. These can be treated in exactly the same manner as those that have been scooped.

Scaling

Unlike most other bulbs, a lily bulb consists of clusters of scales, some of which can be detached for propagation purposes. Increased this way, the scales will take between three and seven years to produce flowering-size bulbs.

Take a deep tray and fill it with John Innes No. 2, with an extra 25 per cent by volume of sharp grit to improve drainage. If, like *Lilium canadense*, the species is a lime hater, select ericaceous soil-based compost. Carefully remove the scales from the bulb, each with a piece of base plate, and insert them into a tray of compost, with the vestige of base plate downwards, so they are completely covered.

Start the scales off in a cold frame and leave them to grow, watering them so that the compost does not dry out, but avoiding over-watering. Depending on the species or cultivar involved, within a couple of months, tiny leaves will appear, at the base of which is a small bulb. Leave the bulbs in the tray through the first winter, transplanting them into a nursery bed early the following spring.

1 *Lily stocks can be increased by removing scales from a sound, healthy bulb. Any damaged or withered scales should be discarded, and plump ones from underneath snapped off with a little of the base plate attached. This technique is useful for propagating hybrid lilies that would not come true from seed, and for the types that do not produce bulbils in the leaf axils.*

2 *Handle the scales carefully by the tips to avoid damaging the base, from which new growth will emerge. Insert them into a pot or tray of compost, base downwards, and water in with a solution of fungicide to help prevent disease. Most types of lily will survive quite well in a cold frame or unheated greenhouse, but the tender types will require more protection.*

Scaling

SPRING BULBS

Garden highlights

A display of spring-flowering bulbs is an excellent way of banishing the winter greyness still hanging over the garden, for bulbs bring colour into the dullest areas and create outstanding focal points. Furthermore, the diversity of bulbs available guarantees something for every kind of situation, from the disciplined bedding display to the informal mixed border.

No other plants herald the coming of spring more than daffodils, with their nodding yellow and white heads. Although primarily used for naturalizing, they are also very useful border plants because, being so bright, they draw the eye away from less sightly areas or, indeed, bare earth. Some careful thought should be given to their positioning so that after flowering their dying foliage is hidden by other plants.

The daffodil season lasts from early to late spring and, with careful selection, it is possible to have a continuous display of flowers. For the early spring, *Narcissus cyclamineus* hybrids can be planted on their own in clumps or grown beneath shrubs. Although delicate-looking, 'February Gold' is one of the first to flower and will tolerate lingering winter weather. With its back-swept, golden yellow petals and slightly darker trumpets, it is a handsome daffodil deserving much attention. Equally attractive is the later-flowering 'Dove Wings', with its creamy white petals and yellow trumpets. The ivory-coloured 'Jenny' makes a lovely focal point planted in a corner with evergreens or, for a more colourful display, it can be grown under the red-flowering currant *Ribes sanguineum* 'King Edward VII'.

PREVIOUS PAGE Similar in general appearance to bluebells, Scilla bithynica *increases by self-seeding and offsets into extensive ground cover.*

LEFT Mixed daffodils look their best naturalized in clumps. If the leaves are left to die back naturally, the display will improve each year.

BELOW This mixture of yellow winter aconites, pinkish-purple chionodoxas, snowdrops and daffodils is an eye-catching spring sight.

The deliciously scented jonquil flowers throughout spring. 'Sweetness', is plain yellow, but 'Suzy' has attractive orange cups. For more of a show, the pretty double-flowering narcissi burst into bloom later on in spring, sometimes continuing into early summer. They come in a variety of colours including white and orange ('Bridal Crown') and yellow and orange ('Tahiti'), and are excellent for mixed cottage-garden-style borders grown among a few pale pink hellebores (Lenten rose), interspersed with primroses, polyanthus and bright green fern fronds. Blue can be introduced in the form of hyacinths, grape hyacinths or bluebells.

The grape hyacinth (*Muscari*) is an invaluable plant for spring-border colour. Used on its own, it is good for edging paths and for uniform ground cover and, if desired, its intense blue can be softened with other plants including daffodils and primulas or, later on in the season, small tulips. It also associates well with hellebores, particularly the green- or pur- ple-flowered *H. purpurascens* or *H. foetidus*; a few clumps of tall-growing snowdrops will lift the display. A long-lasting show can be achieved by planting *Muscari armeniacum* 'Blue Spike' with the silvery, low-growing *Stachys olympica* 'Silver Carpet' (lamb's tongue). Muscari are also useful for planting under trees and shrubs. First-rate combinations involve the deep blue *Muscari neglectum* and *Forsythia* 'Lynwood', and the mid-blue *Muscari tubergenianum* and early-flowering, pale pink viburnums or darker pink camellias.

ABOVE The golden yellow of the daffodils is here complemented by the blue Scilla bithynica.

BELOW A classic spring planting of Narcissus *'February Gold' and acid-green hellebores.*

A simple but successful planting early in the year involves nothing more than grape hyacinths and the winter-flowering heaths (heathers). Heaths like the Springwood varieties and 'Pink Spangles' provide bold, startling groups of colour, with *Muscari armeniacum* 'Blue Spike' mixing well with the blousy *Erica carnea* 'Springwood White' or 'Springwood Pink'.

Small irises and delicate-looking scillas are excellent subjects for underplanting shrubs. For a spectacular highlight, plant a large drift of the chunky blue-flowering *Iris histrioides* 'Major' against an evergreen background of *Olearia* × *haastii* (daisy bush), *Mahonia nervosa* or *Hebe brachysiphon*. A sprinkling of the porcelain-blue *Scilla mischtschenkoana* looks particularly fine growing under the scarlet-stemmed *Cornus alba* 'Sibirica', the red-stemmed dogwood or the orange-stemmed willow *Salix alba* 'Chermesina', and the intense yellow stems of *Cornus stolonifera* 'Flaviramea' look even more vivid when underplanted with dark blue *Scilla siberica* 'Spring Beauty'. This lovely scilla also brings life to a planting of conifers such as *Chamaecyparis lawsoniana* 'Stardust' or *C. l.* 'Winston Churchill', both of which have golden-yellow foliage.

Shrubs like Mollis and Pontica azaleas benefit enormously from a complementary planting of *Chionodoxa luciliae* (glory of the snow). This wonderful spring bulb, with its starry blue and white blossoms, soon forms a dense carpet around the leafless shrubs. The Siberian squill, *Scilla siberica*, creates a similar picture, being of an even more intense blue.

ABOVE A raised bed is ideal for this vibrant planting of Muscari armeniacum *and aubrieta.*

BELOW Narcissus *'Suzy' and* Muscari armeniacum *are in flower; the tulips will bloom later on.*

LEFT A fine formal spring bedding display, with Fritillaria imperialis *'Lutea' towering above the* daffodils and densely planted Anemone blanda.

ABOVE LEFT This vibrant layered effect is made using a foreground planting of muscari, backed with Tulipa greigii *'Toronto'.*

ABOVE RIGHT The dazzling colour of Tulipa *'Orange Wonder' stands out well against the stiff variegated foliage of the irises.*

Fritillaria imperialis (crown imperial) is a truly eye-catching plant for the spring border. When planted in a group with herbaceous plants, it bursts into colour long before its neighbours start performing. A tall, dramatic bulb, its stately character demands a prominent position. For the greatest impact, plant a group among a sea of ground cover. A striking display of colours can be achieved using the clear orange-vermilion 'Aurora' and deep blue grape hyacinths.

In addition to the common orange-flowered fritillary, there are other bolder, brighter types. *Fritillaria imperialis* 'Lutea' has startling brilliant yellow bells which stand out best against a dark background planting of evergreen shrubs such as the fragrant yellow *Mahonia × media* 'Charity'. The same fritillary also creates a fine architectural feature growing in front of the broad-leaved evergreen *Viburnum tinus*, although a more gentle use of colour could include the soft, silvery green of rosemary.

Fritillaria persica 'Adiyaman' is much less vibrant than its imperial relative. An elegant plant, it has spires of rich, dark, plum-coloured blossoms and handsome blue-green foliage. It is ideal for poolside planting, with its image reflected in the water. In such situations, it can be planted among the ground-hugging foliage of *Ajuga reptans* 'Atropurpurea', 'Multicolor' or 'Burgundy Glow', all of which have colourful leaves. *F. p.* 'Adiyaman' is also useful for informal borders grown among silver-leaved plants like *Stachys lanata* and

Artemisia schmidtiana. *Allium oreophilum* provides another good partnership, with the dark purple fritillary bells silhouetted against the deep rose pink umbels of the allium, but the almost black fritillary flowers are best appreciated when mixed with yellow. To create this effect, plant a few of the bulbs behind a cloud of primrose yellow *Cytisus × kewensis* (broom).

There is nothing more lovely than leucojums, or snowflakes, as they are commonly known, to brighten up a damp, gloomy border. *Leucojum aestivum* is one of the best varieties to use, with its slender stems and nodding white, green-tipped bells. Like *Fritillaria persica* 'Adiyaman', it looks spectacular when gracefully overhanging the edge of a pool, and the two can be mixed together, with a foreplanting of *Fritillaria meleagris* (snake's head fritillary). For shady borders with rich soil, the various *Erythronium* (dog's-tooth violet) thrive. The creamy 'Pagoda' and icy white 'White Beauty' are good choices, and 'White Beauty' has splendid dark green, marked foliage that mixes well with Solomon's seal (*Polygonatum multiflorum*).

If daffodils mark the beginning of spring, then tulips bring the season to an end. The Single and Double hybrids make good edging plants in formal borders and, being so elegant, they look excellent in front of low-growing, spreading plants, adding height and form. For a more informal planting, Rembrandt tulips are very colourful, along with smaller red or pink types such as *T. linifolia* and *T. greigii* 'Toronto'.

Bulbs for naturalizing

There is nothing finer than a grassy sward covered with narcissi and crocuses, or a shady, woodland site carpeted with snowdrops and winter aconites. No matter how small your garden, it is well worth devoting at least a part of it to naturalized spring-flowering bulbs.

Although it is perfectly possible to naturalize bulbs in an unkempt grassy corner, they are much better planted in specially prepared areas which have been sown with fine grass. Choose an informal part of the garden for the bulbs must be allowed to die back naturally every year before the surrounding overgrown grass can be cut.

Crocuses are one of the first bulbs to provide spring colour, and the great advantage of naturalized crocuses is that their foliage can be mown as little as six weeks after flowering, making them good for high profile plantings. Single colours can be used, but a more exciting feature can be made by mixing yellow, purple and white types with striped blooms. *Crocus vernus* is one of the best and is often sold in mixed colours; grown with the large, deep golden-yellow *C. flavus* hybrid 'Dutch Yellow' (also known as 'Yellow Giant' and 'Yellow Mammoth), it makes a very colourful scene. Also for grassy areas, *C. tommasinianus* naturalizes well, particularly the deep purple 'Ruby Giant' and the purple and white 'Pictus', both of which can be mixed with snowdrops. One of the most graceful of all bulbs is *Anemone blanda.* If left undisturbed it will naturalize into extensive patches and, being partially shade-tolerant, it is useful for planting under trees and shrubs. It is low-growing, with delicate, dissected leaves, and the daisy-like flowers open wide in the sun to display yellow centres. There are various colours to choose from including dark blue, pink, magenta and white; the paler forms are good for underplanting brightly coloured bulbs such as daffodils. Alternatively, plant a mixed selection to create a multi-coloured sheet of flowers.

LEFT A striking effect is achieved in this lightly wooded area by allowing a variety of different-coloured spring bulbs to naturalize and spread into patches at will. The selection includes pale and dark mauve anemones, snowdrops and daffodils. The mingling of Anemone blanda *and daffodils (INSET TOP) provides a delightful contrast in height as well as colour but, for a single-colour impact planting, crocuses can be used as seen here (INSET BOTTOM) growing in the soil around the base of a tree.*

Galanthus nivalis is a good snowdrop for naturalizing, especially the double form 'Flore Pleno', with its frilly head of acid-green and white petals. The larger-flowered *G. elwesii* is also suitable and left to grow undisturbed will form a dense, ivory white carpet, but it will also mix happily with most other spring bulbs. In the light shade of a tree canopy, snowdrops and winter aconites (*Eranthis*) will thrive, and a few small-leaved ivies creeping in between will create a woodland effect. Bluebells enjoy similar wooded situations and also thrive in deep shade, useful for bringing colour and interest to otherwise dull, dark areas. The English bluebell (*Hyacinthoides non-scripta*) is available in white- and pink-flowered forms as well as the familiar blue. It is the best for naturalizing in large areas as it is so invasive, whereas the smaller Spanish bluebell (*H.*

hispanica) does not spread as much and is suitable for localized areas beneath shrubs.

The narcissus is another favourite bulb for naturalizing, either planted on its own or with a selection of other bulbs in an orchard or meadow. As well as being naturalized in grass, these bulbs can also be colonized in the soil around the base of specimen trees like the chalky white-stemmed birch, *Betula jacquemontii*, and the polished, mahogany-like *Prunus serrula*. Because of their bright colours daffodils are also ideal for growing with rhododendrons and other evergreens like Leyland cypress and yew.

BELOW LEFT Clumps of snowdrops such as these will rapidly grow into extensive patches.

BELOW BOTTOM Double daffodils contrast well with the simpler flowers of Scilla siberica.

There is an overwhelming selection of narcissi to choose from. Some of the best are *Narcissus pseudonarcissus*, *N. obvallaris* (Tenby daffodil) and *N. poeticus* (poet's narcissus or pheasant's eye). Recommended large-flowering cultivars include the lovely sulphurous yellow 'Spellbinder', the golden-yellow 'Carlton' and 'Golden Harvest'. The popular yellow and white 'February Silver' is one of the Cyclamineus narcissi hybrids. These have narrow, pointed, reflexed petals, and are excellent for small areas of grass; they are also weather resistant. 'March Sunshine', Peeping Tom' and 'Charity May' are top of the range, and 'Satellite' makes a colourful

impact with its bright orange trumpets. All of these narcissi flower at much the same time and increase year by year provided their foliage is allowed to die back naturally. In fairly damp ground, hoop-petticoat daffodils, snowflakes and snake's head fritillaries can be planted together for a lovely tapestry of colour.

Although a less familiar sight, scillas will happily naturalize in grass, *Scilla bithynica*, *S. siberica* and its white form 'Alba' being the most reliable. Resembling dwarf bluebells but flowering much earlier on in the season, they produce a delicate spreading carpet of blue or white. If planted in soil with a suitable grass sown over the top, they are likely to seed freely, although the pale porcelain blue *S. mischtschenkoana* prefers to colonize open soil unless naturalized in very fine-leaved grass.

BELOW In this natural-looking planting snowdrops grow among ivy and hellebore foliage.

RIGHT This pink rhododendron provides a vivid companion for the Spanish bluebells beneath.

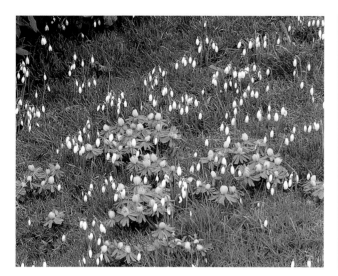

Tulips are not usually associated with naturalized bulbs but the early-flowering *Tulipa kaufmanniana* and its cultivars will colonize grass in much the same way as narcissi. The only disadvantage is that their broad, fleshy leaves smother the grass beneath if the bulbs are planted too close together.

One of the most attractive ways of displaying a collection of naturalized bulbs is in an alpine meadow. Although not naturally occurring in the garden, it is easy to recreate the right conditions. Start the meadow off from scratch: cultivate but do not fertilize an area of soil, plant the bulbs and sow a variety of fine-leaved grass seed over the top. Since typical alpine meadows are fairly damp in spring, incorporate some moisture-retaining organic matter into the dry soil before planting the bulbs. The spring-flowering meadow will be a star feature for approximately six weeks, followed by two months or so of somewhat unruly vegetation and grass for the rest of the year. However, the bulbs can be supplemented with other flowering plants for summer and autumn colour.

ABOVE LEFT A characteristic and delightful spring planting of snowdrops and winter aconites.

ABOVE RIGHT Crocus tommasinianus *is a robust bulb despite its delicate appearance.*

BELOW Though sparsely planted, these tulips lend both colour and form to a grassy area.

RIGHT Scilla bithynica *is often used as ground cover, as seen here in this woodland glade.*

Narcissus bulbocodium conspicuus (hoop-petticoat daffodil) can be planted liberally through the alpine area for a brightly coloured show. Left undisturbed it will form large clusters and clumps. *Fritillaria meleagris*, with its purple or white, pendent, chequered flowers is much more subtle and delicate-looking than the daffodil. It also enjoys alpine meadow conditions, especially rather wet ones; plant a large quantity for the best effect, mixing them with the hoop-petticoat daffodils. Species crocuses and their cultivars will enhance such an area in early spring. Look for the cultivars of the pretty bunch-flowering *Crocus chrysanthus* like 'Cream Beauty', 'Blue Pearl' and 'Zwanenburg Bronze'. *Crocus ancyrensis* 'Golden Bunch' is another possibility, and this crocus will spread quite rapidly to form a dashing golden carpet during early spring, attracting the first of the spring bees and other pollinating insects.

Another exciting feature to establish using naturalized bulbs is a wildlife garden. *Leucojum aestivum* is a native wild plant that enjoys garden conditions along with *Fritillaria meleagris*, and the small-flowering *Allium neapolitanum* is also useful. However, the majority of native bulbs do not require such rich conditions. Instead, use varieties of bulbs that respond well to garden conditions but which look like their wild relatives; for example, plant the wood anemone, *Anemone blanda* 'White Splendour' instead of its native cousin *A. nemorosa* and *Hyancinthoides hispanica* rather than *H. non-scripta*.

FAR LEFT Anemone blanda *comes in a variety of flower colours, from white to deep blue.*

BELOW LEFT A pretty mixture of wild primroses and Cyclamen repandum *for a grassy patch.*

ABOVE The snake's head fritillary, Fritillaria meleagris, *will grow happily in damp meadow conditions.*

BELOW RIGHT Narcissus cyclamineus *is quite at home growing with crocuses.*

Bulbs for bedding displays

Bulbs make excellent spring bedding subjects, massed together on their own or used in association with other spring-flowering plants. With careful selection, colours, heights and flowering can all be co-ordinated for a stunning display.

Hyacinths are among the most useful spring bedding bulbs because of their short, stiff stems. Available in a multitude of colours, the flowers have one of the richest perfumes in the garden and their scent will linger in the air. Arrange the bedding hyacinths in square or rectangular blocks of colour as they are not good for detailed patterns, or use them as dot plants among other bedding plants like polyanthus. The choice of bedding varieties is wide, but the pure white 'Carnegie', the blue 'King of the Blues', the rose pink 'Lady Derby' and the lilac-violet 'Amethyst' are all reliable and tend to flower simultaneously; 'Carnegie' is especially lovely grown beside the primrose yellow 'City of Harleem'.

One of the most striking formal arrangements involves creating a small chequerboard using the pure white 'L'Innocence' and 'Violet Pearl'. Both are of similar height and flower together, as do the later-flowering 'Carnegie' and 'Queen of the Violets'. Hyacinths also look good against dark cultivated soil. For a variation on the theme of bedding, plant them well spaced out rather than close together, so each individual flower stem can be seen. Nothing looks finer than a neat lawn surrounding a bed of widely spaced hyacinths, with a border of dark soil between the bulbs and the grass.

Tulips make equally successful bedding plants, and there is a type of tulip for every colour scheme. *Tulipa kaufmanniana* and its hybrids bloom early on in spring. The lovely red and yellow 'Stresa', the sulphur yellow 'Gluck' and the scarlet 'Brilliant Star' can be grown with the carmine and yellow 'Edwin Fischer', and 'Stresa' makes a dazzling display with rich red polyanthus. Plant a single-colour batch of polyanthus first, and interplant these with a contrasting variety of tulip. 'Heart's Delight' has deep red flowers edged with the palest pink which look stunning interplanted with white 'Crescendo' polyanthus or pink and white double daisies. The pure white tulip 'The First' and blue winter-flowering pansies go well together; a bold blue edging of pansies with a solid centre of white tulips is a sensational sight. The taller, more elegant, later-blooming tulips such as Triumph or Lily-flowering have

LEFT For a traditional bedding display, tulips are planted among forget-me-nots.

TOP RIGHT Any colour of tulip looks well with forget-me-nots. Here, 'Prinses Irene' is used.

MIDDLE RIGHT The pink 'Chestnut Flower' and blue 'Dreadnought' hyacinths make a fragrant show.

BOTTOM RIGHT Primulas can also be planted with hyacinths to create a formal display.

beautifully sculptured flowers and, with Mendel, Single early and Darwin hybrids, are best planted among other spring-flowering subjects with a strong basal colour.

The hybrids of *Tulipa greigii* and *T. fosteriana* are extremely useful for narrow beds where taller-growing varieties are inappropriate. Being much shorter, they are also ideal for exposed positions, but the leaves are rather large so the plants should be well spaced. By mingling them with a boisterous cluster of hybrid polyanthus, they will form a tough, resilient display that can withstand everything from hailstones to gales. The purple and brown splashed and striped leaves of the cultivars derived from *T. greigii* are an added attraction, providing a strong foil for white- or blue-flowered winter pansies at the beginning of the season, before the tulips bloom.

Forget-me-nots (*Myosotis*) have traditionally been used as a base for bedding displays, creating a misty, azure haze through which tulips can be grown. In a formal corner, these schemes are very eye-catching. Try *Myosotis* 'Royal Blue' and the tulip 'White Triumphator' or *M.* 'Blue Ball' and the 'West Point' tulip. Double daisies (*Bellis perennis*) are equally good as companion plants and, when designing a small cottage-garden bed or border with loose, informal plantings, *Bellis perennis* 'Alba Plena' and 'Stafford Pink' make an excellent chorus for the crumpled and ruffled blossoms of the Parrot tulips, especially 'Blue Parrot' or 'Apricot Parrot'. Fringed tulips also work well in bedding schemes with double daisies: try the violet-purple 'Blue Heron', the wine-red 'Burgundy Lace' and the icing-sugar pink 'Bellflower'.

The majority of narcissi are unsuitable for bedding displays, but the versatile shorter-growing *Narcissus cyclamineus* cultivars can be used to provide splashes of bright colour, and once the display is over, the bulbs can be planted in a grassy corner and allowed to naturalize. 'March Sunshine', 'February Gold' and the ivory white 'Jenny' can be bedded out with grape hyacinth, and the very special *Narcissus cyclamineus* 'Foundling', a white dwarf daffodil with deep rose pink cups, makes an excellent dot plant among a bed of forget-me-nots. The multi-headed 'Tête-à-Tête' is a marvellous plant to grow in a solid planting with *Muscari armeniacum* 'Blue Spike'.

BELOW In order to create a light and airy effect, tulips are planted among pale pansies.

RIGHT Tulips, daffodils and Fritillaria imperialis can be seen growing in this rockery.

Bulbs for the rock garden

There are plenty of dwarf, spring-flowering bulbs that enjoy the free-draining conditions of the rock garden. They can be used to fill pockets with startling colour for highlight planting, or a collection can be grown together, with summer- and autumn-flowering alpines to fill unsightly gaps and hide the dying foliage of the bulbs after flowering.

Narcissi make lovely rock garden subjects, and the sheltered conditions offer an ideal opportunity to grow some of the smaller species. *Narcissus asturiensis* is the tiniest of the trumpet daffodils, worth growing in a large clump as a specimen display, and the multi-flowering dwarf *N. canaliculatus*, with its pure white petals, bright yellow trumpets and pleasing fragrance, reproduces freely. The latter should be planted in an isolated position because it will not tolerate any companion plant other than a dwarf shrub or conifer like *Chamaecyparis lawsoniana* 'Minima Glauca' and 'Ellwoodii', or *Cryptomeria japonica* 'Vilmoriniana'.

Narcissus cyclamineus is always popular; it is easy to grow and attractive, with narrow, grassy foliage and charming, swept-back, bright yellow petals and projecting trumpet. Rarely attaining more than 10in (25cm) high, it is perfect for planting next to close-growing carpeting plants like the pink-flowered *Thymus serpyllum* and the red and white cultivars, which will burst into flower just as the narcissi leaves are disappearing. Also worth considering are the downy leaved

T. lanuginosus and the tiny *T.* 'Minimus'. The narcissi will also happily grow with the low-growing arenarias like *Arenaria caespitosa* and the golden *A. c.* 'Aurea'.

Although their natural habitat is an open woodland glade, snowdrops and winter aconites will tolerate a sunny spot in the rock garden if plenty of organic matter is mixed into the compost. Plant a few dwarf azaleas or small rhododendrons first, and then insert some snowdrops and winter aconites into the soil at the base of the plants. The effect of pristine white snowdrops or glowing yellow aconites peeping from among the branches is delightful. Also enjoying shady conditions, cyclamens add colour and interest to the rock garden.

Crocuses provide a long-lasting, colourful display in the rock garden. Try any of the *chrysanthus, biflorus* and *sieberi* varieties. Dwarf irises also look very attractive among rocky outcrops; plant a group of the pale blue *Iris reticulata* 'Cantab' or the rich blue *I. r.* 'Joyce' next to a patch of *Crocus chrysanthus* 'Cream Beauty'. However, for a touch of stark simplicity, try 'Cantab' or the plum-coloured 'J.S. Dijt' in a drift on its own. The purplish-violet *I. histrioides* 'Major' makes a colourful contribution; flowering before its foliage develops, it often appears while snow is still on the ground. The foliage tends to swamp any nearby carpeting plants, so the bulbs should be planted at the edge of the rock garden. Also for the lower areas of the rockery, *Ipheion uniflorum*, with its soft blue flowers, grows well given free-draining, sunny conditions.

Containers, window boxes and hanging baskets

There are many excellent opportunities for growing spring-flowering bulbs in window boxes and containers. Concentrate on those that yield an instant display, like narcissi, tulips and crocuses, or purchase hyacinth that are on the point of flowering. Bulbs like snowdrops or winter aconites should not be used, however, because they will not give a worthwhile display until the second or third year.

For the widest range of colour and interest, nothing surpasses the tulip. The taller kinds are best avoided as they may blow over, but all the other types will thrive in the free-draining conditions of containers and window boxes.

The most useful is the early-flowering *Tulipa kaufmanniana* (waterlily tulip), a stocky plant that is well able to cope with spring gales and even scatterings

ABOVE In a simple wooden container, vivid blue muscari supplies additional interest at the base of the orange Fritillaria imperialis.

ABOVE Single container plantings can be very effective. Here, pots of muscari and hyacinths are displayed with a bowl of pansies.

of snow. The ordinary species is compact, rarely more than 8in (20cm) tall, with cream or pale yellow, pointed blossoms, flushed red, opening out into a dazzling display. The leaves are stiff and formal, giving the plant an architectural appearance. For a mixed window box, plant them through the ivy *Hedera helix* 'Anne Marie', with a foreplanting of *Crocus ancyrensis*. There are a number of hybrids between this tulip and *T. greigii* which make an even more startling show; the multi-flowered 'Toronto' is pinkish-red, 'Shakespeare' is carmine-orange and yellow, 'Berlioz' yellow, 'Stresa' red and yellow, and the ever popular 'Red Riding Hood' is a good red. *T. greigii* and its many varieties have distinctive purplish striped foliage but, since they differ slightly in height and flowering period, it is unwise to mix them together.

Tulipa clusiana is another exciting choice, with white pink-flushed blossoms carried in profusion among crowds of grey-green, rush-like foliage. Like most tulips, it is best seen alone, although it can be mixed effectively with pastel shades of *Aubrieta* tumbling over the edge of the box. The curious-looking *T. acuminata*, with its long, thin, vertical yellow and red petals, is another first-rate choice, especially for gardens with an old-fashioned atmosphere but, for a

less flamboyant choice, select a tulip like the soft yellow *T. batalinii*. The apricot 'Bronze Charm' is enormously popular and, if planted in full sun, will produce a reliable and colourful show. It associates well with hummock-forming plants such as *Armeria maritima* (pink thrift).

Most other tulips only give a short display but they still present a marvellous, if temporary, spectacle. Of the conventional kinds, choose the Lily-flowered cultivars. With their beautifully sculptured blossoms and long straight stems,

they are the aristocrats of the genus. In a round, wooden tub, a bold planting of a single variety, surrounded by single-colour polyanthus, creates a splendid feature. If grown in window boxes, however, the tulips are best planted alone due to lack of root space.

For container planting, hyacinths excel above all other bulbs: not only are they available in an incredible range of colours, but they are wonderfully fragrant. In addition to conventional large-flowered cultivars, the multiflora kinds are well worth considering; try a mixed planting of blue hyacinth 'Bismarck' and blue or yellow pansies, or the pink hyacinth 'Lady Derby' and white pansies. Clumps of polyanthus can also be added, along with a few clumps of narcissi for a multicoloured display.

RIGHT Tulips and hyacinths are planted in plain flower pots and these are placed in attractive glazed containers so they do not show.

BELOW The glowing colours of these narcissi, tulips, pansies and hyacinths are set off beautifully by the terracotta containers.

Narcissus cyclamineus hybrids such as 'Jenny' and 'Peeping Tom' are ideal for container planting as they can cope with adverse weather conditions, an important consideration for window boxes on high, exposed walls. For a bright display of contrasting colours, plant the daffodils among clusters of red polyanthus. Sweetly scented single jonquils or jonquil hybrids, like the red and yellow 'Suzy' or the ivory white and pink-cupped 'Waterperry', make a wonderful, fragrant show, especially when massed together, and the *Narcissus triandrus* hybrids are equally lovely, enjoying the free-draining conditions provided by large containers. 'Thalia' is a very good white variety; planted alone in solid blocks or interspersed with the velvety blue or golden yellow winter-flowering pansies, it is quite spectacular. Another delight is the lemon-flowered narcissus cultivar 'Liberty Bells'.

All the narcissi look good with foliage, especially variegated ivy, because the foliage complements their simple flower heads. More substantial companion plants, however, include small conifers

ABOVE The bright scarlet-orange of Tulipa *'Aladdin' creates a flamboyant splash of colour in these plain clay pots.*

or evergreen shrubs such as *Rhododendron* 'Blue Tit' or 'Blue Diamond' and *Sarcococca confusa*. These can be treated as permanent plants, whereas the daffodils will have to be replaced once flowering is over.

For a colourful mixed planting providing early spring interest, crocuses cannot be bettered. Do not make them too much of a feature, however, because the blooms only last a short time. Simply push the corms into the compost among narcissi, polyanthus, pansies or double daisies and leave them to grow. By distributing them evenly among companion plants the problem of their unsightly, fading foliage and dead flowerheads can be minimized.

Of all the spring-flowering bulbs, few surpass the fritillaries. *Fritillaria meleagris*, the common snake's head fritillary, is one of the most attractive. It has nodding flowers, held on upright leafy stems, and is available in white and various shades of pink and purple. Requiring free-draining soil and full sun or partial shade, the snake's head fritillary is a good window-box subject because its beauty can be enjoyed at eye-level or below.

While relatively few bulbs can be used successfully in hanging baskets, those that are suitable for this type of

ABOVE The spring-flowering ranunculus and multiflora hyacinths here provide cool white container plantings.

container will provide a spectacular show. The scillas are a prime example, but they look best mixed with other spring-flowering subjects. *Scilla siberica* and 'Spring Beauty' look especially fine when contrasted with a blue or white strain of Universal pansy. The smaller narcissi are also very amenable to hanging basket cultivation. The sweet-smelling *Narcissi canaliculatus* and the true *N. cyclamineus* look lovely tucked in among shorter growing winter heathers or creeping variegated ivy, and *N.* 'Tête-à-Tête' makes a fine show grown as a centrepiece in a hanging basket full of plain green ivy like.

LEFT The red ranunculus provides a splash of colour in this cool-looking display of Hyacinthus *'Ostara', muscari and ivy.*

ABOVE This attractive planting consists of narcissi and trailing ivy in a simple wire basket which has been covered with moss.

Indoor bulbs

Provided they are kept as cool as possible, most popular outdoor bulbs can be grown indoors, especially hyacinths. For a really early display, plant the multiflora *H.* 'Borah'. Available in white, blue and pink, it resembles a dwarf bluebell. Good container companions include *Selaginella martensii* and *S. helvetica*, soft, green, fern-like plants. The larger hyacinth cultivars such as 'Delft Blue' and the primrose yellow 'City of Haarlem' can be grown in bowls, top-dressed with green sphagnum moss. The double-flowered hyacinths, which tend to look a little stiff and unyielding in the garden, are most rewarding indoors; one of the loveliest is the deep red, richly scented 'Hollyhock'.

BELOW Inspired use of wood makes a spectacular centrepiece, with narcissi, lily-of-the-valley and Tulipa *'White Dream'.*

ABOVE Hyacinths will grow quite happily in a glass container filled with water, provided it is deep enough to allow the roots to develop.

A good reason for growing tiny Jonquil narcissi inside is their sweet perfume. Both 'Trevithian' and 'Sweetness' are delightful, with pale yellow blossoms. For a small container, try the lemon and white 'Pipet', top-dressed with green sphagnum moss. Generally too tender for life outdoors, the beautiful Tazetta narcissi are also excellent for indoor displays. 'Cheerfulness', with its highly fragrant, creamy white, double flowers, will blossom in the early part of the season. The equally fragrant 'Yellow Cheerfulness' and the orange-cupped 'Soleil d'Or' are also highly recommended.

Tulips can also be grown indoors, and what they lack in fragrance, they make up for in colour. *Tulipa kaufmanniana*, *T. greigii, T. fosteriana* and their popular cultivars are all suitable; for the greatest impact, restrict each container to a single colour. A reliable show is easy to achieve using *T. praestans* or one of its cultivars like 'Fusilier'. These stately, multi-flowered subjects have fine green leaves and upright heads of bright red blossoms, three or four per stem. Unless the temperature is very high, they will last for several days.

There are many dwarf plants which adapt well to indoor cultivation. Grow a single variety per container; mixed

displays will look messy and unruly because each bulb will flower at a different time. The dwarf scillas, known as spring squills, are among the most adaptable, especially the bright blue *Scilla siberica* 'Spring Beauty'. Keep scillas as cool as possible until the flowers start to show colour, then bring them into the house for flowering. Once inside, they should be kept in a cool room to prolong their flowering period. Chionodioxas and puschkinias can also be grown indoors. Like the scillas, they perform best and last longer in cool rooms.

ABOVE If using a wicker basket for planting bulbs it must be lined with plastic before being planted. This basket is filled with muscari.

RIGHT This metal bucket is an unusual but attractive container for a planting of blue hyacinths, seen here in full flower. The decorative twigs add to this striking display.

BELOW This informal-looking arrangement consists of fragrant narcissi and ivy in a simple moss-lined metal basket, with catkin twigs added at random as ornament.

Cut flowers

Provided they have a long enough stem, the majority of spring-flowering bulbs will last well in water. However, the main problem with growing the bulbs for cutting is that the plants are vulnerable to damage from strong winds and hail stones. Even a little warmth, shelter and protection from an unheated greenhouse will radically improve the flower quality.

Daffodils yield first-rate cut flowers, despite the sticky slime which drips out of their stems. This substance can kill other flowers in the same vase, but its

ABOVE Here, Tulipa *'Snowflake', ranunculus,* Hyacinthus *'Carnegie' and lily-of-the-valley are combined with mixed fruit.*

effects can be minimized if the daffodils are stood in water for 24 hours, the stems washed, and a drop of bleach added to fresh water.

Narcissi are best massed together either in single colours or mixed bunches, and placed on a sunny windowsill. The Split corona or Orchid-flowered daffodils are easy to grow and some of the best for cutting. 'Cassata' is a widely grown white kind with a yellow split corona, and 'Baccarat' is yellow, with an orange-red, segmented corona, but both of these narcissi should be grown in the protection of an unheated

ABOVE This informal arrangement of vivid ranunculus is enhanced by the bold colour and design of this striking vase.

LEFT Narcissi are tightly bunched together, tied with garden string and placed in a modern glass vase in this unusual display.

conservatory or greenhouse because their flower heads drop during adverse weather. The Small-cupped daffodils also provide good quality blossoms. 'Barrett Browning', with distinctive orange-red cups, is pleasing both indoors and growing outside, but it must have a little protection or its pristine white petals will turn brown in wet weather. This also applies to the yellow and orange 'Birma', as well as Large-cupped kinds such as the pink 'Mrs R.O. Backhouse' and the pure white, pale lemon-cupped 'Ice Follies'. Some of the best Large-cupped cultivars for cut flowers are the bright

red, edged with yellow, and 'White Triumphator' is snowy white. For something more unusual, however, the Viridiflora types are a real delight for flower arrangers, although they are difficult to place in the garden. They have strange, often feathered, blossoms with green stripes or bands; for example, 'Greenland' is pink with prominent green markings, 'Spring Green' is greenish-cream and 'Esperanto' is more of an oddity, with pink and green shaded flowers and white-margined leaves. All look splendid in a vase on their own, with their unusual blossoms on show.

For smaller displays, florist's anemones are useful at this time of the year, particularly the St Brigid and De Caen strains. A bunch of reds, purples and blues makes a magnificent show. For a mixed posy, place a few snowdrops and hardy cyclamens in a glass with some primroses and ivy leaves. Grape hyacinths can be added, but they will only last a few days in water.

Among the many snowdrop varieties are two large-flowered types: *Galanthus elwesii* and *G.* 'Sam Arnott'. Both are particularly useful for cutting, and 'Sam Arnott' continues to flower late in the snowdrop season. Similar in general appearance to the snowdrops, but with larger flowers consisting of six petals, leucojums (snowflakes) are also good for indoor flower arrangements. Both snowdrops and leucojums look best displayed in plain or coloured glass containers.

For fragrance, hyacinths can be used for indoor displays. If growing the bulbs outdoors for cutting, plant large clumps so the cut flower spikes will not ruin the overall display. It is also possible to cut the flower spikes of forced hyacinth bulbs when the flowers are nearing their end; they will last longer in water.

yellow 'Carlton', 'Golden Harvest', 'Dutch Master', 'Spellbinder' and 'Mount Hood'.

Tulips can either be used to add colour and form in a mixed display, or a few stems can be placed in a vase on their own. Any of the May-flowering hybrids are ideal; 'Golden Harvest' and the silky, salmon pink 'Clara Butt' are both good choices but, for something extra special, try 'Queen of Night', with its velvety, deep maroon flowers. They look spectacular on their own, but the purple-maroon cups also stand out well when mixed with creamy-coloured flowers. 'Sorbet' is one of the best pink-flushed hybrids and, for more of an impact, the red 'Halcro', with its distinctive orange-red edges, is hard to beat. Among the Darwin hybrids, the yellow 'Gudoshnik' and the carmine-red 'Holland's Glorie' both last well in water.

A little later on, Lily-flowered tulips are ready for cutting. 'Aladdin' is scarlet

ABOVE Here, flowering narcissi bulbs are mixed with violets, twigs, candles and an old bird's nest.

BELOW An impression of warm opulence is created by this display of white ranunculus, scarlet-orange tulips and mixed narcissi.

ALLIUM
Ornamental onion

There are many attractive and unusual alliums besides the better known edible species – onions, garlic, chives, shallots and leeks – that flower in spring. They are mostly easy to cultivate and all are hardy, although some of the earlier ones die down over the summer and require a fairly dry position during their dormant period.

Alliums are a distinctive group of bulbs because they produce small, star- or bell-shaped flowers held in spherical or hemi-spherical heads, known as umbels, and they give off an unmistakable smell of onions when cut or bruised. The following species bloom in late spring and are fairly short, less than 12in (30cm) tall when flowering, suitable for the front of a border or rock garden where they can be left undisturbed to form clumps. Since the many species and varieties flower at different times, others are listed in the Summer and Autumn Directories (see pages 150 and 203). Propagation is by offsets which, in some species, are produced quite freely, or by seed, which may take up to three years to produce flowering bulbs. Hardiness zones: 6-8.

A. karataviense (*below*)
This striking plant has attractive, broad, greyish-purple leaves at ground level which spread 8-10in (20-25cm). In late spring, stout, 6in (15cm) high stems carry large umbels made up of many small, pale pink flowers. It is best in a prominent, sunny position and needs good drainage.

A. neapolitanum
This Mediterranean species requires a warm, sunny spot. In mid-spring, its wiry, 8-12in (20-30cm) tall stems bear loosely flowering umbels of small, brilliant white flowers.

A. oreophilum 'Zwanenburg'
This is a good dwarf species suitable for a rock garden, trough or alpine house, requiring sun and good drainage. It has narrow, greyish leaves and 2-6in (5-15cm) high stems which carry large, carmine red flowers in umbels 1½-2¼in (4-6cm) wide.

A. triquetrum (*above*)
This allium is best used for naturalizing in a wild part of the garden, or under trees and shrubs where it can be left to seed and increase at will. An attractive species, it stands about 4-8in (10-20cm) high, with channelled, pale green leaves, and umbels that bear only a few pendent, bell-shaped, white flowers in mid-spring; these have a green stripe on each petal.

A. unifolium (*above*)
Usually sold under the name *A. murrayanum*, this American species produces large, almost flat, pink flowers in mid-spring. The loose umbels grow on 6-12in (15-30cm) high stems above the narrow leaves.

ANEMONE
Windflower

Among the most colourful spring-flowering bulbs, anemones are available in white and shades of red, blue, pink and purple. Although they are unrelated to most other bulbous plants, they do have tuberous rootstocks and are usually obtainable through bulb nurseries. The showy, often many-petalled flowers of the St Brigid types are well-known for their long-lived cut flowers, while the hardier *A. blanda* and *A. apennina* are good rock garden plants. Propagation is by division in autumn. Hardiness zones: 5-8.

A. apennina
This is an excellent plant for semi-shaded areas beneath deciduous shrubs where, when well-suited, it increases into patches. The dissected leaves are topped in mid-spring by 1-1½in (2.5-4cm) diameter blue flowers with up to 20 petals. The stems grow about 6in (15cm) high, and may spread into clumps up to 12in (30cm) or more across. The pure white form is known as 'Alba'.

A. blanda
Like *A. apennina*, this anemone tolerates partial shade and full sun, growing well in a rock garden or when left undisturbed at the front of a border of perennials. Its many-petalled, blue flowers are produced in early spring on 2-4in (5-10cm) long stems, above fern-like, divided leaves. 'Atrocaerulea' (*above*) has deep blue flowers; 'White Splendour' is a good white form; 'Charmer' has soft pink blooms; and 'Radar' has very showy, vibrant, magenta-coloured flowers. Cheaper mixed collections are available, although plantings of one colour tend to look best.

A. coronaria
This is the original species from which the St Brigid and De Caen florists' types have been raised by selection. The hard, knobbly tubers can be planted at almost any time of the year, and may perform better if first soaked in water overnight. Those planted in autumn should flower in early to mid-spring, but they require a sheltered, sunny position and

benefit from being covered with a cloche in cold weather. Subsequent plantings will flower in late spring or summer. The plants grow to a height of about 6-10in (15-25cm) and have leaves like parsley. The large, almost flat flowers in blue, white, red or violet have zones of paler colours and an eye of dark stamens. The St Brigid varieties have a semi-double layer of petals and De Caen are singles. Each plant has a spread of 4in (10cm).

A. pavonina (*above*)

This anemone is similar to *A. coronaria* but has less finely divided leaves; cultivation requirements are the same. It is best known in the large-flowered selections of St Bavo strain; these come in a wide colour range and make as good cut flowers as the St Brigids.

ARISARUM

A relative of the arum, this strange little tuberous-rooted plant is grown for pure curiosity, although the carpet of arrow-shaped, rich green leaves, resembling those of the arum, have some value as ground cover. Propagation is by division in early autumn. Hardiness zone: 7.

A. proboscideum (*above*)

Mouse plant

In mid-spring, small, chocolate-coloured spathes with 6in (15cm) long, tail-like

appendages appear amid the leaves, giving the appearance of a mouse diving for cover, hence the common name. *A. proboscideum* is only 2-4in (5-10cm) high, but can spread by tuber division into patches over 12in (30cm) across. It grows best in a semi-shaded spot in humus-rich soil.

ARUM

Lords and ladies or cuckoo pint

A large and interesting group of tuberous-rooted plants, arums are characterized by having many tiny flowers which are clustered together and enclosed within a hooded or sail-like spathe, on a pencil-shaped spadix; the leaves are often arrow-shaped. The arum lily, *Zantedeschia*, is probably the best-known to gardeners, but there are several other hardy species well worth planting for a touch of the unusual.

A few of these lords and ladies are worth considering for the spring garden and, in some cases, the foliage is a note-worthy ornamental feature. Those mentioned below die down over summer, although some have spikes of berries that ripen to a bright red in autumn. Propagation is by removal of offsets in autumn. Hardiness zones: 6-8.

A. creticum (*above*)

This unusual species is one of the showier arums. It has a bottle-shaped, yellow spathe, the upper part being twisted and reflexed leaving a projecting, yellow spadix. It appears in mid-spring, accompanied by deep green, arrow-shaped leaves. *A. creticum* reaches 12-16in (30-40cm) in height, and slowly increases into a compact clump about 12in (30cm) in diameter.

A. dioscoridis (*next column*)

Being Mediterranean in origin, this dramatic plant needs a warm, sunny position. It grows 12-16in (30-40cm) high and has the usual

arrow-like leaves, but the spathes are either deep velvety-purple or pale green, with striking blackish-purple blotches. Unfortunately, this arum gives off a rather unpleasant smell.

A. italicum

The main value of this hardy species lies in its highly ornamental autumn foliage retained throughout the winter (see page 226) into spring. The leaves are arrow-shaped and shiny green, with a marbling of silvery white veins; they are good for flower arrangements. *A. italicum* grows well in semi-shade, but is less likely to flower than if planted in the sun. In a warm position, it may produce pale greenish spathes in spring, followed by showy red berries in autumn. 'Pictum' (*below*), sometimes known as 'Marmoratum', has particularly fine foliage.

BULBOCODIUM

A small, seldom-seen bulb, *Bulbocodium* is related to *Colchicum* (see page 203) but flowers in spring. It is probably best grown in an alpine house on account of its small height of under 1½in (4cm), but will grow outside in a sunny, raised bed. Propagation is by division in early autumn. Hardiness zone: 4.

B. vernum

Small corms produce pinkish-purple, funnel-shaped flowers about 1-1½in (2.5-4cm) in diameter. These are almost stemless and are accompanied by short, narrow leaves which later elongate. It is a native of the Pyrenees and Alps.

CHIONODOXA; × CHIONOSCILLA
Glory of the snow

These close relatives of the scillas or squills owe their name to the melting snow patches around which they grow in the mountains. They are very hardy and do well in a semi-shaded or sunny position, provided it does not become too hot and dry in summer. When growing well, they seed freely, giving a valuable early spring display, particularly under deciduous trees and shrubs. Chionodoxas have almost flat, star-shaped flowers held in short racemes less than 6in (15cm) high; these are produced between a pair of narrow leaves which die down soon after flowering and seeding. Propagation is by division in early autumn or by seed in autumn. Hardiness zone: 4.

C. luciliae (*above*)

C. siehei is often sold under this name but the true *C. luciliae* has large, upward-facing, pale lilac-blue flowers, only one or two per stem. *C. l.* 'Alba' is a good pure white form.

C. sardensis

The bluest of the chionodoxas, *C. sardensis* has up to 12 rich, deep blue flowers held in a raceme facing outwards horizontally. Each of the flowers has a very indistinct, almost unnoticeable, white eye.

C. siehei (*next column*)

This is sometimes sold as *C. luciliae* or *C. forbesii*. Probably the best garden plant of all, this species is excellent for naturalizing. It has

one-sided racemes of up to 12 lavender blue flowers, each with a large, white eye in the centre. 'Pink Giant' is a vigorous form with rich pink, white-eyed flowers.

× *Chionoscilla allenii* (*below*)

A hybrid between the cultivated *C. luciliae* and *Scilla bifolia*, this bulb flowers very early on in spring, producing a raceme of deep blue, star-shaped flowers approximately 4-6in (10-15cm) high. Like its parents, it grows well in dappled shade and is suitable for planting beneath deciduous shrubs, or in a cool spot in the rock garden. In the perennial border, it associates well with hellebores, pulmonarias and other shade-loving plants.

CORYDALIS
Spring fumitory

Although some of the tuberous-rooted corydalis have been known for centuries, they have only recently become popular, and the new introductions and selections provide some exciting and unusual subjects for the spring garden. They are low-growing plants no more than 4-6in (10-15cm) high when in flower, and produce spikes of white, purple, pink or red, long-spurred flowers over attractively divided foliage. Cultivation is easy: simply

provide a reasonably well-drained soil in partial shade, where the dormant tubers will not become too hot and dry over summer. They should be planted at a depth of about 1-2in (2.5-5cm) in the autumn, and are ideal for naturalizing under and around shrubs, together with snowdrops, winter aconites and wood anemones. Individual plants may eventually make clumps 6-10in (15-25cm) across. Propagation is by division in early autumn or seed sown in autumn as soon as it is ripe. Hardiness zone: 6.

C. bulbosa (**syn.** *C. cava*)

A common European species, *C. bulbosa* produces purple, two-lipped flowers with long spurs. 'Alba' is an attractive white version, and 'Cedric Morris' has white flowers and dark purple bracts. Unlike *C. solida*, the tubers do not often divide, but seedlings are produced.

C. solida (*above*)

The most commonly seen form of this excellent little spring plant has dull purple, long-spurred flowers, but beautiful pinks and reds are available at the more specialist bulb nurseries. 'George Baker' has rich, glowing red flowers, while 'Beth Evans' comes in clear, pale pink. The small, yellowish tubers increase quite rapidly, usually doubling in number each year, and the established clumps can be lifted and divided in early autumn. Seedlings may also appear and will probably have different coloured flowers.

CROCUS

No other group of bulbs epitomizes the early spring to quite the same extent as the crocus, which produces wineglass-shaped flowers in a great array of sizes and colours from late winter onwards. They are mostly easy to grow and increase quite well when given suitable conditions. All require well-drained soil that dries out to some extent in summer, but they are not fussy about the pH, if anything slightly preferring alkaline soils. Most like open ground, their blooms unfolding wide in the spring sunshine, but they can be equally successful in the light shade of deciduous trees and shrubs. The dormant corms are sold in late summer or early autumn and should be planted about 2in (5cm) deep. A few of the species may seed and spread widely, but most produce compact clumps no more than 2-4in (5-10cm) in diameter, barely reaching 4in (10cm) in height. Propagation is by division in late summer or by seed; seed will take three to four years to produce flowering plants. Hardiness zones: 4-6.

C. ancyrensis (*above*)

The Ankara crocus has small, bright orange flowers in early spring, several per corm produced in succession. The commercial variety 'Golden Bunch' is free-flowering.

C. angustifolius (**syn.** *C. susianus*) (*below*)
Cloth-of-gold

A native of the Crimea, this small, bright orange crocus has a bronze stain or stripes on the outside of its petals. In the sun, these roll back to display a shiny orange-yellow interior, hence the name cloth-of-gold.

C. biflorus (*above*)
Scotch crocus

This variable spring crocus comes in a wide range of shades from white to blue, sometimes marked with stripes or stains on the outside of the petals. All forms are attractive and make good rock garden plants, or they can be grown at the front of sunny borders. *C. b. alexandri* has striking, bicoloured blooms, white on the inside and purple-stained outside. *C. b. weldenii* is usually white-flowering, but the cultivar 'Fairy' has a pale, soft lilac-blue tint, while *C. b.* 'Argenteus' is white, with brownish-purple stripes.

C. chrysanthus

An early spring-flowering species, the wild version of this crocus has yellow flowers, although the name is now attached to a range of cultivars with lovely, medium-sized, goblet-shaped, fragrant flowers in a wide colour range. Some are hybrids (*C. biflorus* × *C. chrysanthus*). They succeed in rock gardens, sunny borders and grass, and are also suitable for growing in bowls in the conservatory. When forced for early flowering, move them into the warmth only when the buds are showing colour otherwise they may abort. Most *C. chrysanthus* varieties increase well vegetatively, and the resulting clumps can be lifted and divided in early

autumn. The following are all equally valuable garden plants: 'Blue Pearl' has soft blue flowers and yellow throats; 'Cream Beauty' (*previous column*) is one of the most vigorous, with large, creamy white flowers and yellow throats; 'E.A. Bowles' has deep yellow flowers striped bronze at the base; 'Zwanenburg Bronze' is yellow, shaded bronze over the whole outer surface; 'Ladykiller' is a bicoloured variety, purple outside and white within; and 'Snow Bunting' is a good clean white.

C. corsicus (*above*)

One of the later spring crocuses, this species flowers in mid- to late spring, producing small, lilac flowers which are heavily striped and feathered purple on the outside. It requires a gritty, quick-draining soil.

C. dalmaticus

This mid-season crocus has pale lilac flowers with yellow centres; the outside is biscuit-coloured with a few purple stripes. The leaves are very narrow.

C. etruscus

Very similar in colour to *C. dalmaticus*, often flecked and veined on the exterior, this is a robust, easily grown species for the rock garden. 'Zwanenburg' (*above*) is a selected form with lilac-coloured flowers.

C. flavus

This original wild species has small, deep yellow flowers and is not readily obtainable, but the familiar 'Dutch Yellow' (*above*), also called 'Yellow Giant' and 'Yellow Mammoth', can be found in most bulb catalogues. It is an ancient, large, robust hybrid from *C. flavus* × *C. angustifolius* and does very well in grass and perennial borders and beneath deciduous trees and shrubs. The flowers are large and goblet-like, being deep golden yellow with darker veining at the base.

C. gargaricus (*above*)

An unusual, rarely cultivated Turkish species, *G. gargaricus* is available from a few specialist nurseries. The small, bright orange-yellow blooms appear in mid-spring. It flourishes in a moisture-retentive, humus-rich, gritty soil, but avoid waterlogged areas. The small corms produce stolons and are capable of forming sizeable clumps.

C. imperati

This is a striking late crocus, with large, slender, elongated flowers, buff-coloured on the outside and bright purple within. The vigorous selection 'Jager' has strong purple stripes on the outside and increases well by offsets. It flourishes in open ground, but can also be grown in the conservatory.

C. korolkowii (*below*)
Celandine crocus

A central Asiatic species flowering in mid- to late spring, the yellow flowers of the celandine crocus open wide in the sun to reveal shiny petals.

C. minimus (*below*)

This small, late spring crocus is remarkable for its rich violet, long-tubed flowers that are shaded even darker blackish-violet on the outside. It can be grown outdoors in a well-drained, sunny spot, but its size makes it better for pot cultivation in an alpine house.

C. olivieri

Requiring a hot, sunny situation, this species produces orange-yellow, fragrant flowers in mid-spring.

C. sieberi

Also from Greece, this is one of the best early spring crocuses. The most commonly seen form is lilac-blue with a yellow throat; it is a good choice for a rock garden, for planting in short grass or at the front of a border and, when happy, will increase into clumps. Equally reliable variations include: 'Violet Queen', a robust grower with rich, deep violet-blue flowers; 'Bowles' White', one of

the best of the white crocuses with large, white, yellow-centred flowers; 'Hubert Edelsten', which has a white background overlaid with bands of purple; and 'Tricolor' (*below*), a colourful crocus with rich purple flowers, each with a central yellow eye surrounded by a white zone.

C. tommasinianus

The "tommies" are usually the earliest crocuses to appear, sometimes emerging at the end of winter. The flowers are small and slender, graceful despite any wind and rain, and open wide the moment the sun appears. *C. tommasinianus* is very accommodating and grows in partial shade or full sun, in light or heavy soil, and often seeds profusely across gravel paths and in cracks between nearby paving. It is at its most delightful when seen in large numbers and is never a nuisance since it dies down rapidly after flowering. The common form is pale lavender with a greyish-white exterior, but there are several selections, all equally valuable, including 'Albus', the white-flowering version, 'Whitewell Purple' (*below*), a deeper purplish-blue, 'Ruby Giant', a larger and more robust crocus with deep purple flowers, and 'Pictus', which has purple and white marks on the tips of the lavender-coloured blooms.

C. vernus (*above*)

This common spring crocus of the European Alps is seldom cultivated in its true wild form. Dutch expertise in selection has produced the fine range of large Dutch cultivars that are now available and suitable for forcing gently in pots and bowls, or for naturalizing in grass or borders. They have larger flowers than most of the species crocus and are very robust, increasing rapidly to form clumps which may be divided in early autumn or from late spring to early summer when the leaves turn yellow. *C. vernus* is often sold in mixed colours, white, purple or striped, but is also available in single colours. 'Jeanne d'Arc' is an extremely good white; 'Pickwick' has striking, purple stripes; 'Queen of the Blues' is an excellent rich violet-blue; 'Vanguard' is a soft, silvery, lilac-blue; and 'Remembrance' is one of the best deep purples, with shiny petals.

C. versicolor

A popular 19th-century plant with many known varieties, *C. versicolor* is now seldom seen except for the cultivar 'Picturatus'. It has white flowers with purple veins on all six petals, but the wild forms can vary from lilac-blue to white, usually marked with purple veins or stripes. It does well in sharply drained soil, enjoying full sun.

CYCLAMEN

The highly popular florists' cyclamen sold in winter and spring are tender plants selected from the wild winter-flowering *C. persicum* (see page 226). However, there are several other species which are frost-hardy to varying degrees, all unmistakably cyclamen but subtly differing in flower shape and colour, with different mottled patterns on their foliage. All are dwarf plants, only 2¼-4in (6-10cm) high when in flower, with a spread of some 4-6in (10-15cm). The following are ideal for an alpine house or cool conservatory, or for growing in the dappled shade of a rock garden. They are best planted in light soil with added leaf mould and grit to give good drainage. Propagation is by seed sown in autumn or winter; it takes about two to three years to produce flowering-size tubers. Hardiness zones: 7-8.

C. balearicum (*above*)

One of the smaller species, this cyclamen has silvery, heart-shaped leaves and small, white, fragrant flowers. It is a native of Majorca.

C. creticum

This cyclamen originates from Crete and is very similar to *C. balearicum*, but the leaves are usually a darker green.

C. libanoticum

This Lebanese plant is one of the most beautiful cyclamen with larger flowers than most species. These are soft pink, marked with a jagged carmine zone near the mouth; they have a musty fragrance.

C. pseudibericum (*above*)

This Turkish cyclamen has fragrant, bright carmine-coloured flowers with white and darker purple areas around the mouth. The handsome leaves are variously patterned with light and dark silvery green.

C. repandum

This native of Italy, Greece and Yugoslavia performs later than other species, producing its deep pinkish-red, deliciously fragrant flowers in mid- to late spring above ivy-shaped, deep green leaves. 'Album' is the white form. The subspecies *C. r. rhodense* from Rhodes is similar but has bicoloured flowers that are white with a pink mouth, and the leaves are splashed with silver. Another subspecies, *C. r. peloponnesiacum* (*above*), is like the latter but has pale pink flowers with a dark pink mouth.

C. trochopteranthum

The curious name of this Turkish species refers to the flower shape, each petal being twisted like a ship's propeller. Its flowers are variable, from near-white to pale pink or carmine with a darker stain at the mouth, and they have a musty fragrance. The leaves have various light and dark silvery patterns.

ENDYMION (see HYACINTHOIDES)

ERANTHIS
Winter aconite

Winter aconites are the real harbingers of spring, pushing up yellow to golden, cup-shaped flowers in late winter. They are ideal subjects for dappled shade in soil rich in leaf mould, together with snowdrops and hellebores. The knobbly tubers are either obtained soon after spring flowering while still in growth, in which case they should be planted out straight away, or they can be purchased in a dried state during autumn. In the latter case, they are best soaked overnight or placed in damp peat for several days before planting at a depth of about 1-2in (2.5-5cm). All winter aconites are low-growing, only reaching 2-4in (5-10cm) in height, with the flowers carried on short stems and surrounded by a ruff of deeply toothed leaves. They grow

well in acid soil but prefer alkaline conditions and, when thriving, will self-seed to form extensive patches. Propagation is by seed when ripe, or by division of clumps immediately after flowering while the plant is in leaf. Hardiness zones: 4-5.

E. hyemalis (*above*)
The European winter aconite has greenish-yellow flowers surrounded by a frill of pale green, coarsely toothed leaves. It is a good, cheap purchase and by far the best for naturalizing in large quantities.

E. × tubergenii (*below*)
This hybrid between *E. hyemalis* and the related Turkish *E. cilicica* has bronze-coloured, heavily divided leaves. The hybrid has larger flowers than either parent; they are a rich gold and the young leaves are slightly bronzed. The deep yellow-bronze 'Guinea Gold' is a very attractive, vigorous-growing plant with large flowers.

ERYTHRONIUM
Dog's-tooth violet

Among the most graceful of all spring bulbs, these lovely plants are instantly recognizable. Its curious common name, dog's tooth violet, refers to the long, pointed bulbs which resemble canine teeth.

They have pendent bells, the six petals reflexed rather like those of a cyclamen, held above a pair of spreading leaves. These very hardy plants are suitable for growing in dappled shade beneath or between deciduous trees and shrubs, or in a cool spot in a rock garden. Most of the better-known species have bold, beautifully marbled foliage with light and dark patterns. They are all compact plants, the most vigorous being no more than 12in (30cm) high when in flower. Propagation is by seed or division of established clumps. Hardiness zones: 3-5.

E. americanum
One of the dwarf eastern American species, *E. americanum* has brown-mottled leaves and solitary, yellow flowers shaded bronze on the outside, with petals reflexing in the sunlight. When growing happily, the plants spread to form sizeable patches.

E. californicum
A fine Californian species, *E. californicum* has creamy white, yellow-centred flowers which have a ring of brownish angular marks around the throat. The ornamental leaves are marbled with silvery green patterns. 'White Beauty' is especially vigorous, increasing into clumps by bulb division. It has prominent white stamens, rather than the usual yellow or brownish-purple ones.

E. dens-canis (*above*)
The European dog's-tooth violet is the most popular, easily grown species, and is one of the earliest to flower in spring. It is a dwarf plant, only 3¹⁄₄-4³⁄₄in (8-12cm) high when flowering. The lovely, elliptical, brown- and green-mottled leaves make a good foil to the pinkish-purple or white flowers, which have darker zones in the centre. There are several named cultivars differing in colour intensity. It can be grown in short grass.

E. hendersonii (*above*)
A beautiful and unusual western North American bulb, this species has several lilac, dark purple-centred flowers carried above mottled leaves.

E. oregonum (*above*)
White-flowering and very similar to *E. californicum*, this version has contrasting yellow stamens protruding from the bells. It is a native of western North America.

E. revolutum (*below*)
This western American species is one of the brightest, with elegant, pink, yellow-centred flowers held over brownish-purple-mottled foliage. It seeds liberally. There is a rich pink form in cultivation known as 'Johnsonii'.

E. tuolumnense (below)

This plant has plain, bright green leaves topped by 10-12in (25-30cm) long stems which bear several rich yellow flowers. It is vigorous and increases well by bulb division.

E. 'Pagoda' (below)

This vigorous hybrid reaches up to 12in (30cm) in height with large, bright green, faintly brown-mottled leaves spreading 6-8in (15-20cm) in diameter. It has several pale yellow flowers to a stem, each one marked with a brown zone in the centre.

FRITILLARIA
Fritillary

The pendent, bell-shaped flowers borne near the top of leafy stems give the fritillaries a distinctive appearance, making them instantly recognizable regardless of flower colour. This includes white, purple, pink, green, brown or orange, sometimes in a chequered pattern or striped. The height varies from a few inches to over 3½ft (1m), as in the case of the crown imperial. Most fritillaries prefer well-drained, sunny situations which dry out to some extent in summer, although a few, such as *F. meleagris* and *F. camtschatcensis*, do best in a moisture-retentive soil.

The bulbs should be planted with about 1½-4in (4-10cm) of soil above the top of the bulb; the larger the bulb, the deeper the planting. Being so diminutive, the smaller species are best grown in an alpine house or cold frame, but the more robust ones are suitable for sunny borders where there is little disturbance, or for naturalizing in grass and between shrubs. Propagation is by seed sown in autumn or winter, or by bulblets, which may be removed from the parent and potted up or planted out individually. Hardiness zones: 3-8; most are hardy in zones 4-6.

F. acmopetala (above)

This mainly Turkish species with slender, 6-14in (15-35cm) high stems has alternating narrow, grey-green leaves, and one or two wide, green bells 1-1½in (3-4cm) long; these have recurving tips and are stained brown on the outside. This fritillary grows well in sunny borders.

F. affinis (syn. F. lanceolata) (above)

Robust forms of this species may reach 3½ft (1m) high. The leaves are carried in whorls up the stem; the ¾-1½in (2-4cm) long bells vary in colour from purple to greenish-purple with a chequered pattern, sometimes several in a spike. It is best grown in a deep pot in a cold frame or alpine house.

F. armena

A small species only 2-4in (5-10cm) high, *F. armena* has a few scattered, grey-green leaves and one or two small, conical, deep blackish-purple bells, often greenish-yellow on the inside. It is best grown indoors as an alpine house plant.

F. bucharica (above)

An attractive species from central Asia, *F. bucharica* grows 4-14in (10-35cm) high. It has scattered, greyish leaves and several shallow, cup-shaped, green-tinged, white flowers about ½-¾in (1.5-2cm) long. It is best suited to an alpine house or bulb frame.

F. camtschatcensis
Black sarana

An unusual shade-loving plant from eastern Asia, this fritillary produces up to eight blackish flowers carried on 6in-2ft (15-60cm) long stems, and whorls of glossy green leaves. It prefers cool conditions in humus-rich, well-drained soil.

F. crassifolia (below)

This stocky, 4-8in (10-20cm) high plant has scattered, greyish leaves and up to three green bells about 1in (2.5cm) long, some of which are chequered with brown. It is suitable for an alpine house or bulb frame.

F. graeca

This fritillary varies from 2-8in (5-20cm) in height, and has alternate greyish leaves and up to four wide, bell-shaped flowers, each ¹/₂-1in (1.5-2.5cm) long. These are usually green chequered with brown, with a bold green stripe along the middle of each petal. It is suitable for a sunny position in gritty soil.

F. imperialis (*above*)
Crown imperial

This is one of the largest fritillaries with stout stems up to 5ft (1.5m) high and glossy green leaves arranged in whorls. The several large, reddish-orange bells, about 2in (5cm) long, are carried in a dense cluster and topped by a crown of small, leaf-like bracts. There is a large drop of nectar at the base of each petal. The whole plant has a foxy odour. It is an excellent, striking border plant for a rich, well-drained soil and is particularly good in alkaline conditions. 'Lutea' is a showy variety with large yellow bells; 'Aurora' is a rich orange-red; and 'Argentea Variegata' and 'Aureo-marginata' have variegated leaves.

F. latifolia (*above*)
This Caucasian species up to 14in (35cm) high is suitable for an open, sunny spot. It has scattered, greyish-green leaves and 2in (5cm) long, brownish-purple, strongly chequered bells.

F. lusitanica (**syn.** *F. hispanica*)
This easily cultivated species can be grown in a well-drained position in the open garden. The height varies considerably but rarely exceeds 20in (50cm). It has narrow, alternate leaves and up to three wide, ³/₄-1¹/₂in (2-4cm) long bells in shades of brown and green.

F. meleagris (*above*)
Snake's head

This most widely grown fritillary has slender stems and scattered, narrow, grey-green leaves topped by usually solitary, drooping, bell-shaped flowers 1-1³/₄in (3-4.5cm) long. These are often pinkish-purple and conspicuously chequered, although other forms include the white 'Aphrodite', the purple 'Charon', and the strong reddish-violet 'Saturnus'. This is the best species for naturalizing in grass so long as it is not too dry and baking in summer; it is also suitable for planting in semi-shaded areas between shrubs where the bulbs will not become desiccated when dormant. The snake's head fritillary looks particularly attractive in association with water.

F. michailovskyi (*above*)
This species is small, about 4-8in (10-20cm) high, with a few greyish leaves and up to four ³/₄-1in (2-2.5cm) long striking, bicoloured, bell-shaped flowers, the lower two-thirds

being purplish-brown and the upper third bright yellow. It is ideally grown as a pot plant in an alpine house, although it can be cultivated in sharply drained soil which does not dry out excessively in summer.

F. pallidiflora (*below*)
This central Asiatic species ranging from 6in-2¹/₄ft (15-68.5cm) high is a beautiful plant. It has bold, glaucous leaves and up to five large, squarish, bell-shaped flowers that grow to a maximum of 1³/₄in (4.5cm) in length. The blooms are pale yellow, faintly checked with brown. It requires well-drained, cool growing conditions and is reliably hardy.

F. persica
This is one of the taller fritillaries with large, unpleasant-smelling bulbs. The stems, which may reach up to 5ft (1.5m) in height, are densely clothed with many narrow, grey-green leaves that grow up to the top of the long spike. It has 10-20 smallish, conical flowers, each only ¹/₂-³/₄in (1.5-2cm) long. The colour of the wild version varies from pale straw yellow to dirty brown and deep plum-purple, but 'Adiyaman' (*below*) has dark plum-coloured flowers. *F. persica* comes from the Middle East and requires a hot, sunny, sheltered situation.

F. pontica (*above*)

One of the easier species to grow, *F. pontica* requires a semi-shaded position where the soil does not become too hot and dry. The 6in-1½ft (15-45cm) long stems carry pairs of grey-green leaves, a whorl of three topping the solitary, wide bells. The green flowers are tinged with brown and range from ¾-1¾in (2-4.5cm) in length.

F. pudica

A very small but charming North American species only 2-6in (5-15cm) high, this fritillary has a few scattered, greyish leaves on the stem and one or two deep yellow, small, conical bells 1in (2.5cm) long. In view of its size, it is best grown in an alpine house or cold frame, although it succeeds outside in gritty soil, enjoying an open, sunny position.

F. pyrenaica (*above*)
Pyrenean fritillary

After *F. meleagris*, this is probably the most successful fritillary in the garden, thriving in a range of ordinary soils and sometimes forming dense clumps. Although, like many of the fritillaries, it is not showy, it has good interest value. The 6-12in (15-30cm) tall stems carry scattered, greyish leaves and one or two chequered, blackish-purple bells which flare out at the tips to show a greenish interior. They are about 1in (2.5cm) long.

F. sewerzowii (*below*)

Sometimes known as *Korolkowia sewerzowii*, this central Asiatic species is a fairly stout plant with thick, 6-10in (15-25cm) tall stems bearing broad, almost succulent leaves and a spike with up to 10 green or purplish bell-shaped flowers. The blooms flare out at the mouth and are 1-1¼in (2.5-3.5cm) long. It needs a sheltered position to avoid early spring frosts and does well in an alpine house or cold frame.

F. tubiformis (**syn.** *F. delphinensis*) (*below*)
Slender stems 6-14in (15-35cm) high carry scattered, narrow, greyish-green leaves. The solitary, 1¼-2in (3.5-5cm) long bells are a soft shade of purplish-pink overlaid with grey on the outside, and are noticeably chequered. Plant in a sunny, well-drained spot.

F. uva-vulpis

Sometimes incorrectly called *F. assyriaca*, this fritillary is perhaps best appreciated in an alpine house or frame, although it also enjoys a well-drained position outside. Growing 4-10in (10-25cm) high, it has scattered, shiny green leaves and one or two narrow bells ½-1in (1.5-2.5cm) long. The flowers are a metallic shade of deep purple with yellow tips on the petals.

F. verticillata (*above*)
The cultivated variety of this hardy eastern Asiatic species, *F. v. thunbergii*, is easy to cultivate outside in deep, rich soil and will tolerate an open site or partial shade, but should not be baked over summer. In ideal conditions, it will form large clumps. The slender stems grow 16in-2ft (40-60cm) high, bearing whorls of very narrow leaves that coil at their tips like tendrils. There may be up to six wide, conical, creamy-coloured bells, usually chequered with a greenish pattern, that range in length from 1-1¼in (2.5-3.5cm).

GALANTHUS
Snowdrop

Probably the best-loved of all spring bulbs, the snowdrops carry us through the bleak, late winter into spring; there is even an autumnal one, *G. reginae-olgae* (see page 208), for those who seek the unusual. Despite many variations, the several species and many named selections and hybrids are all unmistakably snowdrops in flower shape and colour. Each delicate-looking flower is composed of three large, white, outer petals and three small, green-tipped, inner ones.

Snowdrops prefer cool growing conditions in partial shade where the bulbs will not bake in summer; a position beneath deciduous trees and shrubs is ideal. Although not especially fussy about soil type, they do particularly well in heavy, neutral to alkaline soil. Since they flower at about the same time and enjoy the same conditions as hellebores, the two make excellent companions.

Snowdrops may be obtained as dried bulbs in autumn or as growing plants in spring while still in leaf. In both cases, plant immediately since they suffer if overdried. In early autumn or spring, either during or soon after flowering, crowded clumps can be lifted and divided into smaller groups,

even down to single bulbs if necessary, provided that they are replanted at once. Snowdrops often seed themselves, but with named clones the offspring will not necessarily be exactly the same as the parent snowdrop.

The following snowdrops grow from 2-6in (5-15cm) high, the vigorous growers sometimes reaching as much as 10in (25cm). Hardiness zones: 4-6.

G. caucasicus (*above*)
This vigorous species produces bold, grey-green leaves and large, rounded flowers in late winter. The earlier variety 'Early Form', sometimes called 'Hiemale', flowers in the depths of winter.

G. elwesii (*above*)
Giant snowdrop
This Turkish species is larger than the common snowdrop and very similar to *G. caucasicus*, with broad, greyish leaves and large flowers, but it can be distinguished by the two green blotches on each of the inner petals, one at the apex and one at the base.

G. gracilis (**syn. *G. graecus***)
Like *G. elwesii*, this species has two green spots on each of the inner petals, but the flowers are smaller and the leaves are much narrower and elegantly twisted lengthways.

G. ikariae (**syn. *G. latifolius***) (*above*)
A distinctive snowdrop, *G. ikariae* has broad, glossy green leaves that accentuate the whiteness of the flowers. It often flowers slightly later than *G. elwesii* and *G. caucasicus*.

G. nivalis (*above*)
Common snowdrop
Compared with *G. elwesii*, this snowdrop is quite small, with narrow, grey-green leaves. It often flowers a little later and is excellent for naturalizing in large quantities. The bulbs normally increase well so that clumps can be divided every three or four years. There are many named selections including 'Flore Pleno' which has tight, double flowers with many extra petals.

G. plicatus
This good, robust species increases well by offsets. It usually flowers a little later in the snowdrop season and has distinctive leaves with down-turned margins. The variation known as *G. p. byzantinus* is similar, but its flowers have two green marks on each of the inner petals.

Named cultivars
Some of the best named cultivars include 'Atkinsii', a particularly graceful snowdrop with stems up to 10in (25cm) high, bearing elegant, long flowers; 'Magnet', a distinctive variety with the flowers held away from the stem on long, thread-like stalks; 'Sam Arnott', with large, beautifully formed flowers held on stout stems; 'Scharlockii', which is easily recognized by its small flowers topped by two spathes resembling a pair of ears; and 'Viridapicis', a snowdrop with green tips to the outer and inner petals.

HERMODACTYLUS
Widow iris
Although not a showy plant, this iris is well worth growing for interest's sake in a hot, sunny, sheltered position such as at the base of a warm, sheltered wall. In autumn, plant the finger-like rhizomes about 2in (5cm) deep in well-drained soil which may be acid to alkaline, although it usually prefers chalk or limestone. The rhizomes can eventually spread into considerable patches over $3\frac{1}{2}$ft (1m) wide. Propagation is by division of the established clumps in autumn. Hardiness zone: 7

H. tuberosus (**syn. *Iris tuberosa***) (*above*)
H. tuberosus is the only species of widow iris and it has characteristic iris-shaped flowers. These are an extraordinary translucent green, with a velvety, black or brownish patch on each of the three larger outer petals (known as the "falls"). The flowers have a delicate fragrance and last for a few days when cut so they are occasionally seen in florists' shops in winter or early spring, although in the garden they flower in mid- to late spring. The stems reach 8-12in (20-30cm) in height and are produced separately from the long, narrow, greyish leaves which have a squarish cross-section similar to those of *I. reticulata*.

HYACINTHOIDES or ENDYMION
Bluebell
Bluebells are often regarded as scillas and the two are indeed very similar, with only slight botanical differences. They are very

good garden plants, suitable for naturalizing under shrubs or for planting in perennial borders where there is little disturbance, and they tolerate a wide range of soil types but dislike hot, dry positions. The bulbs are best planted in autumn at a depth of approximately 2-3¼in (5-8cm); they flower in mid- to late spring and grow 10-12in (25-30cm) high. They spread by bulb division into large clumps and can form extensive patches by seeding. Propagation is by division or seed in autumn. Hardiness zone: 5.

H. hispanica (syn. *H. campanulata*) (*above*)
Spanish bluebell
A robust plant, the Spanish bluebell has fairly wide, shiny green, strap-like leaves and stout spikes of bell-shaped flowers arranged around the stem. It is useful for planting in perennial borders among herbaceous plants where it adds spring colour. The wild form is mostly pale to mid-blue, but large-flowering selections offer flowers that are bright blue ('Myosotis'), pink ('Rosea' and 'Azalea') and white ('Alba' and 'Mount Everest').

H. non-scripta (syn. *H. nutans*) (*above*)
English bluebell
The English bluebell is a smaller, more slender plant with narrower leaves than the Spanish bluebell. The flower spike bends over at the apex and the tubular bells are carried on one side. This bluebell is normally a rich, deep blue but there are pink and white forms. Although a charming plant under the right conditions, it can be quite invasive and is best naturalized beneath deciduous trees and shrubs.

HYACINTHUS
Hyacinth
These beautifully fragrant, colourful spring bulbs are very popular. The colours and types available are descendants of the wild Middle Eastern *H. orientalis*, selected over generations from the time of the Ottoman Turks. Hyacinths are naturally spring-flowering but are also ideal when cultivated in bowls for an indoor winter display. For early winter-flowering purchase "prepared" bulbs; non-prepared, ordinary bulbs flower later and can be used for bedding displays or permanent planting in borders since they are hardy and easily cultivated, requiring only a reasonably well-drained soil in sun or light shade. In addition to the varieties with very large, solid flower spikes, there are some with smaller flowers in loose spikes, such as 'Roman', 'Cynthella' and 'Multiflora'. They vary from 8-12in (20-30cm) in height when flowering. Propagation is by division in early autumn. Hardiness zone: 5.

H. 'Borah'
This is a multiflora hyacinth, with loosely flowering spikes of pale blue flowers.

H. 'City of Haarlem'
A large-flowering variety, this hyacinth has lovely, soft primrose yellow blooms.

H. 'Delft Blue' (*above*)
This is one of the best of the large-flowering blue varieties, with mid-blue flowers that are flushed violet on the outside.

H. 'Hollyhock' (*above*)
This double-flowering hyacinth produces tight, deep red florets.

H. 'Jan Bos'
A large-flowering plant, 'Jan Bos' has dense, compact spikes of crimson red flowers.

H. 'L' Innocence' (*above*)
This is a very good large, white hyacinth.

H. 'Snow Princess'
A multiflora type, 'Snow Princess' has pure white flowers held in loose spikes.

IPHEION
The only species in general cultivation, *I. uniflorum* is sometimes listed as *Triteleia uniflora*, *Milla uniflora* or *Tristagma uniflora*. It is an excellent dwarf bulb for planting in perennial borders or around and under deciduous shrubs since it enjoys partial shade, and is best when left undisturbed to build into clumps. The bulbs should be planted in autumn, in a reasonably well-drained soil which will not become too hot and dry, although it should not be too cool and damp; a depth of about 1-2in (3-5cm) is sufficient. Propagation is simple since offsets are freely produced and can be removed in early autumn when clumps are dug up for splitting. Ipheions also

make interesting subjects for an alpine house or cool conservatory. Hardiness zone: 6.

I. uniflorum

If bruised, this small Argentinian bulbous plant smells of onions. It produces tufts of narrow, pale green or greyish-green leaves, topped in mid-spring by 4-8in (10-20cm) long stems. These bear solitary, upward-facing, flattish, pale blue flowers, each one about 1-1½in (2.5-4cm) in diameter. The colour varies, and apart from the usual form there are deeper violet-blues ('Wisley Blue' and 'Froyle Mill'), an attractive, clear mid-blue ('Rolf Fiedler') and a lovely pure white ('Alba') (*above*).

IRIS

Apart from the many beautiful and popular rhizomatous bearded irises, there are some excellent bulbous ones, some of which are among the earliest spring bulbs, even continuing to the end of the season. There are two groups: the early, well-known Reticulatas and the much less well-known Juno species, which flower later on in the season and have leek-like leaves. The irises belonging to the Juno group are characterized by their strange-looking flowers with very small, horizontal or even downward pointing standards which, in most irises, stand erect.

The cultivation requirements are similar for both types: a well-drained, preferably alkaline soil and an open, sunny position. The best site is in a border or rock garden where there is little disturbance since they are best left alone for a few years to build into clumps, after which they can be lifted and divided in autumn. They also grow well in pots for an early display in an alpine house, cold frame or conservatory, but they require repotting every year and, in the case of some of the Reticulatas,

new flowering-size bulbs should be purchased each year since they have a tendency to split into many small bulbs. Some of the taller Junos can be planted in a sunny herbaceous border, whereas the shorter species and the Reticulatas are best at the front of the border or in a rock garden. Propagate by division in autumn; Junos can also be propagated by seed sown in autumn. Hardiness zones: 4-5.

Reticulata

All the Reticulata irises are about 2-4in (5-10cm) high when in flower, although the leaves much exceed this later on before dying away for the summer. The foliage is quite unlike that of other irises, being very narrow and almost square or round in cross-section.

I. bakeriana (*above*)

Although seldom available in its true form, *I. bakeriana* has been used as a parent with *I. reticulata* to create many of the hybrid cultivars. The flowers have a pale blue background and the three falls are stained a deep violet-blue at the apex of the reflexed blade. This striking feature repeats in the offspring of the plant.

I. danfordiae (*above*)

This very popular, small iris is cheap to buy and best planted afresh each year since the

bulb usually dwindles in size after the first season. It has deep yellow flowers spotted green in the centre, and is unusual because the standards are all but missing. Flowering the second and subsequent years can sometimes be achieved by deep planting at a depth of 4in (10cm) or more, and feeding with a potash-rich fertilizer in spring.

I. histrioides

This is one of the best of the Reticulatas, being a robust grower with very early flowers that withstand inclement weather. Its large, rich blue flowers have conspicuous dark spots and blotches on the falls. 'Major' is particularly fine, and has rich, deep bluish-violet flowers, and 'Lady Beatrix Stanley' is another good choice, with light blue flowers and heavily spotted falls.

I. reticulata

By far the best-known of the Reticulatas, *I. reticulata* is available in a wide range of cultivars. It is good in a rock garden or at the front of a sunny border, and is excellent in pots for an early display; it will only tolerate gentle forcing otherwise it goes "blind" (does not flower). The deep violet-blue flowers of the wild *I. reticulata* have an orange stripe down the centre of each fall and a pleasant scent reminiscent of the primrose. Among the many excellent cultivars are: 'J.S. Dijt', with deep reddish-purple flowers; 'Joyce' and 'Harmony', rich blue cultivars with yellow marks in the centre of the falls; 'Clairette', a paler blue, with dark blue-violet blotches on the tips of the falls and a dark blue-spotted centre; and 'Jeannine', also pale blue, but with a conspicuous orange-yellow ridge in the centre of the falls, spotted and blotched darker blue towards the tips. At the lighter end of the colour range are 'Cantab', a lovely shade of pale blue with a yellow ridge on the falls, and 'Natascha' (*above*), almost white with a faint hint of blue.

I. winogradowii

Although quite rare and expensive, this yellow-flowering Caucasian species is one of the hardiest of the Reticulatas. The bulbs do not have the same tendency to split as *I. danfordiae*, the only other yellow-flowering iris in the group. It flowers early while the leaves are still very short, and is a beautiful soft lemon yellow. It prefers a slightly cooler situation where the bulbs will not get too hot and dry over summer.

I. 'George' (*above*)

This very strong grower produces large, rich, deep reddish-purple flowers early in the Reticulata season.

I. 'Katharine Hodgkin' (*below*)

This hybrid of the blue *I. histrioides* and yellow *I. winogradowii* has flowers in a curious mixture of colours with a yellow background overlaid with blue veining. This extremely vigorous plant grows very well in open gardens.

Juno

These bulbs, also known as Scorpiris, are covered with papery tunics and have rather thick, even swollen, fleshy roots that should be handled with care since they are apt to break. The gutter-shaped leaves initially

resemble those of a small leek but are mostly shiny green on the upper side, with conspicuous white margins. In mid- to late spring, the flowers blossom in the axils of the upper leaves, although in some of the shorter, stockier species they appear almost stemless in the centre of the leaf cluster. All the following are particularly good in alkaline conditions and can be cultivated in sunny borders or rock gardens, in gritty, well-drained soil.

I. aucheri

This stocky plant, with leaves closely packed in a dense cluster at its base, grows only 6-10in (15-25cm) high when in bloom, with up to six pale blue flowers, each about 2¼in (6cm) across.

I. bucharica (*above*)

This somewhat taller plant, 8-16in (20-40cm) high, bears several bicoloured flowers in the upper leaf axils. These are golden yellow to white, with yellow falls, growing about 2¼in (6cm) across. The channelled leaves grow all the way up the stems.

I. graeberiana

Very similar to *I. bucharica* in habit, *I. graeberiana* ranges from 6-14in (15-35cm) in height, and has several bluish-lavender-coloured flowers which are produced in the leaf axils.

I. magnifica

As its name suggests, this is a particularly showy iris. A robust plant reaching 12in-2ft (30-60cm) high, it has many broad, glossy leaves and several large, pale lilac-coloured flowers in the upper axils. The blooms are about 2¼-3¼in (6-8cm) across with yellow stains in the centres of the falls. 'Alba' is an excellent white form with striking yellow-stained falls. It is one of the best of all the Juno irises.

I. × sindpers (*above*)

A compact grower 4-6in (10-15cm) high, this iris produces a tuft of broad leaves with several large, clear, pale blue flowers.

I. × warlsind

In overall size and appearance, *I. × warlsind* is similar to *I. bucharica* but the flowers are pale lilac-blue, with a darker stain on the tip of the falls and a yellow patch in the centre.

IXIOLIRION

Only one type of ixiolirion, *I. tataricum*, is readily available. The bulbs should be planted in a warm, sunny site in autumn, planted at a depth of 3¼-4in (8-10cm) in well-drained soil. Since they are natives of very cold areas they are quite hardy, although they need a hot, dry period in summer while dormant. In cooler climates, either lift and store them or choose a site where they will bake. Propagation is by division in early autumn or by seed in autumn. Hardiness zone: 7.

I. tataricum (**syn.** *I. montanum*) (*below*)

This bulb grows 12-16in (30-40cm) high and has long, narrow, grassy leaves and a loose head of blue, funnel-shaped flowers, each 1-2in (2.5-5cm) long. These resemble small lilies and are excellent for cutting.

LEUCOJUM
Snowflake

These close relatives of the snowdrop differ most noticeably from their better-known cousins in their bell-shaped flowers made up of six petals of equal rather than different lengths. Most flower in spring, although a few of the less common ones flower in autumn (see page 208). All spring-flowering snowflakes have white flowers, usually tipped with green or yellow although, in some cases, they are plain in colour. *L. vernum* and *L. aestivum* are hardy, robust plants for growing outside in borders where they will not become too dry in summer; a fairly damp soil is best. *L. nicaeense* is a tiny plant more suited to pot cultivation in an alpine house or frame where its minuscule charm can be better appreciated. Like snowdrops, leucojums can be planted or lifted and divided while in growth in spring or early summer, or in autumn before growth commences. Propagation is easily done by dividing clumps, but seed is also produced quite freely, although it may be some years before the plants start producing flowers. Hardiness zones: 4-5; 7 for *L. nicaeense*.

L. aestivum (*above*)
Although called the summer snowflake, this plant usually flowers in late spring. The flower stems of this tall, robust species reach as much as $3^1/_2$ft (1m) or more in height and carry umbels of pendent flowers approximately $^1/_2$–$^3/_4$in (1.5-2cm) long. These are white with green-tipped petals. The leaves are long and strap-shaped, reminiscent of a daffodil, as are the bulbs, which require deep planting in damp soil at a minimum depth of 6in (15cm). *L. aestivum* looks particularly attractive planted alongside a garden pond or stream, although it also grows very well in grass and, being a native plant, can be naturalized in a wildlife garden.

L. nicaeense
This tiny species is delightful at close quarters and is therefore best appreciated in a raised, well-drained part of a rock garden, in a pot or a trough. It has very narrow basal leaves often lying on the ground and 2-4in (5-10cm) high stems bearing one or two small, white bells in late spring.

L. vernum (*above*)
Spring snowflake
The delightful snowflake is the earliest flowering leucojum appearing at the same time as snowdrops. It has short, glossy green, strap-shaped leaves which later elongate after flowering. The foliage is topped by 4-8in (10-20cm) high stems which bear one or two large, white, green-tipped bells. It does very well in dappled shade beneath deciduous shrubs but is good in any cool, dampish situation. *L. v. carpathicum* has yellow tips to the petals, and *L. v. vagneri* has two flowers per stem.

MUSCARI
Grape hyacinth

These small, blue-flowering bulbs with their dense spikes of tiny globular flowers are a familiar, colourful feature of many gardens. While some species are not invasive and are even difficult to grow, others increase so rapidly that they tend to be avoided, but even the most invasive ones are valuable garden plants if grown in the right situation. They mostly flower in mid- to late spring, perhaps even early summer in the case of *M. comosum*. Some produce their leaves in autumn and are best planted as early as possible at a depth of 2in (5cm) in any reasonably well-drained soil in a sunny spot, although the common *M. neglectum* flowers in partial shade and is useful for naturalizing under shrubs. In general, the muscari species grow from 4-8in (10-20cm) high and may eventually expand into sizeable areas by division; *M. neglectum* can form extensive patches by bulblets and seed if left to spread. Most grape hyacinth are various shades of blue, although some are white and a less common yellow-flowered species also exists. Propagation is by division in autumn. Hardiness zones: 4-6.

M. armeniacum (*below*)
One of the best garden plants in the group, this grape hyacinth has stout, showy spikes of oblong, mid-blue flowers. Although it will increase into clumps by bulb division, it does not become too invasive. 'Blue Spike' is a curious and showy variation with minute, sterile flowers that appear in a dense mass on fat spikes. It is good for spring bedding displays mixed with yellow, winter-spring-flowering pansies, and for naturalizing in borders as ground cover.

M. azureum (*below*)
This Turkish mountain plant has attractive bright blue, bell-shaped flowers produced in dense spikes on 4-6in (10-15cm) high stems. It is ideal grown in a rock garden or left to naturalize in sunny or slightly shaded borders. The leaves are fairly short, making it a neat, compact plant. It is very hardy.

M. botryoides (*above*)
This grape hyacinth grows approximately 6-8in (15-20cm) high, with narrow, erect leaves and dense spikes of small, spherical flowers that are bright mid-blue with a white rim around the mouth. There is also a white form called 'Alba'.

M. comosum
Tassel hyacinth
M. comosum differs in appearance from the blue grape hyacinth; it has 8-12in (20-30cm) long, loosely flowering spikes of brownish flowers crowned by a cluster of long-stalked, bright violet sterile ones. It usually flowers after most of the other species in late spring or early summer and needs a warm, sunny position with good drainage. 'Plumosum' (syn. 'Monstrosum') is a sterile but showy curiosity with no flowers, the large heads consisting of a mass of purple threads.

M. latifolium (*below*)
This unusual grape hyacinth has one broad, grey-green leaf per bulb and an 8-10in (20-25cm) long stem bearing a dense, bicoloured spike of oblong flowers which have constricted mouths. The lower flowers are mostly deep blackish-violet in colour and the upper ones are paler and smaller. It is an attractive plant for a sunny rock garden.

M. macrocarpum (*below*)
A delightful species but not the easiest to grow, *M. macrocarpum* requires a hot, sunny position with little disturbance since its bulbs produce fleshy perennial roots. It grows 4-8in (10-20cm) high and has dense spikes of oblong-shaped, bright yellow flowers, each with a brown rim around the mouth. The blooms have a delicious, fruity fragrance which is best appreciated when the plant is grown in an alpine house or conservatory. If planted in pots, they must be deep enough to accommodate the roots.

M. muscarimi (syn. **M. moschatum**)
M. muscarimi is related to *M. macrocarpum*. The two species are very similar but *M. muscarimi* has greyish or pale pearly-blue flowers with brown-rimmed mouths, and has a musk-like scent. It requires the same conditions as its relative.

M. neglectum (syn. **M. racemosum**) (*above*)
Grape hyacinth
The most common species of muscari, *M. neglectum* produces long, narrow leaves in autumn that last through to flowering time in mid-spring. The 4-6in (10-15cm) tall stems have dense spikes of oblong or egg-shaped, deep blue to blackish-blue flowers, usually with a group of fragrant, pale blue sterile ones

at the top. A ring of tiny, whitish "teeth" encircle the mouth of each individual bloom. Although increasing to the extent of becoming invasive in some gardens, it is excellent for naturalizing in shrub borders, for example, beneath deciduous magnolias.

M. tubergenianum
This type of grape hyacinth has dense, 6-8in (15-20cm) long, bicoloured flower spikes of very bright, mid-blue lower flowers and pale blue upper ones. It is one of the best of its kind and is sometimes referred to as the Oxford and Cambridge grape hyacinth.

NARCISSUS
Daffodils are the mainstay of the spring garden and come in an ever-increasing array of colours and forms thanks to the skill and patience of plant breeders. The true wild species are also very attractive and many nurseries offer a range of both species and cultivars.

The flowers of all narcissi have a cup or trumpet developed to varying degrees called the corona, surrounded by six petals, known collectively as the corolla. The flowers may be solitary, as in most trumpet daffodils, or number several per stem, as in the case of N. tazetta and N. papyraceus. Through extensive interbreeding, the combination of these features has led to a horticultural classification based on the features of the species. Propagation is by dividing clumps in early autumn. Hardiness zones: 4-6; 7-8 for N. tazetta, N. cantabricus, N. papyraceus and N. romieuxii.

N. asturiensis (syn. **N. minimus**) (*above*)
This is the smallest trumpet daffodil, only 2-4in (5-10cm) high, with narrow, grey-green leaves and small, solitary, deep yellow flowers barely $\frac{1}{2}$in (1.5cm) long. The flared trumpets have crinkled rims.

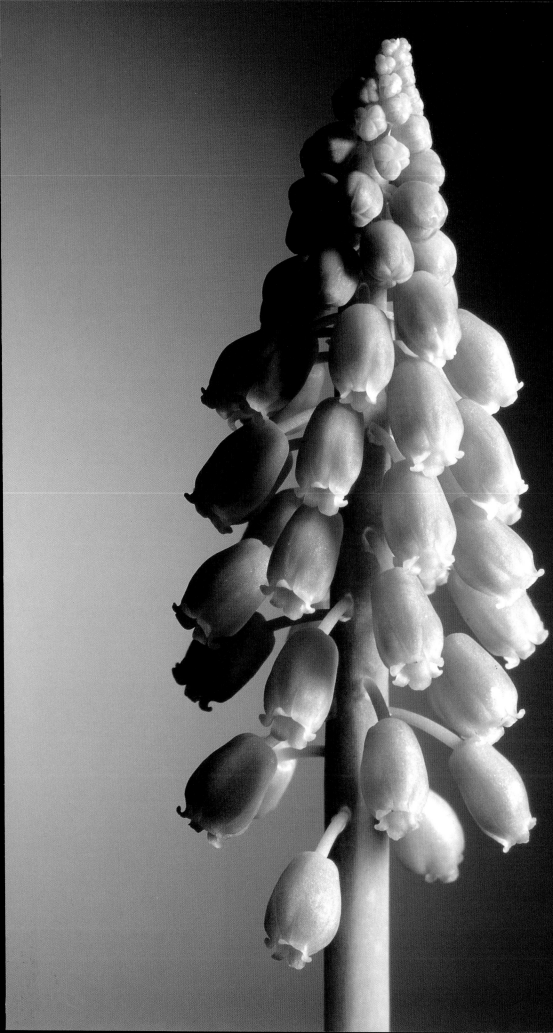

N. bulbocodium
Hoop-petticoat daffodil
This daffodil is commonly known as the hoop-petticoat because of its striking, funnel-shaped trumpets about ¾-1in (2-2.5cm) long which are surrounded by very narrow, rather insignificant petals. The dark green leaves are slender and thread-like. Because the whole plant is less than 6in (15cm) high, it is best grown in a rock garden or alpine house where it will not be swamped by other plants. However, given the right conditions it will also thrive in some grasses; a sloping meadow of fine grasses through which water seeps in the early part of the year is ideal. In these conditions, *N. bulbocodium* will seed very freely to form large drifts. 'Julia Jane' (*above*) is a good pale yellow-flowered selection, blooming early on in the season. There are several variants including *N. b. conspicuus* which has large, deep yellow flowers, and *N. b. romieuxii* (syn. *N. romieuxii*) (see page 107), a more tender, pale sulphur yellow type.

N. canaliculatus (*above*)
This charming plant 8-10in (20-25cm) high requires a hot, sunny place where the bulbs will ripen over summer, as do all members of the Mediterranean Tazetta group. It bears clusters of sweet-smelling, creamy white flowers; these are small and almost flat, with orange cups.

N. cantabricus (*below*)
Another of the hoop-petticoats but with white flowers, this is a more delicate plant requiring alpine house cultivation. Like *N. bulbocodium*, several variants exist differing in corona shape and size.

N. cyclamineus (*below*)
One of the most delightful and distinctive of all the dwarf narcissus, *N. cyclamineus* has a long, slender trumpet which is crinkled and flared at the mouth and the petals are reflexed like a cyclamen. The flower is deep yellow and borne singly on 6-10in (15-25cm) long stems, accompanied by shiny green leaves. It is a very good parent plant for breeding new hybrids, and a race of cultivars bearing similar characteristics has been raised, some of which are mentioned under the Cyclamineus hybrids. *N. cyclamineus* prefers moist conditions and grows well in a damp, grassy area or peat garden.

N. jonquilla
Jonquil
Well-known as a cut flower and for its delicious fragrance, the jonquil is also an excellent late spring garden plant. The deep green leaves are almost rush-like and the rich yellow, long-tubed but smallish flowers,

about ¾-1¼in (2-3.5cm) in diameter, are carried in clusters on 8-12in (20-30cm) tall stems. It prefers sheltered positions and does particularly well on sandy soil.

N. minor (*below*)
Although this small trumpet daffodil is slightly larger than *N. asturiensis*, it is otherwise similar. The 6-10in (15-25cm) high stems bear solitary, deep yellow flowers. *N. nanus* is thought to be a variant.

N. obvallaris
Tenby daffodil
This is very similar to the ordinary wild trumpet species, *N. pseudonarcissus*. It has uniform deep yellow flowers which are slightly smaller than the average daffodil, and grows about 8-10in (20-25cm) high. It is very useful for naturalizing.

N. papyraceus (*above*)
Paperwhite
This much-loved species with a delicious perfume is good for early forcing in bowls or as a winter cut flower (see page 231). Unlike most bulbs which are forced, it requires no skill and will flower in pots or bowls of peat, soil or gravel on a bright windowsill a month or two after planting. *N. papyraceus* can also be grown very successfully in a sheltered,

sunny position outdoors, for instance, at the base of a warm wall or fence where it may form large clumps. One of the cluster-headed species, it has up to 20 pure white, small-cupped flowers to a head and rather broad, grey-green leaves.

N. poeticus (*above*)
Poet's narcissus or pheasant's eye
The very small, yellow or greenish cup of *N. poeticus* has a bright orange or red rim staring out like an eye from the centre of the large, flat, white flower. This robust mountain plant from southern Europe is very hardy and wonderfully fragrant, flowering right at the end of the narcissus season in late spring. Although it can be grown in borders, it is at its best when planted in grass and will do well in relatively damp conditions.

N. pseudonarcissus (*above*)
Daffodil
Most of the trumpet daffodil cultivars have been developed from this species. In its wild form, it is a small plant with bicoloured flowers; the corolla is pale yellow and the $^3/_4$-$1^1/_4$in (2-3.5cm) long trumpet is deeper yellow and flared at the mouth. There are many variations in the wild that have been named separately. It is easily grown in the garden and is best when naturalized in semi-shade or grass.

N. pseudonarcissus moschatus; N. alpestris
These Pyrenean plants are very alike and should be regarded as variations of one species. They are small trumpet daffodils with plain white or creamy-coloured flowers that hang downwards on 6-10in (15-25cm) tall stems. Since the petals do not stand away from the trumpet, they have a rather droopy appearance. Although very uncommon in gardens, they do well in a cool but well-drained position.

N. requienii (**syn.** *N. assoanus*)
This dwarf jonquil has rush-like leaves and small-cupped, fragrant, yellow flowers barely $^1/_2$in (1.5cm) across; it has just one or two blooms on each 6-8in (15-20cm) tall stem. Although hardy enough to be grown in a sunny, well-drained spot, it is easier to see in an alpine house or cold frame.

N. romieuxii (*above*)
A relative of the hoop-petticoat daffodil (see *N. bulbocodium*).

N. tazetta (*above*)
The highly fragrant tazetta has formed the basis of several much-loved varieties, such as 'Soleil d'Or', which are valuable as early cut flowers and for forcing. The wild form grows 6-20in (15-50cm) in height and bears a cluster of up to 20 small, yellow-cupped,

white flowers on a single head. It varies considerably and there are several subspecies. Originating in the Mediterranean, it requires hot, sunny conditions and is unsuccessful in cold gardens as the leaves are vulnerable to frost and the bulbs seldom flower. However, where conditions permit, it is worth trying in a sheltered position at the base of a wall.

N. triandrus
Angel's tears
One of the most delightful species for a cool spot in a rock garden, this narcissus can also be successfully naturalized in the semi-shade of deciduous shrubs. It is only about 4-8in (10-20cm) high with slender, dark green leaves and up to six pendent, creamy white flowers which have a prominent cup and reflexed petals. 'Albus' (*above*) is creamy-coloured throughout, but occasionally the deep yellow *N. t. concolor* is found.

N. watieri (*above*)
This small North African species is perhaps a little too precious to be grown outdoors but it is fairly hardy and might be tried in a well-drained, sunny spot in a rock garden. It stands about 4in (10cm) high with narrow, grey leaves, and has solitary, flat, white flowers about 1in (2.5cm) in diameter with a shallow cup. It is probably best kept in pots where the bulbs can be ripened well in summer.

Garden forms

In addition to the wild species, countless garden forms of narcisi exist. For convenience, they have been classified into groups and a few of each are mentioned here; refer to up-to-date bulb catalogues for a fuller picture of those available.

Large-trumpet daffodils (*above*)
These typical daffodils with long trumpets are available in a wide range of colours, including yellow (the old varieties such as 'King Alfred') (*below*), solid golden yellow ('Rowallane' is an excellent variety), pale lemon yellow ('Spellbinder' ages to near-white with a yellow rim to the trumpet, giving an unusual bicoloured effect), and pure white ('Mount Hood' has a very large, nicely formed flower).

Large-cupped daffodils
These produce a fairly large flower on each stem; the corona, which is shaped like a deep cup, must be more than one-third the length of the petals to qualify as a Large-cupped daffodil. 'Ice Follies' has white petals and a very widely expanded, pale lemon cup that fades to near-white with age. This highly attractive variety mixes well with green-flowering spring plants like *Helleborus foetidus*. N. 'Ambergate' (*next column*) has an orange cup and golden petals which have a curious tint of peach, and 'Mrs R.O. Backhouse' is one of the so-called "pink" daffodils with white petals and a pink cup.

Small-cupped daffodils
The small cup that characterizes this group is less than a third the length of the petals because of the influence of *N. poeticus* in its breeding. 'Barrett Browning' has a large, white flower, ruffled and crinkled at its rim, and is flat except for the small, shallow, orange-red cup in the centre; 'Birma' has sulphur yellow petals surrounding a small, orange cup; and 'Verger' is white with a lemon yellow, orange-rimmed cup. All have solitary flowers on tall stems and often flower slightly later than the Trumpet daffodils, again an influence of *N. poeticus*.

Triandrus hybrids
Here, *N. triandrus* supplies the dominant characteristics: usually a fairly compact habit with more than one flower per stem, each with somewhat swept-back petals. Although robust garden plants, they require slightly drier conditions than the Cyclamineus hybrids. 'April Tears' is a dwarf variety about 6-8in (15-20cm) high, with several pendent, yellow flowers per stem; it increases very rapidly by offsets. 'Hawera' (*above*) is an equally popular dwarf narcissus 8-10in (20-25cm) high, with up to six small, long-tubed, fragrant flowers in a shade of lemon yellow. This particularly graceful and delicate plant is a hybrid, having the small cup and long tube of *N. jonquilla* and the reflexed petals of *N. triandrus*. 'Liberty Bells' is larger, with several nodding, lemon yellow flowers per stem, and 'Thalia' has large, solid white blooms with several flowers to each 8-12in (20-30cm) high stem. Both have the reflexing petals characteristic of the group.

Cyclamineus hybrids
These hybrids bear obvious similarities to *N. cyclamineus* such as the swept-back appearance of the petals. They are rather shorter than the majority of ordinary daffodils and are excellent plants for cooler positions and for growing in grass since they do not mind a little more moisture than most narcissi. 'February Gold' (*above*) and 'February Silver' are probably the best known, but there are many others in a wide colour range. 'Dove Wings' is a delightful variety with reflexing white petals and a pale yellow cup; 'Jetfire' has dramatic golden yellow petals and a conspicuous orange trumpet; and the striking 'Peeping Tom' (*below*) has very long, golden yellow trumpets the same colour as the petals.

Jonquilla hybrids

Members of this group tend to have the upright, narrow leaves of *N. jonquilla* and several fragrant flowers per stem with long, slender tubes. They readily form clumps in the garden and are excellent for cutting. 'Trevithian' and 'Sweetness' reach a medium height of 14–16in (35–40cm) and have pale yellow flowers, the former producing several per stem and the latter usually only one. At the shorter end of the scale, 'Sundial' measures about 6in (15cm) high and has a few lemon-coloured, green-tinged flowers. 'Pipet' (also spelled 'Pipit') is bicoloured with lemon yellow petals fading to white at the base of the lemon and white cup.

Poetaz hybrids

With *N. poeticus* and *N. tazetta* as parents, this group combines the fragrance of both with the cluster-headed characteristic of the latter and the larger flowers of the former. 'Geranium' (*above*) is one of the best, about 14–16in (35–40cm) high, with three to five almost flat, fragrant, white flowers and shallow orange cups. 'Scarlet Gem' has clear yellow flowers with orange cups.

Tazetta narcissi

Although often planted in gardens or pots, these half-hardy daffodils are mostly used for cut flowers or for forcing to create an early winter display. As with the true species, the derivatives of *N. tazetta* have several very fragrant flowers grouped in a cluster. 'Cheerfulness' (*previous column*) is aptly named with its double, creamy-coloured flowers, and the popular 'Soleil d'Or' has highly fragrant, yellow-orange cups. The 'Chinese Sacred Lily' is sometimes available and is like a large-flowering version of *N. tazetta*, excellent for late winter forcing indoors. Tazettas grown outside in the garden should be given a sheltered position where they can bake over summer while dormant. However, the 8–10in (20–25cm) high dwarf 'Minnow' seems to thrive in any well-drained, sunny spot and will also grow in grass. It has several small, lemon-coloured flowers which have deeper yellow cups.

Poeticus narcissi

The most obvious characteristic of these narcissi is the deliciously fragrant, almost flat, white flower with a tiny cup, one per stem. They often flower slightly later in the season in mid- to late spring. 'Actaea' (*above*) has all the features of the group and makes a fine cut flower, very large and pure white with a small yellow cup rimmed orange-red. The popular 'Pheasant's Eye' (*below*) grows well in grass and has smaller, highly fragrant flowers appearing late in the season.

Split corona narcissi

Also known as Collar and Orchid-flowering daffodils, these are a comparatively recent development. They are an unusual shape, rather far removed from the classic daffodil. The corona of this type is split into segments which are pressed back against the petals, forming a flat flower with two layers of "petals". The various cultivars are mostly quite tall, at 1¼–1½ft (40–45cm) high, and have only one flower per stem. 'Cassata' (*above*) has white petals and the split corona segments are yellow; 'Baccarat' is a striking plant with orange corona segments flattened against yellow petals; and 'Orangery' has small, orange segments and large, white petals.

ORNITHOGALUM
Star-of-Bethlehem

Although a large and familiar group of spring-flowering bulbs, only a few ornithogalums are in general cultivation. Many species are natives of Europe, western Asia and South Africa, some of which are not hardy. Since the majority are so alike, there is little point in growing more than two or three types. In general, they have star-shaped, white flowers with a green stripe on the outside of each of the six petals. The spring-flowering ones are all fairly low-growing and can be sited in a rock garden, at the front of a perennial border or in the dappled shade of deciduous trees and shrubs. While they will grow in shade, they do need some sunlight during the day or they do not open, leaving ranks of closed green buds.

For most species, an ordinary, well-drained garden soil is acceptable but avoid very hot, dry spots. These bulbs should be planted in autumn at a depth of about 2in (5cm). Propagation is easy since the plants increase by bulb division and seed, sometimes too abundantly. Hardiness zones: 5-6.

O. balansae (*below*)

This Turkish mountain plant is one of the earliest to flower and is a particularly choice species. It is a dwarf plant, only 2–4in (5–10cm) high, with two or three short, broad, glossy green leaves and a short raceme of white flowers about 1in (2.5cm) across. It is ideal for a rock garden or trough, or an early display in an alpine house.

O. lanceolatum

Although seldom seen in gardens and not readily available, it is worth searching through bulb catalogues for this particularly low-growing species. A rosette of wide leaves spreads out at ground level with a cluster of white flowers nestling in the centre, only slightly higher than the leaves. It needs an open site in well-drained soil.

O. nutans (*above*)
Nodding star-of-Bethlehem

This European species is rather different from most in having spikes of drooping flowers. Its 6–10in (15–25cm) high stems carry silvery white, pendent flowers, the pointed petals suffused with grey–green on the outside and elegantly curved outwards at the tips. An excellent plant for the semi-shade, *O. nutans* is perfect for naturalizing under trees and shrubs.

O. umbellatum (*above*)
Star-of-Bethlehem

From Europe, this is the most common species of star-of-Bethlehem, producing dense clumps of narrow, green leaves that have a white stripe along the centre of the upper surface. The flower stems are 4–8in (10–20cm) high and in mid- to late spring bear flat-topped heads of shiny, white flowers. These will not open out in the shade, and therefore the plant must be grown in a sunny spot. It is good for planting between and beneath shrubs where the sun will filter through; it also does well in grass.

PUSCHKINIA
Lebanon squill

Although attributed to the Lebanon, this relative of the scilla is found in many of the mountains of the Middle East near the melting snow patches. Like the scilla, it therefore requires a cool spot where the bulbs will not become too hot and dry in summer; it is suitable for planting beneath deciduous shrubs in partial shade or in a not-too-dry position in a rock garden. The small bulbs are obtained in autumn and should be planted about 2in (5cm) under ground. The plants die down in summer. Propagation is by division of offsets or seed sown in autumn. Hardiness zone: 5.

P. scilloides (**syn. P. libanotica**) (*previous column*)

This plant grows 2¼–4¾in (6–12cm) high with two leaves at its base and a raceme of pale blue flowers. These have a darker blue stripe along the centre of each of the six petals. Each flower is about ½in (1cm) in diameter, with the segments joined into a short tube. 'Alba' is the white form.

ROMULEA

Romulea is a relative of the crocus. Although many species are widespread and sometimes common in the wild, they are scarcely known as garden plants in spite of being easily cultivated. Unfortunately, some are not very hardy and others have less attractive flowers and require a good, sunny, spring day before they will open. The spectacular species from South Africa can be tried in the warm climates of southern regions of North America, but gardens in cooler climates are restricted to the less striking Mediterranean species. *R. bulbocodium* is, however, worth trying in a warm, sunny, well-drained spot. The small corms are planted in autumn at a depth of about 2in (5cm) and may be left undisturbed for several years to increase into clumps, in which case the flower display improves considerably. It is also a good plant for a mid-spring display in an alpine house. Propagation is either by division of clumps or seed sown in autumn. Hardiness zone: 7.

R. bulbocodium (*above*)

This dwarf romulea is the showiest of the hardier species, reaching 2–4in (5–10cm) high, with thread-like, tough leaves topping funnel-shaped, lilac-blue flowers; these open out 1in (2.5cm) in diameter in the sun. The flower throat is usually yellow but, being a variable plant, there are many colour forms to choose from.

SCILLA
Spring squill

Almost without exception, the spring species of scilla are blue-flowering, apart from a few selected colour variants such as albinos. They are mostly dwarf and hardy plants, flowering from early to late spring, and are generally inexpensive, making it a particularly useful group. Scillas vary in their cultural requirements, but are all best planted in autumn at a depth of 2-2³/₄in (5-7cm), in reasonably well-drained soil. Propagation is mainly by division of clumps in late summer or early autumn since they tend to produce offset bulbs quite freely; seed is also produced, although this is much slower. Hardiness zones: 5-8.

S. bifolia
This small, early spring bulb will grow in semi-shade or full sun and is useful for naturalizing under shrubs or for planting among early perennials such as hellebores. Each bulb produces two leaves and a 2-4in (5-10cm) high stem bearing a one-sided spike of small, deep blue-violet flowers that are flat and star-shaped when fully open. 'Praecox' (*above*) is a vigorous, showier, large-flowering form, 'Alba' is white and 'Rosea' pale pink.

S. bithynica
This is a good squill for naturalizing since it seeds freely and grows in full sun and partial shade, eventually forming sizeable patches up to 3¹/₂ft (1m) or more across under the right conditions. It grows as tall as 6in (15cm), with narrow basal leaves and dense racemes of small, star-shaped, mid-blue flowers, each about ¹/₂in (1cm) in diameter.

S. greilhuberi
This scilla produces long, linear leaves in autumn, and 4-6in (10-15cm) long racemes of star-shaped flowers in mid-spring. The flowers are lilac-blue, with reflexed segments when fully open. It is easily cultivated in the semi-shade, and is ideal for planting under shrubs and trees.

S. italica (*below*)
A useful plant for a sunny spot in a rock garden or the front of a border, *S. italica* makes a good show in mid-spring, increasing into clumps by bulb division and offsets. The thin leaves are accompanied in mid-spring by 6-8in (15-20cm) high stems; these carry rather flat-topped or conical racemes of pale to mid-blue flowers ¹/₂in (1cm) across and almost flat when fully open.

S. lilio-hyacinthus
This version produces tufts of up to 10 broad, glossy green leaves from large, scaly, lily-like bulbs. In late spring, 4-8in (10-20cm) tall stems carry loose racemes of small, star-shaped flowers, pale to lilac-blue, or white in 'Alba'. It requires a cool, semi-shaded spot.

S. litardierei (*above*)
This scilla is better known by its incorrect name *S. pratensis* or its more vigorous form *S. amethystina*. It flowers later than most scillas in late spring or early summer, and has narrow basal leaves. The 4-8in (10-20cm) long dense racemes of *S. litardierei* have up to 30 small, star-shaped, blue flowers, each about ¹/₄in (0.5cm) in diameter. It grows best in the rock garden or sunny border where it can be left undisturbed to form clumps, making a good show after the main flush of spring bulbs has finished.

S. mischtschenkoana (syn. S. tubergeniana)
A delightful and inexpensive scilla, this species is invaluable for planting in groups in a rock garden, between hardy perennials or shrubs and in the semi-shade of trees and shrubs. At flowering time in early spring it has short, glossy, pale green leaves almost hidden by the pale blue flowers that begin to open as soon as they push through the ground. The stems elongate and ultimately grow 4-6in (10-15cm) high when flowering is complete. The individual flowers are about ¹/₂in (1.5cm) in diameter, saucer-shaped and pale blue with a dark blue stripe on each petal; the display lasts for a long period. The clone known as 'Tubergeniana' (*above*) is the best and most commonly sold.

S. peruviana (*above*)
An attractive species when flowering well, this plant requires a hot, sunny spot where the bulbs can bake over summer when dormant. Plant them in autumn with their tips just beneath the surface. The large bulbs

start to produce rosettes of broad, pointed leaves that continue to grow until late spring, when they are accompanied by large, conical heads of up to 100 steely blue, flat, star-like flowers growing $\frac{3}{4}$in (2cm) across. There is also a white version, 'Alba'.

S. siberica (*above*)
Probably the most well-known of the group, this early spring squill is inexpensive and worth planting in patches or drifts in the semi-shade of shrubs where it provides a bold splash of colour. It grows almost anywhere except hot, dry places and is reliably hardy. The glossy green leaves are topped by flowering stems that elongate through the season from 2-6in (5-15cm) in height, bearing up to five bell-shaped, mid- to deep blue flowers, each up to $\frac{1}{2}$in (1.5cm) long. The form most often sold is 'Spring Beauty', a brilliant deep blue; there is also an albino form known as 'Alba'.

S. verna
Spring squill
Not as showy as the similar *S. italica* but nevertheless a charming plant, *S. verna* is well-worth growing in a sunny rock garden or in a pot in an alpine house. It has narrow basal leaves and 2-4in (5-10cm) high stems that carry flat-topped racemes, each with up to 12 small, lilac-blue to violet flowers. These are flat and star-shaped, barely reaching $\frac{3}{8}$in (1cm) in diameter.

TECOPHILAEA
Chilean blue crocus
This appropriately named plant originates from the Andes in Chile. Although it is thought to be extinct in the wild, the Chilean blue crocus is propagated in cultivation and is obtainable from a few bulb nurseries, albeit at a price since it does not increase very rapidly. Tecophilaea is not a difficult plant to grow, requiring only

well-drained soil and a sunny spot, but in view of its rarity and cost it is probably best given the protection of an alpine house, cool conservatory or cold frame. In summer, while the plants are dormant, the corms should be kept dry but not allowed to bake, and then repotted, and watered from autumn until summer. Propagation is by seed sown in autumn or by offsets which are sometimes produced. Hardiness zone: 9.

T. cyanocrocus (*below*)
The almost flat corms produce 2-4in (5-10cm) high stems with narrow, deep green leaves and one or two large, funnel-shaped flowers about 1in (2.5cm) in diameter. An intense deep blue, they rival gentians in colour. *T. c.* 'Leichtlinii' is paler blue with a large, white centre, and *T. c.* 'Violacea' is a deep purple.

TRILLIUM
Wake robin
The first part of the name trillium describes these gorgeous spring flowers because their stems have three leaves held in a whorl and the solitary flowers, one per stem, have three sepals and three petals. Mainly woodland plants, the majority are from North America and are hardy, although the young emerging shoots can be damaged by late frosts. The thick rhizomes should be planted at a depth of 2-4in (5-10cm) with the largest and most vigorous species planted deeper than the small ones. The following recommended types are not difficult to grow, requiring partial shade in a humus-rich soil, and are best if left undisturbed to establish clumps. The flowering period is mid- to late spring. Seed propagation is slow, but clumps can occasionally be lifted and divided in autumn or spring. Hardiness zones: 4-6.

T. cernuum
Nodding trillium
About 10-12in (25-30cm) high, this trillium has white flowers, each one with a maroon-coloured ovary. The blossoms are held just below the rosette of three broad, green leaves in a pendent position. For this reason, it is not easy to see the flowers, so it is best planted in a raised bed where they can be fully appreciated.

T. chloropetalum (*below*)
This beautiful plant carries large flowers held upright and stemless, resting on top of the rosette of three mottled leaves which are carried on a 10-14in (25-35cm) high stem. The flowers have erect petals 2-3$\frac{1}{4}$in (5-8cm) long; they are usually white, although other colours are available.

T. cuneatum (**T. sessile** of gardens) (*below*)
This plant is very similar to *T. chloropetalum* in general appearance but with deep maroon petals over broad, handsomely mottled leaves. When growing well, it may reach 16in-1$\frac{1}{4}$ft (40-53cm) in height and can form large clumps, making it particularly suitable for woodland gardens. The true *T. sessile*, rare in cultivation, is a much smaller, unremarkable plant.

T. erectum

The whorl of plain green leaves is held on 10-16in (25-40cm) high stems and is topped by flowers held on slender, erect or oblique stalks. The most commonly available are deep reddish-maroon and white.

T. grandiflorum (*below*)
Wake robin
Perhaps the best species, wake robin is easy to grow and showy, with its snow white flowers having petals up to 3$\frac{1}{2}$in (9cm) long. They are held on stalks well above the deep green leaves carried on 8in-1$\frac{1}{2}$ft (20-45cm) high stems. The flowers fade to a purplish-pink with age; 'Roseum' is a beautiful form with flowers opening soft pink, and 'Flore Pleno' has tight, double, white flowers. A good flowering clump of *T. grandiflorum* is one of the best spring sights in the garden.

T. luteum (*below*)
Resembling *T. cuneatum*, *T. luteum* has mottled leaves and erect, stemless flowers, but with greenish-yellow petals.

T. nivale (*next column*)
Snow trillium
This dwarf species is rarely cultivated and difficult to grow. It is only 2-4in (5-10cm)

high and has deep green leaves topped by small, white flowers with 1-1$\frac{3}{4}$in (2.5-4.5cm) long petals. It prefers an alkaline soil in sun or very slight shade and is best grown in an alpine house or cold frame.

T. ovatum
This trillium is similar to *T. grandiflorum*, although it generally has slightly smaller flowers and is seldom as vigorous.

T. rivale (*above*)
T. rivale thrives in a cool position in a peat garden or semi-shaded rock garden. It is only 2-3$\frac{1}{4}$in (5-8cm) high, with a rosette of plain green leaves and a small flower 1$\frac{1}{4}$in (3.5cm) in diameter. This is white or pale pink, spotted darker red to varying degrees and sometimes with a darker red eye in the centre. Although a diminutive plant, it forms patches when growing well. It is an excellent subject for the alpine house or cold frame.

TULIPA
Tulip
If crocuses are the mainstay of the early spring bulb display and daffodils of the mid-spring period, then tulips provide the climax in late spring. As well as the many delightful species that are readily available, there are hundreds of selections and

hybrids, from the dwarf Kaufmanniana types to the tall late Darwins, mainly thanks to the skill and patience of the Dutch growers. Hybrid tulips are grouped into horticultural divisions according to distinguishing characteristics; a few of each are described below. Propagation is by division in autumn. Hardiness zones: 5-7.

T. acuminata (*below*)
For those who like curiosities, this strange tulip is tall, 1$\frac{1}{2}$-1$\frac{3}{4}$ft (45-53cm) when in flower, and has slender flowers, each in a mixture of yellow and red with long, tapering petals. Although not showy enough for bedding displays, it is a fine plant for placing in small groups adjacent to neutral foliage that allows the flowers to stand out.

T. batalinii (*below*)
This is a popular dwarf tulip for a rock garden, the front of a border or trough. Given a warm, well-drained position, it is often persistent and will even increase into clumps. It is only 2-4in (5-10cm) high, with primrose yellow flowers 2-2$\frac{3}{4}$in (5-7cm) across, set amid narrow, grey, wavy-margined leaves. There are several colour forms including 'Bronze Charm' which has an apricot-bronze flush to the flowers.

T. clusiana
Lady tulip
A graceful slender species up to 12in (30cm) high, the lady tulip has narrow, grey leaves and elegant, narrow-petalled flowers that open out into a star-shape 4in (10cm) in diameter. They are white with a dark crimson eye in the centre and a strong pinkish-crimson stain on the outside. *T. c. chrysantha* (*above*) is similar but has a yellow background colour instead of white, whereas *T. c. stellata* has white flowers with a yellow central blotch. *T. aitchisonii* is sometimes offered in catalogues but is so similar to *T. clusiana* some botanists consider it identical.

T. eichleri (*above*)
This striking central Asiatic tulip grows to a height of 10-12in (25-30cm) and has broad leaves. The large, orange-red flowers reach up to 4¾in (12cm) in diameter when open, revealing a blackish blotch in the centre.

T. fosteriana
A vigorous, red-flowering tulip that reaches 1½ft (45cm) in height, *T. fosteriana* has bold, grey-green leaves and huge flowers that can measure up to 8in (20cm) across. Each bloom is flushed yellowish-gold on the outside, with a blackish eye surrounded by a narrow yellow zone inside. The best of the group includes 'Purissima', a creamy white turning pure

white with age, 'Madame Lefeber' (*below*), a brilliant glowing red, and 'Orange Emperor', a lovely striking shade of orange.

T. greigii (*below*)
This early tulip is mostly grown for its broad, attractive, purplish-brown striped leaves, a characteristic continued in its hybrids. The true species is 8-16in (20-40cm) high with bright red, black-eyed flowers.

T. humilis
A charming small tulip from the Middle East, this species flowers right at the beginning of the tulip season in mid-spring and is ideally suited to a warm sunny border, a rock garden or alpine house. It is only 2-6in (5-15cm) high, with narrow, greyish-green leaves clustered at ground level and pinkish-purple flowers about 2¼-2¾in (6-7cm) in diameter with a yellow eye. 'Violacea' has rich purple flowers, 'Pulchella' is a rather paler purple-magenta with a deep bluish eye.

T. kaufmanniana (*next column*)
Waterlily tulip
This stocky little dwarf tulip from central Asia is the earliest to flower with broad, grey-green leaves that are fairly short at flowering time. It is a good candidate for ornamental

containers on a terrace or patio, or for planting in a rock garden or sunny border. It can even be grown in pots for an early display in a cool conservatory but should not be forced with too much heat. In the wild, it varies a lot, but the most commonly seen variation has 4-8in (10-20cm) tall stems with cream or pale yellow flowers flushed red on the outside. The leaves are all carried in a tuft at the base making a neat and compact plant when flowering. *T. kaufmanniana* has been hybridized with other species; several are mentioned under Kaufmanniana tulips.

T. kolpakowskiana
This elegant species stands approximately 4-8in (10-20cm) high, with upright, grey-green, wavy-edged leaves and a slender, yellow flower flushed pink on the outside of its pointed petals. Each one opens out 2¼-3¼in (6-8cm) in diameter.

T. linifolia (*above*)
This wonderful dwarf tulip species measuring 4-8in (10-20cm) in height adds a brilliant splash of colour to the rock garden or sunny border in mid-spring. They have narrow, wavy-edged leaves and brilliant scarlet flowers with a small blackish-purple eye in the centre, opening out flat in the sun to 2¼-3¼in (6-8cm) across.

T. marjolettii
Unusually coloured, this species has cream petals flushed purplish on the outside and edged with pink. It generally reaches 14in-1½ft (35-45cm) in height.

T. maximowiczii
Similar in general appearance to *T. linifolia*, this tulip has a white-edged, dark eye in the centre of each flower.

T. orphanidea
Although subdued in colour when compared with some of the gaudy red species, the subtle coloration of *T. orphanidea* has much to recommend it and looks particularly effective with grey- or silver-leaved subjects. It grows 10-12in (25-30cm) high, with up to three dull orange-brown flowers stained green on the outside and opening to approximately 1¾in (4.5cm) in diameter. Its relatives *T. hageri*, with dull red flowers, and the orange-bronze *T. whittallii* are both closely related and sometimes available.

T. praestans (*above*)
The interesting feature of this central Asian tulip is that it produces up to five showy flowers on each stem and has played a part in the development of the "bunch-flowering" tulips. It has rather broad, upright, grey-green leaves and 12in (30cm) tall stems bearing several bright, orange-red flowers up to 4in (10cm) across; just a few bulbs can give a striking display.

T. saxatilis
An unusual species from Crete, *T. saxatilis* requires the hottest, sunniest spot in the garden where it will have room to develop since it increases by stolons to form patches. It enjoys sites such as a border at the base of a warm wall, and grows particularly well on alkaline soil, although this is not essential. The broad, glossy green leaves are

accompanied by 8-12in (20-30cm) high stems bearing up to four pink flowers that have a deep yellow eye in the centre; each bloom reaches 2¼-3¼in (6-8cm) in diameter.

T. sprengeri (*below*)
This is the latest-flowering tulip of all, its smallish flowers appearing well after the others have finished, so late it almost qualifies as a summer bulb. It has erect, shiny green leaves and 1-1½ft (30-45cm) tall stems carrying solitary yellowish-gold buds which open out to reveal bright scarlet flowers. It succeeds in a range of different situations from full sun to partial shade, and also seeds very freely.

T. sylvestris (*below*)
With a height of 8-14in (20-35cm), this small-flowering tulip is easy to grow in open positions or dryish semi-shade, but it is not free-flowering. However, it creates sizeable patches. The yellow flowers, 2¼-3¼in (6-8cm) wide, are suffused green on the outside.

T. tarda (*next column*)
This is a most attractive and popular dwarf tulip for the front of a border, rock garden or trough. The leaves are narrow and produced in a rosette at ground level, almost hidden at

flowering time by the blooms, up to five of which appear on each stem. They open wide to about 2in (5cm) in diameter and are yellow with white-tipped petals.

T. turkestanica (*below*)
A slender species tulip from central Asia, it grows 4-10in (10-25cm) high with narrow, greyish leaves and up to 12 small, white flowers. These are flushed green on the outside with a small yellow eye in the centre.

T. urumiensis (*below*)
Similar to *T. tarda* but with yellow flowers diffused bronze on the outside, this is good for a sunny, well-drained site.

Single early tulips

Like the Double early tulips, these are short and stocky in stature, 8-12in (20-30cm) high, with single, rounded flowers on sturdy stems produced early in the tulip season. 'Apricot Beauty' (*below*) is a mixture of soft salmon and orange and is recommended for forcing in pots for an even earlier display; 'Bellona' has bright golden yellow flowers; and 'Brilliant Star', one of the first to bloom, is a short weather-resistant variety with bright scarlet flowers, suitable for planting out or for forcing in mid-winter.

Double early tulips

These appropriately named tulips flower at the start of the tulip season and have tight, double blooms. They are stocky plants, usually 10-12in (25-30cm) high and, being wind-resistant, are good for container planting to give an early display on a terrace. 'Orange Nassau' is a deep blood red and orange-red mixture, 'Schoonoord' is a pure white, 'Peach Blossom' (*below*) a deep rose pink and 'Mr van der Hoef' a good yellow.

Mid-season tulips (including Mendel and Triumph tulips)

These tulip cultivars bridge the gap between the very early types and the May-flowering

group. They have rounded flowers, sometimes rather angular in bud, on stout, short stems and are usually 1¼-1¾ft (40-53cm) high so they withstand inclement weather quite well. A great range of these tulips is available, including 'Lady Diana', a splendid shade of soft rose-red, 'New Design', a very unusual and fairly new tulip with pink-edged leaves and flowers that are yellowish changing to pinkish-cream on the outside and a yellow interior flushed apricot, 'African Queen', a deep wine colour, the petals having a contrasting narrow white margin, and 'Athleet', an excellent pure white cultivar.

Darwin hybrids

These plants also have large flowers, oval before they open fully, and are derived from crosses between the red central Asian species *T. fosteriana* and the Darwin cultivars. Mostly about 2-2¼ft (60-68.5cm) high, they flower slightly earlier than the Darwin and Cottage (or Viridiflora) types in mid-spring. 'Golden Apeldoorn' (*above*) is golden yellow splashed with red on the outside, and when open reveals a blackish eye in the centre; it is a robust garden variety. 'Gudoshnik' is also yellow but has rather more pronounced red spots and streaks on the outside. 'Elizabeth Arden' is a deep salmon pink, with a slightly darker, reddish-violet band in the centre of each petal, and 'Gordon Cooper' is deep pink on the outside, edged with red.

May-flowering hybrids

Also called Single late or Darwin tulips, these varieties have large, oval to rounded flowers on stout 2-2¾ft (60-84cm) high stems and are very popular for bedding displays. 'Clara Butt' is an old favourite with salmony-pink flowers; 'Halcro' is bright red with the petals edged orange-red; 'Queen of Night' (*next column*) has velvety deep maroon flowers; and 'Sorbet' is almost white with a pinkish

shading, becoming more heavily striped and feathered orange-red with age. A good yellow choice is 'Golden Harvest', with its clear, lemon yellow flowers.

Lily-flowering tulips

These are among the most elegant tulips, with tall, 1½-2ft (45-60cm) high stems carrying slender flowers with pointed petals arching outwards at the tips. They flower late in the tulip season and are weather-resistant. 'Maytime' has dull reddish-purple petals shading at the edge to a narrow band of cream; 'China Pink' is a fine shade of pink mixing well with forget-me-nots; 'West Point' is a highly popular clear yellow with long, graceful, pointed petals; 'Aladdin' (*below*) is an attractive scarlet-red with yellow-edged petals; and 'White Triumphator' is a good pure white.

Viridiflora tulips

This group comprises curiously coloured varieties, all marked with green stripes or bands to varying degrees. They are late-flowering and mostly rather stiff and stocky, about 1½ft (45cm) high. 'Artist' has noticeably pointed, salmon-rose petals with a wide green band along the centre, an intriguing blend of colours. 'Greenland' is predominantly pink with a narrow but conspicuous green stripe along the centre of the rather broad petals. In 'Spring Green', the lower half of the flower is bright green fading to cream at the edges and upper half of the petals. The flowers of the 'Esperanto' tulip are very striking, with the petals a deep rose colour at the edges and the tips shading to strong green in the centre; the leaves have a white margin.

Rembrandt tulips

These are the old single cottage garden tulips with "broken" flower colours, that is to say, the flowers are striped and feathered with contrasting colours. They flower in late spring and are 2-2¼ft (60-68.5cm) high. Few varieties are still commercially available, although mixed Rembrandt tulips can be obtained. 'Cordell Hull', a white flower with red flame-like markings, is generally available, and 'San Marino' is yellow, with similar red flame-like markings.

Parrot and Fringed tulips

These are the exotic end of the tulip range with the bizarre colours of the Parrot group and the crystal-fringed petals of the latter types. They flower late in the season and reach up to 1½-1¾ft (45-53cm) high. Of the Parrot types, 'Black Parrot' (*above*) is one of the darkest, with blackish-purple flowers lacerated at the edges of the petals. 'White Parrot' is the pure white equivalent, and 'Flaming Parrot' is the extrovert with wavy, laciniate-edged, pale yellow petals flamed with red on the outside and bold bright red stripes inside. The Fringed types are more like the May-flowering kind in flower shape but the margins of the petals have a crystalline fringe. 'Blue Heron' is a bluish-violet shade with a whitish fringe of needle-like crystals, and 'Burgundy Lace' is a deep burgundy red with a very conspicuous fringe on the edges.

Double late tulips

This group of tulips flower much later in the season, coinciding with the May-flowering cultivars. They are taller than Double early tulips and need shelter from the wind but compensate by having showy, long-lasting blooms that give them their other name, Peony-flowered tulips. 'Angelique' is a soft pink in a blend of lighter and darker tones, 'Mount Tacoma' (*above*) is a pure white, and 'Wirosa' is deep red with the many petals edged and tipped creamy white.

Kaufmanniana hybrids

These hybrids descend from the waterlily tulip and are therefore mostly compact plants, standing 6-8in (15-20cm) high, with neat, broad, grey-green leaves only partly developed at flowering time. They flower early in the season and are very hardy and weather-resistant, making ideal container plants. Some are hybrids with *T. greigii* and have inherited the striped foliage. 'Stresa' (*above*) is very popular, bright yellow with a smart red exterior to the outer three petals; 'Shakespeare' is a soft mixture of carmine and orange on the outside and yellow flushed pinkish-red inside; 'Gluck' has attractive mottled foliage topped by red flowers edged yellow, which open out to show a yellow interior, and 'Berlioz' is a clear yellow with striped leaves.

Greigii hybrids

These are easily recognized because of the attractive brownish-purple striped foliage, a feature derived from *T. greigii*. They are rather early-flowering and are short and stocky, making them ideal for a rock garden or at the front of a border; they are also well-suited to container cultivation for patios or terraces, and for growing in window boxes. They are mostly about 8-12in (20-30cm) high. 'Red Riding Hood' (*below*) has bright scarlet-red flowers and beautiful purple-striped leaves; 'Corsage' has equally good foliage with flowers of a bright apricot-salmon shade; 'Plaisir' has elegant pointed petals in carmine red edged with pale cream-lemon; and the noteworthy 'Toronto' is a multiflowering variety with up to three pinkish-red flowers per stem.

Multiflowering tulips

A few varieties of Multiflowering tulips with several flowers per stem are available. This is a characteristic of *T. praestans*, from which they have partly been developed. They flower fairly late in the season. Apart from the red 'Toronto' (see Greigii hybrids), there is an excellent yellow, 'Georgette' (*below*), which provides a great splash of colour despite its small individual flowers.

SUMMER BULBS

Garden highlights

Bulbs are exceptionally good at providing summer highlights in the flower garden, being easily used to fill awkward gaps in the border without disturbing surrounding plants. They can also be poked into corners and tucked in among the roots of shrubs to provide mid-summer colour.

Of all the summer-flowering bulbs, lilies provide the greatest opportunity for spectacular displays. Indeed, they look so exotic that many gardeners think they are too difficult to grow. However, nothing could be further from the truth, for the popular garden varieties like *Lilium regale* and *L. marta-gon* are both readily available and easily raised.

Lilies are very versatile bulbs and come in a range of colours, from white and pale yellow to dark pink. Some are also wonderfully scented. They are best grown in small groups in a mixed border, with their roots in the shade and their flowers in the sun. Lilies are often seen flowering alongside roses, where they will continue to bloom after the roses have finished their season. It is also worth growing the scented types under a window or in a sitting-out area, either in flower beds or in containers.

Among the most widely grown lilies are hybrids, an extensive range of the Asiatic and Asiatic trumpet lilies with flowers that are good for both border decoration and cutting. They are robust plants with strong stems that rarely need staking, and they can be combined in a number of ways for many different effects. For a bold look, grow a group of upright-flowering orange 'Enchantment' in a border against a background of tall, spiky, soft yellow *Verbascum olympicum* (mullein), or mix a few hybrids together in a colourful mass for more of a cottage-garden look. Also popular, the species

PREVIOUS PAGE A bed full of lilies is a dazzling sight, and on warm summer evenings they will perfume the air.

LEFT In summer, nothing equals the majestic appearance of Lilium regale, *with its deliciously scented white flowers.*

BELOW A striking effect can be achieved by planting brightly coloured lilies, such as this Oriental hybrid, with mixed nicotianas.

L. auratum and *L. regale* have magnificent trumpet-shaped blossoms on towering stems up to 5ft (1.5m) high which must be securely supported. They are among the most spectacular of summer-flowering lilies, especially effective when grown against a dark backdrop; dark green conifers, shrubby, evergreen loniceras (honeysuckle) or broad-leaved evergreens like *Osmanthus, Ligustrum* (privet) and *Cotoneaster* are all appropriate. For a terrace site, plant a mixture of *Lilium regale* and a low-growing shrub such as *Viburnum davidii,* with a soft foreground planting of *Felicia* and a background of scented evergreen osmanthus.

Lilium candidum (madonna lily) has an old-fashioned charm, as does the rich orange *L. lancifolium*. Both are easygoing species that look lovely in a mixed border when associated with unruly hardy annuals such as annual cornflowers, Virginian stocks and toadflax. *L. speciosum* is another good choice as its flowering season extends beyond the first frost. The fine crimson and white blossoms look their best when peeping from among shrubby evergreen ground cover such as *Sarcococca confusa* (Christmas box) and ivies like *Hedera helix hibernica*, both of which provide an attractive foil to the flowers. They can also be grown among low-growing shrub roses and hardy fuchsias; fuchsias will act as a support to the lilies as well as lend colour to the scheme.

Galtonia (summer-flowering hyacinth) is good for lifting a mixed border display. The showy, white-flowered *G. candicans* is particularly effective, being similar to a giant hyacinth but taller, with pendent, creamy bells spaced further apart. Being of sunny disposition, it associates well with bright red border plants; a planting of *G. candicans* and *Lychnis chalcedonica* is quite startling and the perfect combination for a sunny corner. Galtonias also mix well with yellow-flowered *Hemerocallis* and *Lilium candidum*; try them against a background of dark blue ceanothus.

The ornamental onions (alliums) provide some of the best examples of summer-flowering bulbs, producing their brightly

LEFT Nothing is better than a cool, serene planting of white flowers. Use the white-flowering Galtonia candicans *and phlox towards the back of the border, with African daisies grouped in front.* Gladiolus × colvillei 'The Bride' *(TOP INSET) is another excellent subject for a white garden; it is more delicate-looking than some of its relatives. For a completely different effect, however, plant a clump of* Zantedeschia aethiopica *(BOTTOM INSET).*

coloured flowers from late spring until mid-summer. Plant the bulbs in autumn; they are not too demanding and prosper under most conditions and soils, although the majority of the striking, colourful kinds prefer an open, sunny position. They can be grown with any plants that do not require very damp soil conditions but, because of their slightly ragged, faded foliage, they look best tucked away among other plants in a colourful mixed border rather than grown as a feature.

Allium moly is the cheapest, most cheerful ornamental onion, with dense umbels of starry, bright yellow blossoms. It reproduces rapidly in most conditions and creates a perfect carpet beneath summer-flowering shrubs such as *Philadelphus* (mock orange), which produces deliciously scented white flowers. *Weigela*, with its red or pink trumpet-shaped blooms, and the bright pink-flowered *Kolkwitzia* (beauty bush) are equally suitable. *A. moly* does not tolerate too much shade but quickly becomes established among the roots of mature woody plants.

Allium sphaerocephalon has a very different appearance from *A. moly*, and is perfect for providing extra interest in the shrub border. With dense umbels of dark purple, bell-shaped flowers, it is a versatile plant that prospers in sun or partial shade. Allow it to grow up through low-growing plants such as *Ajuga* and *Lysimachia nummularia* 'Aurea' (creeping Jenny) for especially good foliage contrasts. For a strong sculptural statement, grow *A. sphaerocephalon* with domes of lavender 'Hidcote' or *Santolina chamaecyparissus* (cotton lavender). The rich purple *Allium aflatunense* looks very attractive grown in a sunny border with *Achillea taygetea* or the yellow Welsh poppy, *Meconopsis cambrica*.

Sun is the main requirement of *Allium rosenbachianum*, a large, dark purple-flowered onion with rounded heads of blossom held on stout, upright stems. It is rather formal in character but excellent for filling gaps in the mixed or herbaceous border during high summer. The giant *A. giganteum* also provides a startling addition to a mixed planting but is much better as a single focal point. A wonderful plant, it thrusts up bold flower stems which are topped with a large, perfectly spherical head of rosy purple-coloured blossoms 4in (10cm) in diameter. It is best positioned at the end of a walkway or

TOP LEFT The delicate blue of Allium caeruleum *is brought out by the striking pinky-orange lilies and the pink rose 'Queen of Denmark'.*

BOTTOM LEFT For a cottage-garden planting, Allium christophii, *with its loose umbels of starry flowers, mixes perfectly with roses.*

MIDDLE LEFT Pictured here with pink phlox, Allium sphaerocephalon *has dense umbels of pinkish-purple flowers held on tall stems.*

RIGHT The pink flowers of Allium aflatunense *are perfectly complemented by the dark parrot tulips growing in front.*

used as a highlight between tall, shrubby plants. As the leaves are often fairly scruffy, place the bulbs behind a low, dense shrub like *Potentilla* or *Spiraea*.

Dutch irises have similar requirements and, although more frequently used for cut flowers, they can make a useful contribution to the border if carefully arranged. There are many different-coloured hybrids available. Plant a minimum of 20 bulbs in a group, allowing no more than 4in (10cm) between any two bulbs, and they will appear as a bold column of foliage and flowers in early summer when the border is lacking interest. They look particularly striking reflected in water although they dislike water-logged soil but will tolerate the dry soil around the edge of artificial pools.

Crocosmia are delightful summer-flowering bulbs, with arching stems of brightly coloured flowers. The bright red 'Lucifer' and soft yellow 'Solfatare' are particularly attractive, and can also be established almost anywhere, the most logical place being a herbaceous border where they add height as well as colour, although few plants look finer than 'Lucifer' when reflected in water. However, that does not mean crocosmias enjoy wet soil; on the contrary, to obtain the best results, provide a free-draining medium that does not dry out completely during summer and incorporate plenty of well-rotted organic matter into the soil. Crocosmias associate well with gladioli when used to intensify colour schemes; *Crocosmia* 'Citronella' and the soft apricot-coloured *Gladiolus* 'Tesoro' are good companions, as are *Crocosmia* 'Lucifer' and *Gladiolus* 'Black Lash'.

Tigridia is a beautiful orchid-like garden highlight, so bright and colourful that it does not associate easily with other plants and so should be planted alone. These bulbs have vivid, colourful blossoms in almost every hue and combination imaginable and resemble tropical butterflies. Choose a bright, sunny spot and a free-draining soil for the best results, isolating the plants in a narrow border or pocket, or in a terrace flower bed. The warmer and sunnier the spot, the better the flowers will be; under favourable conditions, they will continue well into autumn. Individual blossoms last a day but are produced in such quantities that the plants seem to be permanently in flower.

Watsonia is a greatly under-rated summer-flowering bulb. Elegant plants of similar appearance and temperament to the small-flowered gladioli, but perhaps a little less hardy, they prosper in a warm sunny spot in free-draining soil. Except

TOP Mixed Dutch irises are very versatile in border plantings. They are easy to grow and a familiar sight in many gardens.

RIGHT For real impact in the summer border, nothing is better than crocosmia, the dazzling flowers of which always attract the eye.

for *Watsonia pillansii*, they are likely to need lifting and storing during the winter. For good colour combinations, tuck the red, orange and soft pink flowers into groups of silver- and grey-leaved plants. Unlike other *Watsonia* species, *W. pillansii* tolerates the damp, although it must be grown in full sun. With a mostly unbranched stem up to 3ft (90cm) high, it produces a dense spike of large apricot or orange-red flowers and makes a gorgeous splash of colour that gives any display a lift. It also looks very eye-catching when planted with leafy geraniums or billowing white masses of gypsophila in a large mixed border.

The deep pink *Watsonia densiflora* is not as suitable for general border cultivation as *W. pillansii*. Nevertheless, it is well worth growing, the plants looking best when planted among grey-leaved plants like *Artemisia schmidtiana* and *Helichrysum angustifolium* (syn. *H. italicum*) to create a harmonious colour combination of pink and silvery grey. White-flowering watsonias always look good alongside dark or evergreen foliage plants; small, dark green conifers such as *Chamaecyparis lawsoniana* 'Forsteckensis' and *C. l.* 'Minima' are suitable. The graceful, long-flowering *W.* 'Arderne's White' requires a free-draining, sunny spot and *Arbutus unedo* (strawberry tree) and *Laurus nobilis* (sweet bay) are perfect companions for this particularly good watsonia.

The dappled shade under deciduous trees offers the opportunity to grow another summer-flowering highlight, the truly eye-catching giant white lily *Cardiocrinum giganteum*. This hardy Himalayan plant loves a rich, leafy medium in a woodland glade and grows well beneath a tree canopy where the ground is not too congested with roots. A single tree will suffice, birch, mountain ash and flowering ash being good choices. A giant of a plant up to 8ft (2·4m) high under perfect conditions, it produces the most spectacular spires of white, semi-pendent, trumpet-shaped blossoms. Once they fade, the bulb dies, leaving a cluster of offsets which will not flower for another year or two. With this in mind, plant the bulbs every two or three years in order to secure a constant succession of spires.

Cardiocrinum does not mix well with other plants as it is a stately character which demands planting alone, perhaps at the edge of a winding woodland path. It looks especially fine when emerging from a short, grassy sward but this is not always possible since quality grass does not necessarily grow in the shade of trees. As an alternative, plant the giant lily among a shade-tolerant, low-growing scrambler like *Lysimachia nummularia* (creeping Jenny).

Although gladioli are mostly grown for their cut flowers, they are very popular garden plants in their own right. It is easy to see why, for they are available in many colours including pure white, lemon yellow, pale orange, pale mauve, bright red, strong yellow and dark pink. There are also multicoloured hybrids which have contrasting patches of colour on their lower petals and throats.

Gladioli can be used in mixed herbaceous and shrub borders because they are tall and vigorous enough to withstand the competition of neighbouring perennial plants. Grow the large-flowering, taller types at the back of a border where they will lend height as well as colour. They look particularly attractive rising up behind clumps of phlox, campanula and achillea. The smaller-growing gladioli can be grown in small clumps towards the front of the border, mixed with silver-leaved plants such as artemisia and stachys.

Gladioli can also be grown with other bulbs which enjoy the same sunny, fertile, well-drained conditions, such as alliums and crocosmia. Alliums are especially good for mixing with gladioli because their stark, spherical heads show off the more complicated multi-flowering gladioli spikes.

While the majority of summer-flowering bulbs demand hot, sunny conditions in free-draining soil, there are plants for damp conditions, the exquisitely beautiful *Nomocharis* being

ABOVE Of all the gladioli available, Gladiolus communis *subsp.* byzantinus *is one of the most attractive, with delicate-looking, vivid magenta flowers. It is a highly desirable member of the border because, being early-summer flowering, it lends colour and form to the area before the main show begins. It is also a hardy bulb, meaning that unlike other gladioli which may need lifting over winter, the bulbs can be left in the garden all year round. If left undisturbed,* G. c. byzantinus *will grow into large patches.*

one of the best. A high mountain bulb from Asia, it likes rich, cool, damp soil but not waterlogging. It associates well with delicately fronded hardy ferns such as *Athyrium filix-femina* (lady fern) and *Polystichum setiferum* (soft shield fern), and other finely cut foliage in different greens which off-set the exotic-looking blossoms perfectly.

The easiest *Nomocharis* to grow is *N. mairei*, a lovely plant rarely reaching more than 2½ft (76cm) high. The drooping, saucer-shaped flowers in icy white are liberally splashed and spotted with deep rose-purple, most lovely when seen peeping out from a ferny carpet of low-growing *Polystichum*

setiferum 'Proliferum' or the scrambling, dark olive green fern *Dennstaedtia punctiloba*.

Both *Nomocharis saluenensis*, with its bowl-shaped blossoms of red or rose-pink, and the pale pink, spotted *N. pardanthina* are a little taller than *N. mairei*, attaining at least 3ft (90cm) in ideal conditions. They are bulky plants which look best when grouped together, especially when they are planted as sentinels in a sea of green fern fronds. The short-growing form of the common lady fern, *Athyrium filix-femina* 'Minutissimum', is a fine companion, with palest pea green fronds borne in great profusion.

ABOVE For an informal display of contrasting but muted colours, the orangy-apricot Gladiolus 'Perky' *is here grown against a background planting of soft pink-flowered* Lavatera olbia. *The abundance of surrounding foliage helps tone down the colours of the bulbs.*

LEFT The main colour in this border is supplied by Gladiolus communis *subsp.* byzantinus *and* Iris 'Wild Echo', *along with the pink rose growing behind them. The introduction of red strengthens the whole colour scheme and gives it some variety.*

Bulbs for naturalizing

The naturalizing of summer bulbs is not given the attention it deserves. Most gardeners are familiar with a mass of spring-flowering golden daffodils standing proud in the grass, but less so with a carpet of naturalized summer-flowering, magenta-crimson *Gladiolus communis* subsp. *byzantinus*. When grown in the appropriate grass, the effect of this naturalized bulb is quite spectacular.

It is important to select the right grass when naturalizing summer bulbs since some types of grass can easily swamp the bulbs, which is not a problem with spring bulbs. Ordinary coarse grasses in unkempt corners of the garden cannot be used for this type of cultivation; instead, the bulb should be planted and fescue grass grown over the top, so that the two root systems do not compete for space and nutrients.

A number of lilies can also be naturalized in fine grass, *Lilium martagon* (martagon lily) being a fine example. Although not the most striking lily, with its pendent, Turk's cap blossom in pinkish-purple or wine red, it is still one of the easiest to grow even though it is slow to mature from seed. Growing to a height of approximately 3ft (90cm), it is ideal for open glades among trees; by the time the bulb flowers, the grass will have grown tall enough to mask the stems of the lily. In addition to the common species, there is an even lovelier white-flowered selection called 'Album' which is of similar habit and disposition. Unlike many other lilies, it tolerates lime and, with a natural distribution including Siberia and Mongolia, is unusually hardy. Along with *L. duchartrei*, it prospers in a fine grassy sward in the light shade of a few trees, lending itself well to woodland situations, perhaps interplanted with soft clumps of *Milium effusum* 'Aureum' (wood millet).

The lovely *Lilium hansonii* also responds well to naturalizing, despite being more commonly associated with mixed cottage-garden plantings. The thick-petalled blossoms in deep yellow-orange are similar in appearance to *L. martagon*, although taller. It is lime tolerant and after a year or two spreads quite freely to form sizeable groups.

In damp areas, *Lilium pardalinum* makes a good show, spreading by means of a horizontal rhizome-like growth around which whitish bulbs are clustered. It flourishes in a damp spot but does not enjoy waterlogging, preferring heavy damp soil. In favourable conditions, it produces bold flower stems up to 5ft (1.5m) high which support nodding masses of pale reddish-orange blossoms in mid-summer. Use it as a background plant among other tall plants like meadowsweet and *Aruncus dioicus*.

Being mostly a native of wet meadows, *Camassia* also grows well in damp locations, but is not noted for coping with vigorous grass in garden conditions, and cultivated grass must be a fine variety of fescues and bents. *C. leichtlinii* is a strong grower, well suited to naturalizing. It has spikes of blue or violet-blue flowers, occasionally cream or white.

The summer-flowering *Ornithogalum arabicum* can also be used for naturalizing. With its stout spikes of flower stems sporting up to a dozen pearly-white flowers rising out of handsome, dark green leaves, it is best planted as a bold drift. Given a free-draining soil and a sloping site in a sunny spot, without a heavy growth of grass, it should do well. For a more shady position, try growing *Nectaroscordum siculum* subsp. *bulgaricum*; the pendent, bell-shaped white flowers, flushed red and green, look particularly good when sited in dappled shade among other foliage.

ABOVE Lilium martagon *looks better on the edge of woodland than in a border, while* Lilium 'Pink Sensation' *(ABOVE CENTRE), is at home in either.*

The delicate-looking Gladiolus papilio *(ABOVE RIGHT) holds its own in fine grass where, if left undisturbed, it will spread into sizeable colonies.*

RIGHT It is easy to create the impression of a naturalized flower bed by growing hybrid lilies at random, here pushing up among misty blue lavender.

Bulbs for bedding displays

Summer-flowering bulbs can be used as bedding plants, planted close together to form a dense, colourful carpet, or mixed with other bedding subjects and dotted around to add height to a scheme. Most bulbs depend upon an open, sunny situation and free-draining soil which, in the case of mass plantings, should be of reasonably even structure and fertility to ensure uniform growth over the planted area.

Tuberous-rooted begonias are the most useful and versatile bedding subjects. They are available in a wide array of strong colours, with blossoms that vary from the simple single and double kinds to the carnation-type; attractive frilled varieties are also available. The strong, fleshy foliage provides an excellent foil for the blooms, and the plants completely cover the soil. The double tuberous begonias with smaller flowers, popularly sold by colour, are perfect for bedding. They have individual blossoms up to 3in (7.5cm) across and are weather resistant. Different coloured begonias should be from the same series or strain, and among the most useful are the non-stop colour forms, all of uniform height and stature.

There are also a few named varieties grown by enthusiasts which are rather expensive, especially when used in large quantities. The majority of these have long, flouncy flowers that are too heavy to tolerate life outdoors, being easily damaged by wind and rain, and they tend to be favoured by indoor gardeners as house plants.

Single colours are the best for making an impact. Begonias of one colour can be massed together, with an occasional highlighting dot plant to give the display a lift if it appears a little oppressive for the site. Colour can also be used to create illusions. Mixed colours make a bed look bright, busy and very much smaller; the same bed planted with a single colour looks much bigger. Tiny corners can be made to appear larger by a single light colour such as a subtle shade of yellow or pink, but darker colours like red will make an area appear smaller than it is.

Dot plants in bedding displays of begonias should be selected with care. To avoid unsightly colour clashes, brightly coloured dot plants should be used sparingly only in particularly vivid planting schemes in spacious gardens. The best dot plants are those with fine foliage that complement the heavy leaves and blooms of the begonias. A well-grown *Kochia scoparia* (burning bush) is an ideal choice; it forms a lovely mound of delicate foliage of the palest green, turning fiery red or purple in the autumn. With its rounded form, it always looks good in a circular bed. *Grevillea robusta* (silk oak) can also be recommended for mixing with begonias in any open bed. However, it needs to be a few years old before it is tall enough to make enough impact among other plants. With its finely divided, dark olive-green foliage, it is worth retaining for four or five seasons, after which time quality will deteriorate and the plant should be replaced. For a large, formal bedding display, plant *Canna* × *generalis* 'Black Knight' among deep crimson begonias, surrounded by scarlet-flowered begonias with copper-coloured foliage. Lighten the shades of begonia towards the edge of the bed: fade deep orange into clear yellow, finishing off the display with an edge of primrose yellow. A more restrained planting consists of white-flowered begonias planted around the edge of a bed of *Crocosmia* 'Citronella' and white galtonias, with a centre-piece of deep golden *Gladiolus* 'Peter Pears' or *Lilium* 'Amber Gold'.

In formal gardens, tuberous-rooted begonias can be grown in the manner of annual bedding plants, arranged in fanciful shapes and surrounded by a neatly mown lawn. For a

LEFT Tuberous begonias are ideal for summer bedding displays, where their opulent flowers make a real impact.

ABOVE With regular dead-heading and feeding, begonias make a long-lasting focal point in a formal bed.

more adventurous approach, plant a chequerboard of contrasting colours or recreate various motifs and emblems. Such complicated arrangements only work with large, clearly defined arrangements so do not be tempted by elaborate shapes; simplicity is the keynote. These patterns are best achieved with contrasting or complementary striking colours used in bold strokes; strong central colours bordered by a band of a lighter hue are very effective. In fact, tuberous begonias often look very much more attractive when bordered by a different type of plant, and bright green dwarf box edging is ideal. Alternatives include the blue-green 4in (10cm) high grass *Festuca glauca* (blue fescue) and the silver *Chrysanthemum hosmariense* and gold *C. ptarmiciflorum*.

No other group of bulbs is as good for mass bedding, except perhaps some of the modern lilies, which can also be used as highlights or complementary plants to annual bedding subjects. However, lilies do not yield the same quality and continuity of flowers produced by tuberous begonias, and the cost of a large lily display is also prohibitive.

The cannas or Indian shot plants, with their large, green or bronze, banana-like foliage, are very popular dot plants. While they are noted for their handsome foliage, cannas also produce bright yellow, orange, pink or red spikes of blossom that have a superficial likeness to a gladiolus.

Cannas associate well with a wide variety of summer bedding plants, two recommended choices being a bold green-leaved variety among a solid bed of red geraniums or salvia, and a purple- or bronze-leaved kind grown with lemon-flowered French marigolds.

Zantedeschia aethiopica (arum lily) can take on the role of a dot plant in a bedding scheme although it is more usually associated with bogs or water gardens. Use it in the same way as a canna, utilizing the fine green leaves to give height and a hint of tropical elegance to a small bedding display. Mix it with the bright colours of French marigolds, impatiens,

Although they are not really bulbous plants, having tough, fleshy rootstocks, cannas are regularly sold by bulb merchants during early spring and are worth considering. While a few named varieties are available, cannas are normally sold by flower and leaf colour; a handful of plants is usually enough for a bedding display. As the foliage shrivels in frosty weather, planting out should only occur in more clement periods, and since this also applies to companion bedding plants, both should be planted out together.

ABOVE To create an informal, single-coloured bedding display, plant a mixture of Crocosmia *'Citronella', antirrhinums, tagetes and African marigolds.*

RIGHT The canna lily is a familiar sight in many bedding displays, where it adds height to a uniform base planting. Here, Canna × generalis *'Wyoming' is used.*

tagetes or antirrhinums or, for a cool green and white display, surround a large clump of *Galtonia candicans* with several clumps of *Zantedeschia aethiopica* 'Crowborough', and underplant with three or five plants of lime green nicotiana.

Bulbs for the rock garden

There are several small summer-flowering bulbs that do well in the rock garden, mostly varieties that require a hot, sunny, well-drained position. Either plant them in the soil, in which case you run the risk that some of the more unpredictable characters may rot away during the winter, or plant them in pots inserted in the spaces that have been left by the old pots of spring-flowering bulbs.

Sparaxis is the most successful of the short-growing summer bulbs. Popularly known as harlequin flowers, they produce delicate, brightly coloured blossoms on slender, wand-like

as *Thymus serpyllum* 'Coccineus' and the grey-leaved *T. lanuginosus*, or among the clump-forming *Allium narcissiflorum*. *Ixia* (corn lily) is also unpredictable when planted directly in the rock garden and is more reliable grown in pots plunged into a vacant space. These brightly coloured African plants produce exotic, star-shaped blossoms on strong, wiry stems which show up clearly against a background of millstone grit and limestone, especially grey Westmorland, but they do not associate well with sandstone. Since the flowers only open during the afternoon and evening, be sure to place the plants in a position that receives sun at this time of day.

stems. These delightful plants, with a pink, peach or reddish hue, often prosper in the open ground of the rock garden in a well-drained pocket. However, since they shoot very quickly and the emerging growth is vulnerable to frost damage, they are much more reliable when grown in pots buried in the soil and later removed over winter.

Sparaxis is best displayed against dark, flat stones which also provide some shelter. They are difficult to associate with other plants but can be grown through creeping thymes such

Rhodohypoxis can be grown the same way in pots, but where conditions are favourable outside and the soil is free-draining, plant them directly into the ground where they will often continue from year to year. In more sheltered areas, *Anomatheca* will establish itself in the open rock garden in a hot, sunny spot, but it is much happier and more reliable grown in pots. It is usually planted alone as it is easily swamped by other plants; by its very nature, it looks better when set against the hardness of rock or grit.

Containers, window boxes and hanging baskets

Although there are fewer opportunities for growing bulbs in containers, window boxes and hanging baskets in summer than in spring, plenty of imaginative summer plantings are possible.

The most useful group of plants for container planting are begonias. The pendulous kinds, either a single cultivar or a mixed variety, are especially well

ABOVE Begonias are available in a wide range of bright colours. Here, the tumbling red flowers create a soft, informal effect.

suited to hanging baskets due to their drooping flowers, particularly if grown alone or with tuberous begonias. They should not be used in mixed plantings, however, because they demand rich organic compost, such as a peat-based, soilless type, which many other plants dislike. Grow a single cultivar of one colour, inserting one or two tubers into the side of the basket and on top. Pendulous begonias also look marvellous tumbling out of window boxes. In a large window box, the taller-growing, double-flowered tuberous begonia cultivars provide height and a good background, the pendulous kinds being used to fill the foreground and spill over the edge. Each type benefits from regular dead heading and the removal of faded leaves.

In another window box, grow *Oxalis*, although avoid planting it in hanging baskets, which it dislikes. Its neatly mounded growth permits taller plants to grow through it. Brightly coloured, upright antirrhinums associate well with oxalis, as do the various kinds of sweet-scented stocks. However, a group of oxalis alone makes a good show, and is especially useful for filling narrow window boxes where there is little root room or for planting in terracotta pots with limited compost space. Plant the fleshy rootstock in spring, ideally in a soil-based compost as the plants are likely to rot if grown in soilless composts, which may result in complete defoliation.

Sunny summer window boxes can be filled with vivid purple, rose and red blossoms of *Achimenes*. Although it is usually regarded as an indoor subject, if this plant is provided with a little protection from the wind and is grown in an organic growing medium, it will prosper.

ABOVE A mixed group of icy white Lilium regale *'Album' and creamy coloured* Lilium *'Mont Blanc' highlight a dark corner.*

However, achimenes do not mix well with other plants, although the inclusion of a few nephrolepis ferns will set off their blossoms to perfection.

While *Babiana* (baboon root) is normally planted in autumn for spring flowering in the greenhouse or conservatory, if it is planted in a window box in spring it will flower in summer. Like begonias, babianas must have a sunny spot and ample moisture, although great care must be taken to see that during the early stages of growth the compost does not become too wet. Being a vividly coloured plant with exotic-looking, bright blue, cream or crimson blossoms, babinia is difficult to team up with other flowering plants. Use foliage plants instead; the various grey-leaved helichrysums, if kept under control, are the most suitable companions.

LEFT Gladioli are ideal for a formal, elegant container display, here planted with begonias and softened with trailing ivy.

RIGHT The exquisitely fragrant Lilium regale, *with its purple-streaked white petals, is one of the easiest lilies to grow and propagate.*

ABOVE Warm shades of pink make this a charming summer display, with begonias, dahlias, dianthus and ivy in a simple terracotta container.

There is an equally varied choice of bulbs suitable for containers, lilies being an essential ingredient for larger pots. 'Citronella' is certainly one to try; it grows up to 5ft (1.5m) high and has beautiful bright yellow flowers. For a base planting around this lily, try the tender perennial *Bidens ferulifolia* (bur marigold), which has fennel-like leaves and is liberally covered with yellow, daisy-like flowers. Regular pruning will promote bushy growth. Highly scented varieties of lilies benefit from being grown on their own in pots, say three bulbs to each container, as the pots can be moved about to perfume different areas of the garden. 'Star Gazer' (crimson-pink trumpets), 'Black Dragon' (white inside and maroon outside), 'Imperial Gold' (shiny white speckled with red and yellow stripes) and 'Pink Perfection' (bright pink) can all be relied upon to produce a heavy, sweet perfume. Gardeners new to lilies and keen to try one fail-safe variety should opt for *Lilium regale*, an outright winner that never disappoints. At the other extreme, the splendid *L. duchartrei*, with white flowers flecked maroon, can be quite tricky and needs damp, shady conditions and plenty of peaty soil. If you prefer a slightly more unusual lily then *L. × testaceum* is both easy to grow and rarely seen, producing gorgeous pale peach, scented flowers.

Cannas are invaluable for containers and placed on a patio or terrace will create an exotic, sub-tropical atmosphere. They look good in square or round terracotta pots and the leaves are every bit as exciting as the spires of brilliantly coloured blossoms. If the flower spikes are removed as soon as they appear, most of the plant's energy will be channelled into the foliage.

As cannas enjoy a moist, rich growing medium, associated plants must be chosen with care. One of the finest combinations is the widely popularized

LEFT This classical-style urn filled with yellow lilies and begonias needs a sheltered site to protect the lilies from any inclement weather.

blue *Scaevola* and the bronze-leaved canna; the tumbling succulence of the scaevola provides a particularly pleasing basal planting in a dark wooden tub. Bronze- or copper-leaved cannas also look good when planted with lovely rosette-forming echeverias. These have rounded, symmetrical, often olive-grey fleshy leaves. Since they will not thrive in the same heavy soil conditions as cannas, plant them in pots of free-draining compost and bury the pots in the soil around the base of the cannas.

Zantedeschia is too tall and bulky to rest easily in small containers but is a first-class subject for large pots. Boldly decorated terracotta pots and vases with deep, narrow necks are especially appropriate; choose those evocative of North Africa, the plant's homeland. These bulbs add a rich touch to any surrounding with their bold, dark green foliage and contrasting snow-white spathes. The shorter-growing *Z. aethiopica* 'Crowborough' and the popular white cultivar *Z. aethiopica* are very reliable when provided with a rich, heavy compost, plenty of water and a sunny position. Mix them with *Lysimachia*

BELOW Daring in its simplicity, this planting relies on the perfection of the zantedeschias and a simple planter for a stylish effect.

ABOVE Pendulous begonias are ideal for hanging baskets because their graceful drooping stems and flowers can be admired easily.

nummularia (creeping Jenny), a moisture-lover with slender stems of bright green, rounded leaves which are studded with yellow buttercup-like flowers in summer. This easily grown, tumbling plant has a softening effect when it is used as a base planting in a large trough full of zantecheschia.

The large purple-flowered *Allium giganteum* is a big, brash plant that requires a bold companion plant. Given its height and the architectural value of its rounded heads, the under-planting should be short but capable of dominating the container when the allium has faded. Herbaceous tradescantias such as *Tradescantia virginiana* 'Isis' (spiderwort) are an excellent choice, providing short, bright green foliage when the allium is blossoming. As the summer progresses and the allium heads slowly dry out, the tradescantia produces bright blue flowers which look very pleasing when set against the skeletonized heads of the allium.

The starker members of the arum family, such as *Sauromatum venosum* (voodoo lily) and *Dracunculus vulgaris* (dragon arum), have a sinister appearance; when planted in a bold group they look very effective. Both have dark

hooded spathes and gloomy leaves with boldly marbled stems that need the solidity of an antique-style lead container, perhaps a square solid tub with simple ornamentation. The same container, however, can provide a different mood if filled with the summer hyacinth, *Galtonia candicans*. This is an altogether looser and more joyful plant than the arums and is a delight when seen growing through a carpet of the golden-leaved *Soleirolia soleirolii* (mind-your-own-business).

Dierama pulcherrimum is an excellent character for a permanent planting, its graceful, arching stems and pendulous pink or rose blossoms associating well with neighbouring soft green or warmer silver and grey plants. The dierama is a plant best suited to a large trough or container where it can be left to grow undisturbed, as it dislikes being uprooted and moved.

Mixed tub plantings with a cottage-garden feel should utilize a number of bulbs which do not justify being grown as single specimens. The bulbs will provide invaluable highlights for several weeks of the year, retiring gracefully among the foliage of companion plants when flowering is over. *Nectaroscordum siculum*, a curious member of the onion family, is one of the most useful members of a mixed planting. Looking ill at ease in most parts of the garden, this bulb produces tall flower stems some 3ft (90cm) high and individual greenish-white and maroon blooms arranged in loose umbels. If they are allowed to remain after flowering, the umbels turn into large seed capsules which are perfect for drying for winter flower arrangements. *Nectaroscordum siculum* does not associate very well with brightly coloured plants and looks much better planted with attractive foliage plants such as herbs like thyme, hyssop, harehound and marjoram.

Indoor bulbs

There is a wide and interesting collection of summer-flowering bulbous and tuberous plants that is well suited to the unheated greenhouse, sun lounge, conservatory or porch. A generous proportion of these also tolerate life on the windowledge.

The most useful and adaptable group of indoor bulbs are the achimenes, known as hot-water plants. Grow these brightly coloured subjects in well-drained, richly organic compost, either in a pot on a windowsill or in a hanging planter. Provided they are not mixed with other plants, they will prosper. Plant the strange-looking rootstocks during early spring in the warmth of a living room: place several in a single container or put them all in a tray of compost until they have sprouted and then replant them into pots or containers, matching those of even growth.

ABOVE This container-planting of white begonias and creamy-coloured dahlias creates a cool, refined summer display.

RIGHT Arum lilies, here planted in a moss-lined container decorated with larch twigs, lend themselves well to dramatic arrangements.

Once established in their pots, achimenes require little attention but they must never be allowed to dry out as wilted foliage is almost impossible to revive. The plants can be staked with twigs to support their drooping leaves and, if the twigs are positioned as soon

as the plants begin to shoot, the plants will naturally cover them. Trying to support the full-grown shoots is difficult to do without making the plants appear rather stiff and formal. When growing achimenes in a hanging pot, allow them to tumble naturally over the edge of the container.

Chlidanthus fragrans is a beautiful and richly fragrant bulb from Latin America that is easy to grow in a greenhouse or sun lounge. Use a soil-based compost and plant the bulbs in pots during early spring; the nose of the bulb should only be sparingly covered. Staking is not necessary as the flower stems rarely exceed 12in (30cm) in height and are borne in a small, loose umbels.

Albucas also enjoy life indoors. The waxy white flowers are striped with red and have a distinctive fragrance. If given a late-summer or early-autumn resting period, they provide a reliable display every year. The bulbs are sold during the autumn and should be planted in a good soil-based potting compost in individual pots. When they start to grow, feed them regularly using a high potash fertilizer; an application every three weeks or so is adequate. Albucas do not normally require staking even though they can become a little unruly, especially *Albuca nelsonii*.

ABOVE Begonias make adaptable and effective houseplants; select a flower colour to blend in with the colour scheme of the room.

ABOVE The velvety blooms of assorted gloxinias are a familiar sight, and a long succession of flowers can be achieved with a little care.

For a more startling display of indoor flowers during the summer months choose *Haemanthus*, which is best planted as a solitary bulb. Of tropical and exotic appearance, they are really quite simple to grow if provided with a free-draining potting compost and a large pot. The most popular type is the shaving brush plant, *Haemanthus albiflos*. A lovely bulb, it has bold white or greenish flower-heads and upright protruding stamens that resemble a shaving brush. The blossoms continue for a number of weeks, and where the bulbs are well established there is usually a succession of flowers from daughter bulbs which develop in congested groups. These small bulbs need separating out periodically if the plants are to maintain their vigour. *Haemanthus coccineus* is rather different, with short, stiff, mottled stems supporting large heads of bright coral-red blossoms. These are followed by very showy, strap-shaped leaves which lie flat against the compost. The blood flower, *H. katherinae*, has even larger, rounded heads of bright scarlet blossoms held on stems reaching up to 1½ft (45cm) high. Its leaves are not as coarse and leathery as *H. coccineus*. It is an excellent plant for the sun lounge or conservatory.

Although not quite as showy as *Haemanthus*, *Hymenocallis* can also be grown indoors in a conservatory or heated greenhouse. The best species is *Hymenocallis narcissiflora*, known as the sea daffodil, with exotic, pure white blossoms carried on stout stems up to 1½ft (45cm) high. In addition to this popular species, the hybrid 'Sulphur Queen', with blossoms of pale sulphur yellow, is also worth cultivating. Both plants look best when tucked into a planter containing evergreen foliage and, being easy-going subjects, they will tolerate the compost and growing conditions of most other indoor plants.

Sprekelia is a much loved indoor bulb that can be grown almost anywhere, from the greenhouse to the windowledge. Popularly referred to as the Jacobean lily, it produces startling, bright red, orchid-like blossoms on strong stems 12in (30cm) high. These are followed by dark green, narrow, straplike leaves. The bulb should be grown in a free-draining potting compost, in a container that is large enough to accommodate its extended root system; a pot 6in (15cm) in diameter is adequate for a single mature bulb.

Another striking indoor plant, *Gloriosa* is a genus of climbing lily-like plants which can be grown, given enough support, in a pot, but is better when allowed to scramble up wires fixed to the wall of a greenhouse or conservatory. Plant the tubers during early spring in an organic-rich compost; soilless compost is to be recommended. Put two or three tubers into a single pot to ensure a good display and provide enough warmth (55-65°F/13-18°C) to start them well into growth. Cultivation is simple, the plants being kept moist, but not too wet, and regularly sprayed with both a systemic fungicide and insecticide to prevent the outbreak of mildew and to control aphids.

Gloriosa superba is the most popular species that will tolerate the coolest conditions. The deep orange and red blossoms look rather like an exotic Turk's

ABOVE Lilium longiflorum, *with its exotic appearance and heady scent, is used here for a glamorous display.*

cap lily but with much thinner petals. *Gloriosa superba* 'Rothschildiana' is even finer, its scallop-edged crimson flowers being marked with yellow. Both have broadly lance-shaped, shiny green leaves and tendrils which enable them to cling to supports.

Sandersonia aurantiaca is closely related to the gloriosa and behaves in a similar way, producing scrambling stems some 2ft (60cm) high. However, it can be grown in modest surroundings where space is limited. The stems are sprinkled with soft orange, pendent, urn-shaped flowers in summer. Plant the tubers in pots filled with a rich, organic compost, provide a simple plant support or twiggy stakes and keep well watered. The more tender *Littonia modesta* is similar in habitat to the sandersonia although it can sometimes grow to a height of 6ft (1.8m) in favourable conditions. It will tolerate an unheated greenhouse in summer provided it has been started into growth by warmer conditions. Plant the bulbs in a richly organic medium and keep them moist; as long as they are given sufficient light, the plants will produce a mass of bright orange-red, bell-shaped flowers throughout the summer months.

Polianthes tuberosa, the tuberose, is an underrated bulb that is only found in the catalogues of specialist bulb growers. One of the finest florist's flowers, it has beautiful racemes of white, waxy blossoms which have a delicious sweet scent. Although the species is a single-flowered bulb, the plant that is most usually offered to gardeners is the old-fashioned, fully-double cultivar called 'The Pearl'. For the average home gardener who may only have an unheated greenhouse, summer cultivation is recommended for polianthes. Plant the bulbs during spring in a soil-based compost, several to each pot, and insert metal plant supports.

Cut flowers

There are several favourite summer-flowering bulbs which are excellent for cutting. For traditional flower arrangements, the stems can be placed in a variety of vases, both ceramic and glass, or informal every-day containers such as mugs and jugs. A more ambitious approach, however, might include summer fruits and vegetables worked into a floral display – an ideal arrangement for a table decoration.

ABOVE This harmonious arrangement in shades of purple consists of freesias, irises, scillas, Solomon's seal and hosta leaves.

Bulbs for cutting can either be grown in a mixed border or separately in a corner of the vegetable plot depending upon how many cut flowers are needed. A few stems taken here and there will not ruin a border arrangement, but sustained cutting requires a special patch where the bulbs can be grown without regard for their overall display. Such a patch is best arranged on a more formal and regimented basis which gives easy access for cutting and, if necessary, staking.

Gladioli provide one of the finest summer cut flowers. The large-flowered cultivars are a good example of plants that grow best well away from a mixed border because their large blossoms

rarely fit the scale of a modest-sized garden. However, as cut flowers, with their colourful, long-lasting blooms, they are quite special and certainly repay the extra attention given them.

Select cultivars like the lovely scarlet 'Trader Horn' and 'Hunting Song', the delicate pink 'Chanson', and the rich orange 'Esta Bonita'. 'Early Yellow' (soft lemon yellow), 'Nova Lux' (primrose yellow), 'Green Woodpecker' (lime green and red-throated), and the pure white ones like 'Lady Godiva', 'Ice Cap' and 'White Friendship' are also popular. For a really special cut flower, look out for the lilac-rose 'Vidi Napoli' and the cyclamen-purple 'Fidelio'.

Gladioli do not have to be large-flowered and long-stemmed to make good cut flowers as many of the shorter-stemmed and smaller-flowered cultivars are lovely in a mixed arrangement. For the small garden, they can serve a dual purpose – as cut flowers and as part of the mixed border – and, if planted close together, they will not need staking.

Whereas with formally grown gladioli a planting distance of 6in (15cm) between corms and 1½ft (45cm) between rows is essential, with more informally planted, smaller-growing varieties a planting distance of 3in (7.5cm) is adequate. Groupings in a mixed border require a minimum of 20 corms in an irregular patch. This dense arrangement not only helps to produce a pleasing, practical display but also permits every other flower spike to be cut without ruining the overall effect.

The best smaller-flowered gladioli for cutting come from the early-flowering Nanus group. These subjects of the gladioli kingdom are sometimes treated as cool greenhouse plants, the corms being planted in pots of free-draining compost over autumn to gain a late-spring or early-summer flush of blossoms. However, they are more frequently planted in spring at the same time as the large-flowered kinds, blossoming slightly ahead during mid- to late summer. There are innumerable cultivars to choose from, 'The Bride' (pure white), 'Peach Blossom' (shell pink) and 'Amanda Mahy' (deep salmon pink) all being proven and reliable. Best of all, however, is 'Nymph', a highlight of any summer garden or cut flower arrangement. This is a most wonderful snowy

LEFT Gloriosa, lilies, gladioli and irises make up an impressive display that is eminently suitable for a large room or hallway.

BELOW Nectarines and grapes have been added to this colourful show of Gloriosa superba, Lilium 'Star Gazer', *freesias and foliage.*

white cultivar, each flower displaying a rich crimson throat.

Being large and imposing, gladioli are best used on their own in arrangements or with complementary foliage. The white 'Ice Cap' looks good with the silvery leaves of eucalyptus but, for a more colourful show, combine the striking red blooms of 'Hunting Song' with branches of dark red-leaved prunus. For an impressive, formal display, place the arrangement on a pedestal.

While gladioli generally hold court among the cut flowers of summer, many of the popular lilies are also excellent for cutting and will last up to two weeks inside. When grown specifically for this purpose, they should be allocated their own corner in the garden as nothing looks worse in a border than the basal remains of decapitated lilies. The plants need not be grown in rows but can be planted in a patch and picked at will. Ensure that the soil is in good condition, incorporating plenty of well-rotted organic matter, and eliminate perennial weeds.

Lilies are elaborate, decorative flowers with a sense of majesty and opulence. They are very adaptable in flower arrangements and can be mixed with other summer blooms such as irises, gladioli and Solomon's seal but, for the greatest effect, they can be used on their own in a simple container. There are innumerable cultivars of lily hybrids to choose from, but Mid-century hybrids like 'Enchantment' are highly popular. A number of seedling strains like the Bellingham hybrids are also useful, as are species and their varieties like *Lilium lancifolium*, *L. hansonii* and the late summer-flowering *L. speciosum* 'Album' and *L. s.* 'Rubrum'.

Dutch irises can also be cut for indoor use, although they will only last a maximum of five days in water. Along with their later-flowering English

counterparts, they are easy to grow, requiring only regular watering and a weed-free environment. Few pests or diseases trouble them, although it is best to scatter some slug pellets around emerging shoots in spring. The bulbs can be planted at a depth of 3in (7.5cm) during the autumn so that a root system can be established quickly, but in cold areas, especially on heavier soils, an early-spring planting is preferable. If grown in a border, plant the bulbs at random 4in (10cm) apart; if for cutting, plant the bulbs in rows 1½ft (45cm) apart, at 4in (10cm) intervals.

The light blue 'Wedgwood' and the dark blue 'Imperator', together with

ABOVE The fabulous Casablanca lily is thrown into relief by the finely etched lines of contorted willow in this candle decoration.

'White Superior' and 'Yellow Queen', are the most frequently grown irises, while 'Blue Giant' and 'Mont Blanc' feature among the best-known English types. Although the beauty of the flowers is best appreciated when they are used on their own in vases, either in single colours or in various shades, irises also lend themselves well to mixed arrangements. Successful plant and colour combinations include dark blue irises and yellow roses, mid- and light blue irises with lime green *Nicotiana*

and variegated periwinkle or hosta leaves, or mixed white and yellow irises with yellow lilies. For more of a cottage-garden look, combine blue irises with pink roses, mixed sweet peas and creamy white-flowered honeysuckle.

Ornithogalum thyrsoides (star-of-Bethlehem) is almost exclusively grown on its own for cutting, although it can be highly effective when planted in a mixed border. It demands full sun and free-draining soil and, like gladioli, must be lifted and stored to survive the winter months. When used for cutting, the bulbs will only be good the second year round if only the flower stems are removed, and the foliage is left to build up next season's food supply.

Star-of-Bethlehem will last for up to three weeks indoors. Bearing dense, conical spikes of delicate white flowers, it is rarely used on its own but adds much to a mixed arrangement. A colourful display might include cornflowers, dianthus, lavender and *Alchemilla mollis*. *Ranunculus*, another favourite of florists, grows in sunny, sheltered, well-drained spots. These gorgeous flowers should be planted in succession for near-continuous summer flowering. A clump will produce abundant blooms so that individual stems can be picked for the house without ruining a border display.

Such colourful flowers should be used to make a statement: create a bold, vibrant arrangement using ranunculus, marigolds and poppies. The addition of dark green or grey foliage will intensify the hues; try to select plain-shaped leaves like hostas to complement the blooms. Different-coloured ranunculus can equally well be displayed on their own, bunched together in a brightly coloured vase.

RIGHT White lilies, gladioli and ornithogalum are here combined with various fruits and vegetables to create this tree-like arrangement.

ACHIMENES
Hot-water plant

These lovely summer-flowering tubers for the windowsill or conservatory produce a long succession of colourful, tubular flowers. There are many species, the most available being selections or hybrids. The maggot-like tubers are obtained in spring and potted in a standard proprietary potting compost; they look best if planted several to a pot. Place the plants in a light position and keep them moist and warm, at a temperature of 16-18.5°C (60-65°F). At the end of summer, they can be dried off in their pots over winter and repotted the following spring; most will produce extra tubers. They are very easy to increase by division or by seed, if available, in spring. Hardiness zone: 10.

A. longiflora

This species has been used as the parent for many hybrids. The violet-blue, long-tubed flowers are held on hairy stems, which grow to a height of about 12in (30cm). The leaves are oval and toothed, with purplish-stained undersides. The variation *A.* 'Paul Arnold' (*above*) has large, rich purple flowers; 'Flamingo' is an excellent deep red; 'Tarantella' has soft pink flowers; 'Snow White' is one of the best of the whites available; and 'Peach Blossom' has pale peach-pink flowers, which are slightly darker towards the centre.

ACIDANTHERA

Although listed under the name of *Acidanthera* in catalogues, this bulb is regarded as a gladiolus, as it is very similar in growth habit, although the flowers are more distinctive. Originally from tropical Africa, it is not hardy, but the bulbs can be grown successfully if they are planted in spring and lifted and stored over winter in a dry, frost-free place. Propagation is by freely produced offsets. Hardiness zone: 7.

A. bicolor (syn. *Gladiolus callianthus*)

This grows to a height of approximately 3ft (90cm), with erect, sword-shaped leaves and spikes of large, white flowers which are about 3in (7.5cm) across. Each flower has a purple blotch in its centre, and a long, curved tube $3\frac{1}{2}$in (9cm) in length. 'Murielae' (*above*) is a slightly larger, more robust cultivar.

ALBUCA

This little-known African genus is grown more for its rarity than for its display. Although not frost hardy, the summer-flowering species can be planted out in late spring and lifted and stored over winter in a dry, frost-free place. A sunny position in well-drained soil is suitable, but it can also be grown in pots in a greenhouse or conservatory. Albucas have flower spikes that consist of three outer spreading petals and three inner ones that are held together to form a tube. Propagation is by seed in spring and by offsets when dormant. Hardiness zone: 10.

A. canadensis (*below*)

Flowering in late spring or early summer, *A. canadensis* has narrow, lance-shaped, erect basal leaves and 6in (15cm) tall spikes of small, yellow flowers. Each petal is marked with a green stripe along its centre.

A. humilis

A dwarf plant only 2-4in (5-10cm) high, this albuca has up to three white flowers, each petal having a green stripe on the outside. It can be grown outside all year in mild areas.

A. nelsonii

This is a robust plant that reaches a height of 3ft (90cm) at flowering time. The spikes carry large, white flowers which have a brownish or greenish stripe on each petal.

ALLIUM
Ornamental onion

Alliums are very popular because they have attractive, showy flowers and the bulbs are easy to grow. Most of those listed below can be grown in full sun, in well-drained, acid or alkaline soil. The bulbs are best planted in autumn at a depth of approximately 2-4in (5-10cm) according to bulb size; those sold as pot plants should also be planted in spring. There are also a few spring- and autumn-flowering alliums (see pages 87 and 203).

The small flowers are held in umbels on top of the stems, and the plants look most striking when planted in a group. The taller species are known as "drumstick" alliums because they tend to lose their leaves by flowering time; these types look better planted among other low-growing plants so the basal part of the bare stems is hidden. Most of the plants smell of onions, but only if the bulb is cut or bruised. Propagation is by offsets which, in some species, are produced quite freely, or by seed, which may take up to three years to produce flowering bulbs. Hardiness zones: 4-6.

A. aflatunense (*above*)

A robust species from central Asia, *A. aflatunense* grows up to 3ft (90cm) in height, with many tiny, rich purple flowers held in globular umbels 4in (10cm) in diameter.

A. altissimum
Very similar to *A. aflatunense*, this species has attractive purple "drumsticks" held on long, bare stems.

A. amabile
This Chinese species has small umbels made up of a few funnel-shaped flowers; these are a rich, deep reddish-pink in colour. *A. amabile* grows into grassy clumps approximately 4-6in (10-15cm) high, and is suitable for growing in the rock garden.

A. atropurpureum
This species reaches up to about 3ft (90cm) in height at flowering time. It has basal, strap-shaped leaves and bare stems, which carry almost flat or hemispherical umbels of dark purple flowers. Each umbel is 2-3in (5-7.5cm) across.

A. beesianum (*below*)
A lovely blue-flowered species, *A. beesianum* is suitable for a cool position in the rock garden. It grows to a height of approximately 6-8in (15-20cm), the wiry stems carrying small umbels of pendent, bright blue bells. The linear leaves are grey-green. Grown in a group, they form clumps of slender, bottle-shaped plants.

A. caeruleum
Very similar to *A. caesium*, this clump-forming allium has narrow, erect leaves on the lower third of slender flower stems, which bear umbels of star-shaped, blue flowers 1½in (4cm) in diameter. There are 30-50 flowers per umbel.

A. caesium
This unusual "drumstick" allium has dense umbels of blue flowers, each umbel growing 1¾in (4.5cm) in diameter. The wiry stems grow up to 2ft (60cm) in height.

A. cernuum (*above*)
This American, clump-forming species is very hardy. It is 1-2ft (30-60cm) tall, and has reddish-purple, pink or white, bell-shaped flowers held in a drooping umbel.

A. christophii (**syn.** *A. albopilosum*) (*above*)
This bulb produces a large, symmetrical, spherical umbel that grows 6-8in (15-20cm) in diameter. The umbel is made up of star-shaped, purple flowers held on a stout, 6in-1½ft (15-45cm) tall stem. At the end of flowering, the petals become dry and spiny and the umbels can be used for winter flower arrangements.

A. cyaneum
The pendent, deep blue, bell-shaped flowers of *A. cyaneum* are held in small umbels. The stalks of this clump-forming bulb reach a height of 5-10in (13-25cm); they are useful plants for the rock garden.

A. cyathophorum farreri
Another clump-forming plant, this 6-12in (15-30cm) tall allium is also suitable for the rock garden. It has reddish-purple, bell-shaped flowers held in small umbels.

A. flavum (*next column*)
One of the few yellow-flowering alliums, *A. flavum* has slender, wiry stems that reach up

to 12in (30cm) in height. The loose umbels of small flowers are held on long stalks; these are upright at first but arch downwards with the weight of the flowers.

A. giganteum (*below*)
As its name implies, this is an enormous plant. It has broad basal leaves and a thick stem that grows up to 6ft (1.8m) high. The round umbels are made up of countless tiny, rosy purple flowers measuring about 4-6in (10-15cm) in diameter. *A. giganteum* needs a hot, sunny position.

A. macleanii (**syn.** *A. elatum*)
Rather similar to *A. giganteum*, this allium is usually slightly smaller.

A. macranthum
A clump-forming species, *A. macranthum* grows to a height of 10-12in (25-30cm). It has loose umbels of up to 20 large, purple, bell-shaped flowers, each about ½in (15mm) long, held on slender stalks.

A. mairei
This slender dwarf allium forms grassy clumps of 4-6in (10-15cm) long stems. These carry small umbels of up to 20 pink, funnel-shaped flowers.

A. moly (*above*)
This plant is very easy to cultivate and enjoys both semi-shade and sun. In early summer, its broad, grey leaves are topped by umbels measuring 2-3in (5-7.5cm) in diameter. The star-shaped flowers are bright yellow.

A. nigrum (*below*)
This allium has broad, strap-shaped basal leaves and a stout stem up to 3ft (90cm) high; this carries a large umbel 3-4in (7.5-10cm) across. In the centre of each white flower, there is a blackish ovary which produces a dark eye. The allium sold in garden centres as *A. multibulbosum* is almost certainly a form of *A. nigrum*.

A. pulchellum (**syn.** *A. carinatum* **subsp.** *pulchellum*)
An attractive slender species, *A. pulchellum* seeds freely, although surplus seed can be collected or the seed heads removed to prevent it spreading. It grows to a height of 12in-2ft (30-60cm), and has loose umbels of pendent, bell-shaped purple flowers carried on long, arching stalks.

A. ramosum
This clump-forming allium grows 10-16in (25-40cm) tall. The umbels are about 1-2in (2.5-5cm) in diameter and consist of white

flowers; each petal is marked with a darker vein along its centre. Although not as striking as other alliums, it is easy to cultivate.

A. rosenbachianum (*above*)
Another of the central Asian "drumstick" types, this allium has long, tough stems up to 3ft (90cm) high. The spherical umbel is 3-4in (7.5-10cm) in diameter, and has small, dark purple flowers.

A. schoenoprasum (*above*)
Chives
Although a useful culinary plant, this decorative allium is worth growing as an ornamental plant among other small perennials. It is a clump-forming allium, with many narrow, cylindrical leaves and, in mid-summer, dense umbels 2in (5cm) across. The showy flowers vary in colour, being shades of pale purple and pink; the selection known as 'Forescate' has rosy pink flowers and is a particularly strong grower.

A. schubertii
This is an extraordinary plant, with stout stems reaching 2ft (60cm) high. It carries a loosely flowered but enormous umbel up to 1½ft (45cm) across. The star-shaped flowers are pale pinkish-purple in colour, and they can be cut and dried for a winter flower arrangement. It requires a hot, sunny spot.

A. sikkimense (*above*)
A clump-forming plant, this species has very narrow, grassy leaves and 4-8in (10-20cm) long stems. These carry small, pendent umbels of blue flowers in late summer. *A. kansuense* may be synonymous.

A. sphaerocephalon
An easily grown "drumstick" allium, *A. sphaerocephalon* has long, wiry stems 2-3ft (60-90cm) high. The dense umbels, about 1½in (4cm) in diameter, are made up of many dark purple flowers. It can be dried for winter flower arrangements.

A. stipitatum
One of the tall Asiatic "drumsticks", this species has large umbels 3-5in (7.5-13cm) wide. The individual flowers are small and star-shaped; they are mostly pale purple but a white form is available.

A. tuberosum (*below*)
Chinese chives
A. tuberosum can be grown as a culinary plant, although it is worth growing for decorative purposes as well. The 1-2in (2.5-5cm) wide umbels consist of attractive, star-shaped, white flowers and, at flowering time, the stems grow to a height of 12in-2ft (30-60cm). It is a clump-forming plant.

ANOMATHECA

An interesting little South African plant, *Anomatheca* has freesia-like corms that are planted about 2in (5cm) deep in spring for mid-summer flowering. Although they withstand slight frost in cold areas, where the ground freezes for long periods, it is best to lift the dormant corms in autumn and store them in dry, frost-free conditions over winter. The corms produce offsets, but it is just as easy to propagate the plant by seed. This is produced freely and seed-raised plants may flower in the same season if sown under glass in early spring. A sunny position in fertile garden soil is suitable. Hardiness zone: 9.

A. laxa (syn. *Lapeirousia cruenta*)

This species has narrow, upright, sword-shaped leaves and short spikes of bright red flowers, each with a long tube. The petals open to about 1in (2.5cm) in diameter, the lower ones being marked with a darker red blotch. The plant reaches 6-12in (15-20cm) in height when in flower.

ARISAEMA

This fascinating group of tuberous-rooted plants is related to the arums (see Spring Directory, page 88) but, unlike a number of the aroids, it does not have an unpleasant smell. They are winter-dormant tubers and, although many are very hardy, some of the Himalayan and eastern Asiatic species start to grow rather early in the year and may get frost-damaged. The more tender ones can be lifted in autumn and kept frost-free over winter for planting out the following spring. They require dappled shade and must be planted at a depth of approximately 6in (15cm), in a well-drained, humus-rich soil.

Like the arums, arisaemas have tiny flowers which are produced on a pencil-like spadix and enclosed within a hooded spathe. The spadix may have a long tail-like appendage hanging out of the spathe and, in some species, it is the spathe itself which has the "tail" at its apex. Spikes of red berries may be produced in autumn and these are best sown in winter, although it may be easier to propagate by detaching offsets which form on the tubers of some species. It does not require much space at flowering time, but many types develop large leaves, with a spread of up to 3ft (90cm). Hardiness zones: 4-8.

A. amurense

An Asian species about 1½ft (45cm) high, *A. amurense* has five-lobed leaves and hooded spathes striped purple, green and white.

A. candidissimum (*below*)

This Chinese species is one of the most attractive and is very hardy. Appearing above ground in early summer, the pale pink, white striped, cowl-like spathes, approximately 6in (15cm) long, are produced just before the leaves appear. The leaves, up to 12in (30cm) across, consist of three broad leaflets; this plant tolerates full sun.

A. consanguineum (*below*)

This very robust Himalayan plant may reach 3ft (90cm) in height. It has a stout, dark-spotted or blotched stem which carries an umbrella-like leaf made up of 12-20 narrow leaflets. The 6-8in (15-20cm) long spathe is carried just beneath the leaf and is purple with whitish stripes. It has a tail-like tip.

A. dracontium

A North American species, *A. dracontium* has a greenish spathe with a long, protruding, whip-like spadix. The leaves are divided into 7-15 leaflets, and are carried on stout stems up to 2½ft (75cm) tall.

A. ringens

This eastern Asiatic species has a green or purplish spathe with a paler stripe. The darker purple edge flares out into a wide hood at the apex, and is topped by three lobed leaves. An early-flowering arisaema, it may need protection from late frosts.

A. sikokianum (*above*)

This striking Japanese species has a deep purple-brown, tubular spathe out of which protrudes a thick, white, club-like spadix. The whole plant is about 12in-2ft (30-60cm) tall, and the leaves, which appear after the spathes, divide into three to five leaflets.

A. tortuosum

This Himalayan species is so-called because the long spadix has an "S"-shaped bend as it emerges from the green spathe. It grows 2-4ft (60cm-1.2m) in height, with leaves that divide into as many as 17 leaflets.

A. triphyllum
Jack-in-the-pulpit

A popular North American species, the three-lobed leaves are held on 12in-2ft (30-60cm) tall stems. The slightly shorter, green or purplish-flushed spathes are hooded at the apex. *A. atrorubens* is very similar and is regarded as a synonym of *A. triphyllum*.

BABIANA
Baboon root

These freesia-like, South African corms are normally winter- or spring-flowering, but they are sometimes offered by nurserymen for spring planting so they will flower in summer. However, if planted in spring, they will probably only grow during the first summer before reverting to their natural cycle of starting into growth in autumn and dying down in spring. If planted in spring, a sunny, well-drained position is required, with the corms buried at a depth of 2in (5cm). They are not frost-hardy and must be lifted over winter but, in mild areas, they can be planted out permanently and are likely to behave as winter-spring growers. Few of the babianas are in general cultivation, and they are likely to be offered as a mixed collection. They vary in colour from cream to yellow and pale to deep blue or violet. Propagation is by seed in autumn. Hardiness zone: 9.

B. rubrocyanea (*below*)
One of the most colourful varieties, the short spike has funnel-shaped flowers that are 1½in (4cm) long. The blooms are red in the centre and bright blue at the tips of the six petals. It reaches about 6-8in (15-20cm) high at flowering time.

BEGONIA
The majority of the very familiar indoor or bedding begonias are fibrous-rooted, but there are also tuberous types which are sold in spring bulb catalogues. Because they are not very hardy, they are only intended for planting out as soon as the frosts are over, but they can be grown as pot plants in a conservatory, or in containers for a dramatic terrace or patio display. Propagation is by stem cuttings taken in summer or by division in spring. Hardiness zones: 10 for *B. grandis*; 9 for *B. sutherlandii* and tuberous hybrids.

B. grandis (**syn.** B. evansiana)
One of the hardiest of the tuberous begonias, *B. grandis* may be planted out permanently in areas that receive only light frosts, provided they are given a sheltered position in dappled shade or full sun, and humus-rich soil. This begonia grows 12in-1½ft (30-45cm) high, and has large, pinkish-tinged leaves and sprays of pink flowers, each one measuring about 1in (2.5cm) across.

B. sutherlandii
This graceful begonia grows to a height of 6-12in (15-30cm). It has leafy branches that spread out horizontally, reaching 12in (30cm) or more across. The light orange flowers are produced over a long summer period; *B. sutherlandii* makes an attractive container plant when grown as a single specimen.

Tuberous hybrid groups
Sometimes known as *B.* × *tuberhybrida*, there are many types and cultivars, a few of which are described below to give some idea of the range available.

Camellia-flowered begonias
These begonias are so-called because of the tight, double flowers similar to camellias. They produce upright stems, with large flowers varying in shades of pink, red, orange and yellow; there is also an attractive white version available.

Double-flowered begonias
These begonias are upright in habit, producing very large, double flowers in a range of colours and shades including red, orange, copper, pink, yellow and white.

Non-stop begonias
These tuberous begonias are a race of compact-growing hybrids, reaching 6-8in (15-20cm) in height. They start to flower earlier on in the season than other types, continuing for a very long period. There are many colours to choose from, including orange, apricot, pink, yellow and various shades of red.

B. 'Bertini' (*above*)
The hanging stems of this tuberous hybrid make it ideal for hanging baskets or containers placed on pedestals. The flowers are carried in loose clusters and are red or orange, with pointed petals.

B. 'Bouton de Rose'
This upright-growing begonia is a Picotee type, reaching up to 1½ft (45cm) in height. The double, white flowers are edged red.

B. 'Fimbriata' (*below*)
Of upright habit, this begonia has wavy-edged leaves and large, double flowers. The petals are crimped at the margins, giving the effect of a double carnation.

B. 'Madame Helen Harms'
This is a double-flowering, multiflora begonia, with large, yellow flowers. It grows 12in-2ft (30-60cm) tall.

B. 'Madame Richard Galle'
This upright, multiflora begonia grows 12in-2ft (30-60cm) in height. It has large, double, copper-coloured flowers.

B. 'Marginata Crispa'
There are various colour forms of this bicoloured type, such as white with red margins and yellow with red margins. The petals are strongly frilled or crimped around the edges. An upright plant, it grows 12in-2ft (30-60cm) in height.

B. 'Marmorata'
This tuberous begonia has carmine-coloured flowers with a white marbled pattern; each petal is waved and crimped at the margins. Of upright growth, it reaches a height of 12in-1½ft (30-45cm).

B. 'Pendula'
These types of tuberous begonia are good for hanging baskets because their slender stems hang down almost vertically, bearing clusters of large flowers throughout the summer. The flowers are usually semi-double, although some are singles; colours include red, pink, yellow, white and orange.

BRIMEURA

A small, graceful, bluebell-like plant, *Brimeura* flowers in late spring or early summer, depending upon locality. The bulbs should be planted in autumn in dappled shade, at a depth of about 2ir (5cm), in humus-rich soil; several to a patch gives the best display. Seed is normally produced quite freely and, when growing happily, the bulbs will soon form a colony. Hardiness zone: 6.

B. amethystina (syn. *Hyacinthus amethystinus*) (*below*)

This aptly named bulb has a one-sided raceme of bright blue, pendent, tubular bells. These are held on stems 6-8in (15-20cm) high, each flower reaching ½in (1.5cm) in length. 'Alba' is the pure white variant.

BRODIAEA (including DICHELOSTEMMA and TRITELEIA)

The overall appearance of these early summer bulbs is like an allium, since both types of corms have star-shaped or tubular flowers held in an umbel on top of a bare stem. Unlike the allium family, however, *Brodiaea* does not have the characteristic smell of onions.

There is a considerable number of species, but few are generally available. These North American plants, mostly from California, are reasonably hardy and may be grown in sunny positions, in soil which will dry out during the summer months. The corms, resembling those of the crocus, are planted in autumn at a depth of 2-3in (5-7.5cm). Because the leaves look untidy and turn brown at flowering time, they look best when placed behind low-growing plants; any small alpines or dwarf shrubs are suitable companions. Propagation is by offsets or by seed sown in autumn. Hardiness zones: 7-8.

B. ida-maia (syn. *Dichelostemma ida-maia*)
Californian firecracker

This is a very striking bulb that is not as easy to grow as most species. It reaches a height of 12in-1½ft (30-45cm), and has a dense umbel of up to 12 tubular flowers, each about 1¾in (4.5cm) long. The lower half of the flower consists of a bright red tube and the upper part is made up of six reflexed, green lobes.

B. ixioides (syn. *Triteleia ixioides*) (*above*)

This is one of the best-known species, with a 4in (10cm) diameter umbel of star-shaped flowers. It grows to a height of 12-15in (30-38cm).

B. lactea (syn. *Triteleia hyacinthina*)

This bulb has dense 2-3in (5-7.5cm) diameter umbels of white flowers, each one about 1in (2.5cm) wide across the mouth. The stems grow 9-12in (23-30cm) high.

B. laxa (syn. *Triteleia laxa*) (*below*)

A striking plant, *B. laxa* has long-lasting, large, blue flowers. The wiry stems are 12in-1½ft (30-45cm) tall, and carry loose umbels, each one up to 6in (15cm) in diameter. These are made up of funnel-shaped flowers which measure 1in (2.5cm) across at the mouth. It increases well and provides good cut flowers.

B. × tubergeniana

A hybrid involving *B. laxa*, this is very similar to its parent plant. It has large, lilac-blue flowers and is a vigorous grower.

B. 'Queen Fabiola' (*above*)

Again very similar to *B. laxa*, *B.* 'Queen Fabiola' has rich, deep blue flowers.

CALOCHORTUS
Mariposa lily; cat's ears; globe lily or fairy lantern

These beautiful North and Central American bulbs are some of the most striking of the lily family, although they are not widely cultivated because it is generally difficult to grow them outside beyond their native lands without protection. The flowers consist of three large, inner petals and three much smaller, pointed, outer ones. The mariposas have large, upward-facing flowers, with gaudy zones of colour in the centre; the cat's ears have smaller, upright flowers that are densely clothed, with hair on the inside; and the globe lilies, or fairy lanterns, have pendent, almost globular flowers.

Although many are fairly hardy, they require a dry, warm period if they are to ripen after flowering in early summer, and are best grown in pots under glass or planted in a bulb frame. The bulbs are potted or planted in autumn, in a sharply drained soil mix, at a depth of 3½in (9cm). They require as much light as possible so that they do not become too elongated.

Propagation is mainly by seed, which germinates very rapidly when sown in the autumn, producing flowering bulbs in three or four years. Hardiness zones: 4-6.

C. albus

One of the fairy lantern types, *C. albus* has several attractive pendent globes carried on about 12in (30cm) high stems. The flowers

are mostly a translucent, creamy white colour, but are sometimes pinkish or reddish, each one measuring approximately 1in (2.5cm) across.

C. amabilis

This is very similar in flower shape and size to *C. albus*, but is deep yellow.

C. barbatus (syn. *Cyclobothra lutea*) (*above*)
This Mexican species does not flower until late summer and is dormant in winter. It requires different treatment from the other calochortus, and the bulbs should be planted in spring. It grows to a height of 9-12in (23-30cm), and has pendent, bell-shaped flowers 1-1½in (2.5-4cm) across. These are a deep yellowish-mustard colour, with a lining of hairs on the inside.

C. luteus (*above*)
One of the upright-flowering mariposas, *C. luteus* has bright yellow flowers, often with brown markings at the centre, which reach 2in (5cm) in diameter. The stems are 10-12in (25-30cm) high.

C. splendens

Another mariposa, *C. splendens* has lovely 2in (5cm) wide, upright flowers. These are pale purple, with a darker blotch at the base of each inner petal.

C. superbus

Also a mariposa type, the stems of *C. superbus* are 2ft (60cm) tall, carrying upright flowers about 2in (5cm) in diameter. The colour varies from white or yellow to lilac, with brown and yellow zones in the centre.

C. uniflorus

This is one of the easiest species of calochortus to cultivate. It grows about 6-12in (15-30cm) high, and has several erect, lilac-coloured flowers that measure approximately 2-2½in (5-6.5cm) in diameter and are held in an umbel.

C. venustus (below)

This mariposa has huge, upturned flowers measuring nearly 3in (7.5cm) across. The white, yellow, purple or red flowers are usually marked with a contrasting deep red, yellow-edged blotch at the base of each petal. It may grow as tall as 1½ft (45cm) in ideal conditions.

C. vestae (below)

Very similar to *C. venustus*, *C. vestae* differs in the shape of the hairy nectar area at the base of the petals. The flowers are white or pale purple, with dark brownish-red patches in the centre.

C. weedii

The several erect, yellow flowers, about 2in (5cm) in diameter, are speckled brown and hairy on the inside.

CAMASSIA

These summer-flowering bulbs from North America have clusters of long, narrow leaves held in basal tufts, and long racemes of star-shaped flowers. They require fairly damp situations, and enjoy growing in rough grass, between shrubs or alongside ponds. Propagation is by division of clumps or seed in autumn. Hardiness zones: 4-5.

C. cusickii (*above*)
The 2-4ft (60cm-1.2m) high stems carry a raceme of many pale blue flowers, each one 1-2in (2.5-5cm) in diameter when completely open. It has long, greyish leaves.

C. leichtlinii
A vigorous plant reaching up to 4½ft (1.4m) in height, *C. leichtlinii* has striking racemes of six-petalled, large flowers, sometimes reaching as much as 3in (7.5cm) across. These flowers range in colour from deep violet-blue to white. 'Alba' is a creamy white form that shows up well against a dark background, and 'Atrocaerulea' (*above*) is one of the deeper purple colour forms.

CANNA

The showy cannas, from the warmer parts of North and South America, add a touch of the tropics to any garden. In many regions, they are not hardy enough to be left out in the ground for the winter months, and may need lifting and storing in a frost-free place. The flowers have a complicated structure and are somewhat orchid-like, being produced in spikes or racemes over large, bold, ornamental foliage. Propagation is by division in spring. Hardiness zones: 9-10.

C. × generalis

This name is given to a range of hybrid cultivars with varying flower and foliage colour. 'King Humbert' (syn. 'Roi Humbert') is an old variety, with bright red flowers and brown leaves, reaching a height of about 4-6ft (1.2-1.8m). 'Black Knight' also has red flowers and bronze-coloured foliage, but is a shorter plant, growing up to 4ft (1.2m) tall. 'Lucifer' (*below*) is a very striking red canna, with yellow-edged petals accompanied by purple-coloured leaves. It grows 3-4ft (90cm-1.2m) high at flowering time. 'Wyoming' has bronze foliage with orange flowers, and grows approximately 4ft (1.2m) high.

C. indica

This wild species is more slender than the hybrids. It has green leaves and 5-6ft (1.5-1.8m) high stems which carry racemes of small, bright red or orange flowers. The lower lip of each flower is mottled and streaked darker red on an orange or yellow background.

CARDIOCRINUM
Giant lily

These enormous plants are closely related to the true lilies and, when flowering, are very similar to the long, white, trumpet lilies, although their leaves are completely different, being broad and heart-shaped. The very large bulbs are monocarpic, dying after flowering, but two to three small offsets are produced which can be grown on and will flower two to three years later.

Cardiocrinums require deeply-dug, humus-rich soil and a partially shaded area where they will not dry out too much in summer. They die down in winter and, in cold districts, are best given a mulch of loose straw to protect the resting bulbs from frost. They should be planted in autumn or early spring, with the tips of the bulbs just beneath the surface. Each bulb can occupy a considerable space when in leaf; if planting more than one, space them a minimum of 3ft (90cm) apart. Propagation is by offsets in autumn, or by seed in autumn or winter; seed is very slow and may take up to seven years to produce flowering-size bulbs. Hardiness zone: 7.

C. giganteum (*above*)

Growing up to 8ft (2.4m) tall when in flower, *C. giganteum* has broad, glossy leaves, some of which reach as much as 1½ft (45cm) across, diminishing in size all the way up to the flowers. Each flower stalk has up to 20 6in (15cm) long, semi-pendent, fragrant trumpets; these are white, with a purplish stain inside the tube and a green flush on the outside of the petals.

CHASMANTHE

These perennials, resembling crocosmia, have large, almost flat corms that yield tufts of erect, sword-shaped leaves and spikes of brightly coloured tubular flowers in early summer. They are not very hardy and, in cold-winter areas, must be grown under slightly heated glass, at a minimum temperature of 45°F (7.5°C), or in containers that can be moved outdoors when the last frosts are over. They require a light, sandy soil and, if grown in containers, should be repotted each autumn. The corms naturally increase quite rapidly; propagate by division in autumn and replant the clumps at a depth of 3in (9cm). Hardiness zone: 9.

C. aethiopica (*below*)

The narrow leaves, up to 2ft (60cm) long, are topped by spikes of tubular, red flowers. These are 2in (5cm) in length, with a long, hooded upper petal like a small gladiolus flower. All the flowers on the spike face the same way.

C. floribunda

Similar to *C. aethiopica* in flower shape, *C. floribunda* has much wider leaves and orange or scarlet flowers that face in opposite directions rather than the same way.

CHLIDANTHUS

The bulbs of this South American plant are usually sold in spring, and are planted with their necks just protruding from the soil. Chlidanthus may be cultivated in the open garden in mild areas but, in regions with frosty winters, it must be lifted and stored in dry, frost-free conditions. Alternatively, it can be grown in containers and brought into a greenhouse in autumn, where it is dried off until spring. It is best grown in a sunny, well-drained position. If grown in pots, use a loam-based potting medium with extra sand and, once in growth, feed the bulb once a fortnight with a liquid tomato fertilizer. In mild areas where they are planted permanently, the bulbs can be planted at a depth of 2-3in (5-7.5cm) below the surface. Propagation is by division of clumps of bulbs in spring at repotting time. Hardiness zone: 9.

C. fragrans

These daffodil-like bulbs produce strap-shaped, greyish leaves and 4-12in (10-30cm) long stems, which carry umbels of two to five fragrant, yellow flowers. These are funnel-shaped and 1½-2½in (4-6.5cm) long; the tips of the petals are curled back.

CROCOSMIA

This group of attractive perennials from South Africa form tufts of erect, sword-shaped leaves, and their red, orange or yellow, funnel-shaped flowers are carried in branched, arching sprays. The modern hybrids have superseded the old cottage garden favourite *C. × crocosmiiflora* ('Montbretia'), although this is still a useful plant for difficult areas of the garden, since it tolerates a wide range of conditions which most other plants will not. However, the more highly developed cultivars can be tricky to grow in cold areas. Since the corms increase into patches, the plants are easy to dig up and divide. Division is best in spring just before growth starts, but the clumps may take a year or more to settle in. In very cold areas, it is wise to cover the plants with a layer of straw in winter. Hardiness zone: 7.

C. masonorum (*above*)
This very robust plant grows up to 5ft (1.5m) high. It has bold, prominently veined leaves and arched stems, which bear many reddish-orange flowers. These are long-tubed, with spreading petals and conspicuous stamens.

C. paniculata (syn. *Curtonus paniculatus*)
Similar in growth to *C. masonorum*, the tubular, orange flowers of *C. paniculata* are longer and carried on zig-zag stems.

Cultivars

The more highly developed cultivars are not always so hardy or easy to grow in cold areas,

requiring light, sandy soils rather than cold, heavy clays, and a well-drained, sunny position. However, they are attractive, colourful plants; 'Bressingham Blaze' has wide, funnel-shaped, brilliant red flowers, 'Emily McKenzie' has orange flowers with brown markings on the throat, and 'Lucifer' (*below*) has deep red flowers carried on 3ft (90cm) stems over sword-like foliage.

CYPELLA

A South American, iris-like plant, cypella is worth growing for interest in mild areas, where it can be planted outdoors in a sunny position. In cold areas, it needs to be lifted and stored over winter, or grown in a frost-free greenhouse or conservatory. Seed is produced freely and will grow into flowering-sized bulbs in only one or two years. Hardiness zone: 9.

C. herbertii (*above*)
This cypella produces erect, sword-shaped leaves and loosely branching flower stems, which carry upright, mustard-yellow flowers. These resemble small irises, with three large, outer petals and three smaller, inner ones. Although each flower is short-lived, the bulb produces a succession of blooms over several weeks. The plants grow to a height of 9-12in (23-30cm).

DIERAMA
Angel's fishing rod or wand flower

These lovely, graceful perennials produce long, wiry stems that arch over at the apex so that the spikes of bell- or funnel-shaped flowers hang downwards. The stalks grow from corms and have long, narrow leaves that are very tough and do not die back completely in winter, eventually forming sizeable tufts when growing well. *Dierama* requires a sunny position that is well-supplied with moisture but not waterlogged in summer when the plant is in growth; it looks particularly effective when growing near water. Since it dislikes disturbance, it is best to raise new plants from seed and plant them in their permanent positions as young pot specimens. Hardiness zones: 7-9.

D. dracomontanum (*above*)
This is a short, clump-forming plant, with pink flowers about 1in (2.5cm) in length. It is sometimes wrongly called *D. pumilum*, which is very rare and quite different.

D. pendulum (*above*)
Reaching 3-6ft (90cm-1.8m) high, *D. pendulum* has branched, pendent spikes of wide, bell-shaped, pale pinkish-purple flowers which are each about 1½-2in (4-5cm) in length.

D. pulcherrimum (*above*)
This bulb grows up to 6ft (1.8m) in height, and is similar in appearance to *D. pendulum*, but has narrower bells approximately 2¹/₂in (6.5cm) long, in shades of deep reddish-purple or magenta.

DRACUNCULUS

This small group of arums have the same characteristic form as others: an enlarged cowl or sail-like spathe enclosing a pencil-like spadix, which carries the minute flowers at its base. The spathe is tubular in the lower part and expands into a very large, flattened blade, leaving the thick, protruding spadix erect. It is good for growing in small clumps in a sheltered sunny position; it will tolerate either acid or alkaline soil as long as it is free-draining. The tubers are planted in autumn, at a depth of about 6in (15cm), and covered with a layer of straw or bracken for winter protection. Offsets are produced readily and, when a clump has built up, it can be divided in late summer. Hardiness zone: 9.

D. vulgaris (*above*)
Dragon arum
The stout, blotched and striped stems of this plant reach nearly 3ft (90cm) high, and are crowned by attractively divided leaves, some of which have a spread of 12in (30cm). The

spathe can grow up to 1¹/₂ft (45cm) in length, and is a velvety, deep maroon-purple, with a darker maroon spadix projecting from it. Unfortunately, when in flower, it gives off an unpleasant smell that attracts flies.

EUCOMIS (*above*)
Pineapple flower
These interesting South African bulbs are described in the Autumn Directory (see page 207) because often they do not flower until this time. However, in mild areas they may start to flower earlier in mid- to late summer.

FREESIA

Freesias are naturally winter or early spring-flowering, and a selection will be found on page 228. However, corms are sometimes available in spring for planting outdoors for summer flowering. If left in the ground, they will try to revert to their normal rhythm of growth, appearing in late autumn and growing through the winter. Being tender plants, they will not survive in cold-winter areas. From a spring planting, it is possible to lift the corms in late summer after flowering, keeping them dry and warm for the winter to prevent growth. They can then be replanted next spring, although this is not always successful. On the whole, they are best grown for their valuable, fragrant, winter flowers. Hardiness zones: 9-10.

GALTONIA

These tall, graceful, bulbous plants from South Africa have a cluster of long, strap-like, basal leaves and loose racemes of bell-like flowers produced in mid- to late summer. They are very easy to cultivate, requiring a sunny position, adequate moisture and fertile soil with a good humus content. The bulbs are planted in spring at a depth of about 4in (10cm) or, in cold areas, they can be started into growth in

pots under glass and then planted out when the soil has warmed up. If the soil is liable to freeze deeply in winter, it is best to lift the bulbs in autumn and store them in a frost-free place.

Galtonias look best when planted in clumps of at least five bulbs, at intervals of about 3¹/₂-4in (7¹/₂-10cm). Propagation is by seed sown in spring, or by offsets removed from the parent bulb at planting time. Hardiness zones: 6-7.

G. candicans (*above*)
The most freely available species of galtonia, the stems reach 4-5ft (1.2-1.5m) in height, and carry a long raceme of pendent, white, short-tubed flowers a minimum of 1in (2.5cm) in length.

G. princeps (*below*)
Similar to *G. candicans* but with slightly smaller flowers less than 1in (2.5cm) long, the bell-shaped flowers of *G. princeps* have longer tubes. The blooms are green tinged.

G. viridiflora
An attractive plant, *G. viridiflora* has a spike of pendent, funnel-shaped flowers in a shade of soft green. It has rather shorter and broader leaves than either *G. candicans* and *G. princeps*.

GLADIOLUS

Gladioli are very popular, widely grown cormous plants. Most of those cultivated are hybrids derived from South African species, although there are also a few northern hemisphere ones worth growing which are much hardier and need to be planted in autumn. The South African species and their hybrids are planted out in spring, when the danger of frost is over and the soil has begun to warm up. There are very few species of gladioli in general cultivation, and most of those available are hybrids that have been classified into groups determined by height, flower size and shape. Propagate by removing the young cormlets after lifting in winter or early spring, store them in frost-free conditions and plant them later on in spring. Hardiness zones: 9 for the large-flowered hybrid groups; 5-6 for *G. communis* subsp. *byzantinus* and *G. italicus*; 7 for *G. × colvillei* and *G. nanus* cultivars.

G. callianthus (syn. *Acidanthera bicolor*)
See *Acidanthera bicolor* (page 150).

G. × colvillei and G. nanus
These two gladioli are very similar, if not synonymous. They are hardier than the large, late-summer gladioli, flowering earlier in the season and only reaching about 1½-2ft (45-60cm) in height. They also have fewer wide, funnel-shaped flowers on each spike. In mild weather, the bulbs can be planted after purchase in autumn but, in areas where the soil freezes deeply, it is best to pot them and keep them in a frost-free greenhouse until spring, after which they can be planted out. Sometimes corms can be obtained in spring, in which case they can be planted out directly.

G. (colvillei) 'The Bride' (*above*)
An old variety, 'The Bride' has white flowers with greenish markings on the lower petals.

G. (nanus) 'Amanda Mahy'
This has deep salmon pink flowers, with dark purplish splashes on the lower petals.

G. (nanus) 'Nymph' (*below*)
This also has white flowers, but with pink markings on the lower petals.

G. communis subsp. byzantinus (*below*)
A Mediterranean species for planting out in autumn, this gladiolus produces robust, 2-3ft (60-90cm) high stems, with long spikes of bright reddish-purple flowers in early summer. It produces a fan of sword-shaped, erect basal leaves.

G. italicus (syn. *G. segetum*)
This slender species, widespread in Europe and Asia, is also for autumn planting in warm, sunny situations. It has pinkish-lilac-coloured flowers alternately facing in opposite directions up the spike.

Larger-flowered hybrids
These are derived from South African species and also require spring planting. They are available in almost every colour, and the flowers grow to 2½-5½in (6.5-14cm) or more across when fully open. For show purposes, this type subdivides into groups based on

flower width: Giant, Large, Medium, Small and Miniature. The following is a very limited selection of those available.

Giant
'Trader Horn' (*above*) is a rich, deep scarlet and 'Rose Supreme' has rose-pink flowers, streaked darker pink, with white throats.

Large
'Fidelio' (*below*) is an interesting shade of purple, and 'Peter Pears' (*above*) is soft apricot-orange, with darker red blotches in the throat.

Medium
'Aristocrat' is a late variety, with velvety, garnet-purple flowers. 'Green Woodpecker' comes in lemon-yellow, with a reddish throat.

Small

'Dancing Doll' has creamy-coloured flowers which are suffused with pink and blotched red on the lower petals; 'Bluebird' is a rich blue-violet, and appears rather early in the season; and 'Claret' is rose pink.

Miniature

'Greenbird' has sulphur-yellow flowers which are tinged green with red throats. 'Bo Peep' is altogether more subtle, with attractive almond-coloured flowers which have yellow flecks on them.

Butterfly hybrids

This is the name given to a group of small-flowered hybrids in dramatic hues, usually with contrasting patches of colour on the lower petals. 'Camborne' (*above*) has lilac flowers which are stained with deep violet; 'Avalanche' is a pure white form; 'Mykonos' (*below*) has salmon pink and yellow flowers with red markings; and 'Pamela' is a coral pink gladiolus, each flower having a yellow centre marked with a red patch.

Primulinus gladioli

This group is partly derived from the wild species known as *G. primulinus*, and has a similar flower form. The blooms are funnel-shaped, with the arching upper petal forming a hood. The flowers are not so densely packed together on the spike as with larger-flowered types. 'Anitra' is a good deep red; 'Leonore' (*below*) has bright yellow flowers; 'Lady Godiva' is white; and 'Columbine' has cyclamen-pink flowers, which have a white patch in the throat.

GLORIOSA
Flame lily or glory lily

Suitably named, this is a most spectacular plant, very unusual among bulbous plants because it is a climber. Being a winter-dormant plant, the misshapen tubers are usually obtained in spring for summer growth and flowering. Occurring naturally in Africa and India, it is not hardy in cool areas, but makes an excellent container plant for a conservatory, in which case the tendrils must be given plenty of support from twigs or trellis.

One tuber will require a container that is at least 8in (20cm) in diameter; plant it about two-thirds of the way down, in standard potting medium. They are best started into growth in spring, at a minimum temperature of 55-60°F (13-16°C) and, once showing above ground, should be given liquid feeds once every two weeks. In early summer, they can be placed outdoors for flowering, after which they can be dried off and stored in a frost-free place over winter. The tubers will increase slowly by division, although propagation by seed is also possible if it is sown under glass in spring and kept at the above temperature. Hardiness zone: 10.

G. superba (*next column*)

The weak stems grow up to 6ft (1.8m) in height, and bear scattered, oval leaves with tendrils at their tips. A single flower is carried in each of the upper leaf axils; they are very striking, colourful blooms, with six reflexed petals that are wavy at the edges. Some forms have crimson-red petals with yellow margins and bases, while others are yellow, some plain and some tinged orange-red. They may be listed in catalogues as 'Rothschildiana', 'Carsonii' and 'Lutea'.

GLOXINIA (syn. SINNINGIA)

Although a genus of plants called gloxinia exists, few of the species are in general cultivation. The name gloxinia is used for a race of hybrids in the genus *Sinningia*, involving *S. speciosa* and others. These are very tender, tuberous-rooted subjects, usually treated as summer pot plants, that should be dried off over winter and stored in a frost-free place. In early spring, the tubers are planted in trays of damp peat and sand and started into growth at a temperature of approximately 60°F (16°C). When they start to sprout, plant them at a depth of 1in (2.5cm) in pots containing open potting soil consisting of loam, sharp sand and leaf mould or old rotted compost in equal parts. Place them in a light position but avoid direct sunlight. Throughout summer, they require liquid feeds once a fortnight; it is best to avoid wetting the hairy leaves when watering.

Propagation is by seed sown in spring, or by cutting up the tubers in spring before they start into growth, making sure that each division has a growing point. The following cultivars have a rosette of oval, toothed, soft, hairy leaves and short stems. They are compact plants, with clusters of showy, large, nearly upright, funnel-shaped flowers. They make ideal pot plants. Hardiness zone: 10.

S. 'Tigrina'

This is a name given to speckled or dappled forms of gloxinia in pink, blue or red, one of which is called 'Tiger Red'; this has cerise

flowers with white throats speckled red. 'Mont Blanc' (*below*) has pure white flowers, frilled at the edges of the petals; 'Princess Elizabeth' is blue with a contrasting white throat; 'Blanche de Meru' is a rich red with a cream throat; and 'Emperor Frederick' has crimson flowers with white-edged petals.

HABRANTHUS

These attractive bulbs, mostly from South America, can only be grown in mild, frost-free areas, so are best treated as pot plants for a cool greenhouse or conservatory. They should be kept quite dry when dormant and started into growth in spring, the bulbs being planted half-way down a pot filled with well-drained, loam-based medium. Plant about five bulbs per 6in (15cm) diameter container and, instead of repotting them every year, remove the surface layer of soil and top-dress with new medium. If growing them outdoors, choose a warm, sunny position and plant the bulbs about 3in (7.5cm) deep, in well-drained soil. Propagate by offsets or seed in spring. Hardiness zone: 10.

H. robustus (*above*)
The large, funnel-shaped, pale pink flowers are 2¹/₂in (6.5cm) long, appearing just before the narrow, grassy leaves.

H. tubispathus (*above*)
This is the hardiest species of habranthus which will grow in areas of slight frost. It has small, yellow flowers, about 1in (2.5cm) long, which are tinged a coppery brown or reddish-brown colour on the outside. Propagation by seed takes a year or two to produce flowering-size bulbs.

HAEMANTHUS AND SCADOXUS

Haemanthus is now split into two genera, *Haemanthus* and *Scadoxus*, although most are still found in catalogues under the name *Haemanthus*. These showy bulbs from tropical Africa and South Africa are best treated as conservatory subjects, although they may be grown outside on a patio or terrace during warm summer months. The large bulbs produce broad leaves, either in a cluster or lying flat on the ground, and a dense flower head. The umbel is usually spherical, but some are conical or brush-shaped, each one consisting of 50-100 or more individual, small flowers. They should be potted in spring, with the tip of the bulbs just level with the surface, in a sandy, loam-based compost, and started into growth at a temperature of 55-60°F (13-16°C). During the growing season, they need plenty of water and a liquid feed every two weeks; *H. albiflos* remains in leaf during the winter rest period.

Propagate by removing offsets when repotting in spring, although haemanthus are best left undisturbed for as long as possible since they seem to flower better when pot-bound. Hardiness zone: 9.

H. albiflos
An evergreen bulb, *H. albiflos* has broad, hairy, pale green leaves and small, white flowers held in a dense, brush-like umbel up to 3in (7.5cm) across. The stem reaches a height of 6-12in (15-30cm). It is very easy to cultivate as a house plant.

H. coccineus (*below*)
This bulb has a spotted stem 12in (30cm) high, carrying a dense umbel up to 4in (10cm) wide. This is made up of small, red or pink flowers, the whole head being surrounded by a whorl of broad, pinkish-red bracts. This is followed by a pair of elliptical leaves, often spotted or banded purple, which lie flat on the ground.

H. [Scadoxus] multiflorus (*below*)
Blood lily
The stout stem growing 12in-1¹/₂ft (30-45cm) high is crowned by a spherical umbel measuring 4-6in (10-15cm) in diameter. This consists of up to 200 small, red flowers with long, protruding stamens. The erect basal tuft of broad, bright green leaves expands slightly later. *H. katherinae* (syn. *H. multiflorus* subsp. *katherinae*) is very similar but more robust, growing up to 3ft (90cm) high, each flower having wider petals and a longer tube.

H. pubescens
The broad, hairy, almost flat leaves are produced after the red flowers. These are borne in a dense umbel 2-2¹/₂in (5-6.5cm) in diameter, on a stout, 6-10in (15-25cm) tall stem, and are surrounded by red bracts.

H. [*Scadoxus*] *puniceus*
Royal paintbrush

The 12in-1½ft (30-45cm) tall flower stem carries a shuttlecock-shaped umbel which grows 4-6in (10-15cm) in diameter. The small flowers vary in colour from pinkish-red to orange-red, and are surrounded by reddish- or greenish-coloured bracts. The broad, upright leaves form a separate cluster alongside the flower stem. *H. magnificus* is now considered a synonym of *H. puniceus.*

HERMODACTYLUS
Widow iris

A curious iris-like plant with finger-shaped tubers, the widow iris should be planted in autumn, at a depth of 3-4in (7.5-10cm) in well-drained, preferably alkaline soil. It requires a hot, sunny position where it will sun-bake after its dormant mid-summer period. Widow iris tubers increase quite rapidly and can eventually form extensive patches up to 3-4ft (90cm-1.2m) across. Propagate by division in late summer or early autumn. Hardiness zone: 6.

H. tuberosus (syn. *Iris tuberosa*) (*above*)
This bulb produces 6-12in (15-30cm) tall stems and long, narrow, greyish leaves with a square-shaped cross-section. Each stalk bears a single, iris-shaped flower; this is translucent green or yellowish-green in colour, with a dark, velvety, blackish-brown tip to the three larger, outer petals. In mild areas, it will flower in late spring. The unusual, fragrant flowers are good for cutting.

HYMENOCALLIS
Spider lily or Peruvian daffodil

These tropical or warm temperate bulbous plants of the amaryllis family have fragrant, white or yellow flowers. These resemble daffodils in structure, but the cups from which the long stamens arise are larger and the petals narrower. They

are best treated as pot plants for a heated conservatory or greenhouse, with a minimum summer temperature of 60°F (16°C). In warm areas, the hardier types may be grown outside, either planted or in containers, and overwintered under glass. The large bulbs are potted in spring, planted about half-way down a 6-8in (15-20cm) diameter pot containing a light, open compost of equal parts loam, sharp sand and leaf mould or peat, with a well-balanced fertilizer. During the summer, they need plenty of water and liquid feeds every two weeks, after which they must be dried out over winter at a minimum temperature of 50°F (10°C). The evergreen species require a little water in winter. Propagation is by removal of offsets at repotting time. Hardiness zones: 9-10.

H. amancaes (*above*)
A deciduous species, *H. amancaes* has long, strap-shaped basal leaves and flower stems up to 2ft (60cm) high. These carry an umbel of large, fragrant, yellow flowers with a frilly-edged cup and narrow, spreading petals.

H. × *festalis* (*above*)
This deciduous hymenocallis produces long, strap-like leaves and 2-3ft (60-90cm) tall flower stems. The large, white, fragrant flowers are 6-8in (15-20cm) in diameter.

H. × macrostephana

This evergreen plant has an umbel of white, creamy white or pale greenish-yellow flowers.

H. narcissiflora (syn. *Ismene calathina*) (*above*)
The 2ft (60cm) tall stems of this bulb bear up to five fragrant, white flowers with a frilly-edged cup; it is deciduous.

H. speciosa

An evergreen from the West Indies, *H. speciosa* requires warm conditions of 60-65°F (16-18.5°C). It has up to 10 very large, fragrant white or greenish-white flowers, each with a funnel-shaped cup and narrow, spreading petals. The flowers grow 7-12in (18-30cm) in diameter.

H. 'Sulphur Queen' (*above*)
This deciduous bulb has primrose yellow flowers with a green stripe inside the cup. The flowers are carried on 2-3ft (60-90cm) high stems.

IRIS

Most of the bulbous irises are associated with spring, but the Xiphium group, comprising the English, Spanish and Dutch types, normally flower in early summer, although they can be forced under glass to bloom much earlier for cutting. They all have rather long, narrow leaves which are channelled on the upper surface, and one or two large flowers on top of strong stems. The bulbs are obtained in autumn and need to be planted 3-4in (7.5-10cm) deep. They require an open, sunny position in well-drained, acid or alkaline soil, and look good placed in groups among herbaceous perennials. In areas without a warm, dry period in mid- to late summer, the Spanish and Dutch types are probably best lifted and stored dry until autumn, whereas the English iris should be lifted and replanted in a moisture-retentive soil. Propagation is easiest by removal of offsets when established clumps are dug up for replanting in early autumn, or else by means of seed sown in autumn. Hardiness zones: 5-7.

I. latifolia (syn. *I. xiphioides*)
English iris

In spite of its name, this plant is from the Pyrenees. It is a robust grower, reaching about 3ft (90cm) in height, with varying shades of violet-blue flowers in mid-summer. Each of the three outer petals (the "falls") are marked with a yellow line in the centre. They are usually available as mixed collections rather than single-colour forms.

I. xiphium (*above*)
Spanish iris

Growing 2-3ft (60-90cm) high, this slender-looking plant has slightly smaller flowers than *I. latifolia* and each petal is narrower. The flowers are a pale, clear blue, yellow or white, with a deep yellow band in the centre of each of the outer petals. The Spanish iris is produced earlier than the English iris.

Dutch iris

This group name represents a wide range of hybrid Xiphium irises, which flower slightly earlier than the Spanish ones. They are frequently used for forcing to provide cut flowers in winter, but also make excellent garden plants. They grow to a height of 2-3ft (60-90cm) at flowering time. Good cultivars include: *I.* 'White Excelsior', with white flowers and yellow marks on the falls; *I.* 'Bronze Queen', a curious mixture of gold, bronze and purple; *I.* 'Golden Harvest', a good deep yellow throughout; *I.* 'Wedgwood', a clear mid-blue flower with a yellow stripe on each of the falls; and the attractive *I.* 'Professor Blaauw' (*below*), which has a rich, deep gentian-blue stripe and is yellow on the falls.

IXIA
Corn lily

These colourful plants are South African in origin and not very hardy, since they naturally grow during the winter months and flower in spring. However, some nurseries keep the corms in storage and offer them for spring planting to flower in summer. This may work for the first season, but afterwards they will try to revert back to their normal growth cycle. They should be lifted for the winter and kept warm and dry until spring. They are best planted in a warm, sunny position in well-drained, preferably sandy soil, at a depth of 3in (7.5cm). They are best grown in a clump, with the corms 1½in (4cm) apart. In areas with mild, frost-free winters, they can be planted and left in the ground.

There are many species of ixia, but few are generally available, the most likely being mixed, unnamed collections. They have slender, wiry stems with tough, narrow leaves and spikes of star-shaped, brightly coloured flowers. Propagation is by offsets detached when the corms are dug up, or by seed, which takes two to three years to produce flowering-size corms. Hardiness zone: 8.

I. maculata

This corn lily produces stems that reach 1½ft (45cm) high, with spikes of flattish, 1-2in (2.5-5cm) diameter, star-shaped, yellow or orange flowers; these have brownish or black centres.

I. viridiflora (*above*)

A spectacular species, *I. viridiflora* has 12in-1½ft (30-45cm) long spikes of green flowers, each 1½-2in (4-5cm) in diameter. The flowers are marked with a blackish-purple-coloured eye in the centre.

LILIUM
Lily

The lilies are some of the most beautiful and stately bulbs, valuable for planting among perennials or shrubs. The flowers come in many different forms, for example, trumpet-shaped, Turk's cap, flattish, pendent, upright and horizontal (usually referred to as "outward-facing").

Many are easy to cultivate but, if the soil or climate does not suit them, they make excellent container plants for a patio or terrace, often growing much better here than in the open ground. Some bulbs are sold in autumn, while others are lifted and stored until spring. It is best to purchase them as soon as they are on the market and to plant them immediately. With autumn planting in cold areas, it may be necessary to pot up the bulbs and keep them in a cool, frost-free place until spring, when they can be planted out. Most lilies do well if their bases are shaded by other lower-growing plants, leaving their flowers to push up into the sunlight, but they also enjoy dappled shade provided by taller trees and shrubs.

Before planting, prepare the soil by digging in well-rotted compost or leaf mould, with added sharp sand if necessary to improve drainage, and a well-balanced fertilizer. For the larger-growing lilies, allow 2ft (60cm) in diameter for three bulbs, and plant them in a triangle at a depth of 4-8in (10-20cm) depending on size. *L. candidum* is the exception; these bulbs only need to be just below the soil level. Most lilies can be grown on acid or alkaline soil, but alkaline soil must have humus incorporated at planting time.

Lilies can be propagated in many ways. Either lift and divide established clumps in autumn, or pick the bulblets or bulbils produced by some plants on their stems or in their leaf axils in late summer, and plant them in pots or boxes, or in a nursery bed of fertile soil for growth the following summer. They normally take one to two years to reach flowering size. Bulb scales can also be used to increase lilies and this is quite a simple and rapid method of propagation: break off a few scales any time between mid-summer and early autumn or when dormant without harming the parent, and place them in a polythene bag of slightly damp perlite, vermiculite or clean sharp sand, placing them in a warm room at about 70°F (21°C). In about three to five weeks, remove the small bulbs and grow them on in the same way as the naturally-produced bulblets and bulbils. Hardiness zones: 4-7

L. amabile

This Korean species grows 1½-3ft (45-90cm) high. It has many scattered, narrow leaves and up to 10 pendent, red flowers usually spotted black; these are Turk's cap in shape, with rolled-back petals and protruding brown stamens. *L. a. luteum* (*above*) is yellow.

L. auratum (next column)
Golden-rayed lily

This spectacular Japanese species is known as the golden-rayed lily because its 12in (30cm) wide, saucer-shaped, fragrant, white flowers

have a yellow band along the centre of each petal, and are also spotted red to varying degrees. There are usually 5-10 flowers per stem, the height of the stem varying from 3-5ft (90cm-1.5m). *L. auratum* performs best in a lime-free soil.

L. bulbiferum
Orange lily

One of the oldest lilies to be cultivated, this European species grows up to 5ft (1.5m) high, with upward-facing, cup-shaped flowers. These are bright reddish-orange, usually spotted brown inside. The leaf axils hold bulbils, although the variety *croceum* (*below*) does not. *L. b. croceum* is similar in most respects to *L. bulbiferum*, but with orange rather than reddish flowers.

L. canadense
Canada lily or meadow lily

This very graceful North American species has a creeping rhizome-like bulb, and stems up to 4ft (1.2m) high, bearing whorls of leaves. The pendent, bell-shaped flowers have outward-curving tips, and are available in a range of colours, from yellow through to orange or red, often spotted darker inside. It needs fairly moist rather than waterlogged soil conditions.

L. candidum (below)
Madonna lily

A very distinct lily from the eastern Mediterranean, *L. candidum* is a well-known symbol of purity. Unlike most lilies, it needs to be planted in early autumn, since this is when it makes a new set of overwintering leaves. The 3-5ft (90cm-1.5m) high flower stems appear in early summer and carry many erect leaves, and up to 15 white, wide, funnel-shaped, deliciously fragrant flowers. It needs a warm, sunny situation.

L. cernuum

An eastern Asiatic lily, *L. cernuum* grows up to 2ft (60cm) in height, with many narrow leaves and one to seven pendent, scented flowers. These Turk's cap blooms are pinkish-purple, spotted dark purple on the inside of the flowers.

L. chalcedonicum (below)
Scarlet Turk's cap lily

A slightly scented, scarlet-flowered Turk's cap lily from Greece, *L. chalcedonicum* needs a sunny, well-drained position and prefers alkaline soil. The 3-4ft (90cm-1.2m) long stems have lance-shaped, silver-margined leaves which are densely packed all the way up to the flowers.

L. concolor

A Chinese species 12in-3ft (30-90cm) high, *L. concolor* has scattered, narrow leaves and up to 10 smallish flowers. These are almost flat and held upright; they may be red and either with or without darker spots, or yellow and unspotted.

L. davidii (*below*)

This lily is a native of China. It has many very narrow leaves packed on to the 3-5ft (90cm-1.5m) tall stems, and up to 20 pendent, Turk's cap flowers standing out horizontally on long stalks from the main stem. Each flower is bright orange, with black spots inside. The variety *willmottiae* is more vigorous, with up to 30 reddish-orange-coloured flowers.

L. duchartrei (*below*)
Marble martagon lily

A beautiful but small-flowered lily from China, *L. duchartrei* has slender stems up to 4ft (1.2m) high, carrying scattered leaves and up to 12 pendent, white flowers. The flowers have a Turk's cap shape similar to that of the martagon lily, and are spotted and veined reddish-purple, hence the comparison with marble. It will grow in semi-shade, in acid or alkaline, humus-rich soil.

L. formosanum

This lovely but rather tender trumpet lily from Taiwan grows up to 5ft (1.5m) tall. It has a few very fragrant, funnel-shaped flowers 6-8in (15-20cm) long; these are pure white inside and flushed wine-purple on the outside. It is not a frost hardy plant and is best grown under glass. The variety *pricei* (*below*) originates from higher altitudes and is much hardier; it is a dwarf plant, often only reaching 6-12in (15-30cm) in height.

L. hansonii (*below*)

A distinctive eastern Asiatic lily, *L. hansonii* has whorls of broad leaves held on a 3-5ft (90cm-1.5m) high stem. The deep yellow, Turk's cap flowers are spotted brown on the inside, and the reflexed petals are very thick and waxy.

L. henryi (*next column*)

This Chinese lily is one of the easiest of all to grow. It is a graceful plant up to 7ft (2.1m) high, with broad leaves that diminish in size towards the top of the flowers. There are 10-20 or more pendent, Turk's cap flowers which are bright orange spotted darker towards the centre, with prominent, hair-like projections. It will grow in the semi-shade, in neutral or alkaline soil rich in leafmould.

L. lancifolium (**syn.** *L. tigrinum*) (*below*)
Tiger lily

This familiar species is unfortunately very susceptible to virus diseases. It reaches 5ft (1.5m) in height, with narrow, dark green leaves bearing bulbils in their axils. It has 10-20 or more pendent, orange-red flowers that are spotted black in the centre. The variety *flaviflorum* is clear yellow, and *fortunei* is more robust, with orange-scarlet flowers.

L. langkongense (*below*)

This elegant lily from China grows 3-4ft (90cm-1.2m) high. It has many leaves and up to 15 large, Turk's cap flowers; these are pale pink, spotted dark reddish-purple.

L. leichtlinii

An eastern Asiatic lily, *L. leichtlinii* is usually seen in the variety known as var. *maximowiczii* or *L. maximowiczii*. It has 4-6ft (1.2-1.8m) high stems bearing Turk's cap flowers that are orange-red, spotted darker red inside. It is easy to grow and resembles the tiger lily.

L. longiflorum (*above*)
Easter lily or Bermuda lily

This well-known, white trumpet lily is from eastern Asia. It is so easy to grow that it is cultivated on a vast scale and is often used as a cut flower in floral decorations. A very tender species, it requires frost-free conditions, and may be raised from seed to flowering in just one growing season. The elegant, pure white, funnel-shaped flowers are about 6-8in (15-20cm) long and are pleasantly fragrant; occasionally more than one flower per stem is produced.

L. mackliniae (*above*)
Manipur lily

A choice lily from Burma, this is suitable for growing outdoors in a cool, semi-shaded position in soil rich in peat or leafmould. A very distinct lily, its 12in-2¹⁄₂ft (30-76cm) high stems carry one to five pendent bells about 2in (5cm) long; these are white, flushed pinkish-purple on the outside.

L. martagon (*above*)
Turk's cap or martagon lily

This European lily is one of the oldest in cultivation. It is easily recognized by its racemes of up to 20 small, dull pinkish-purple flowers that are spotted darker in the centre, with the petals rolled back to give the Turk's cap shape. It has whorls of broad leaves growing up the stems. A very hardy species, it is suitable for naturalizing beneath and between shrubs, or in grass. There are several variations worth growing, including 'Album', the lovely white-flowered form, and the interesting 'Dalmaticum', which has almost black flowers.

L. monadelphum (*above*)

This is a large Turk's cap lily from the Black Sea region. It is about 4-5ft (1.2-1.5m) high, with stems carrying several large, pendent flowers of a lovely pale yellow, spotted dark purple on the inside. The petals are less rolled back than those of *L. martagon*. *L. szovitsianum* is very similar to *L. monadelphum*, with only slight botanical differences; for the most part, choice depends upon availability.

L. nanum

A tiny lily from the Himalayas, *L. nanum* requires cool, damp growing conditions in summer and almost dry winters. It is usually only 3-12in (7.5-30cm) in height, with a solitary, bell-shaped flower approximately 1¹⁄₂in (4cm) long. These are normally shades of pinkish-lilac, although there are other variants available.

L. nepalense (*below*)

A beautiful Nepalese lily, but unfortunately rather tender, this bulb requires cool greenhouse cultivation in cold-winter areas. It grows up to 4ft (1.2m) high, and has one to three pendent, funnel-shaped flowers with recurved tips to the petals. They are a curious greenish-yellow colour, stained with purple on the inside. The stems may grow as much as 2ft (60cm) underground before emerging, so the plant may not appear where it was originally planted.

L. pardalinum (*below*)
Leopard lily

This very striking and easily cultivated western American lily requires a damp situation in humus-rich soil. It has whorls of leaves on its 5-7ft (1.5-2.1m) high stems, and several large, pendent Turk's cap flowers. These are a brilliant orange-red in colour, shading to darker red at the tips of the petals, with deep brown spots towards the centre of each flower.

L. parryi (*above*)
A western American species, *L. parryi* grows 2–5ft (60cm–1.5m) high, with lovely yellow fragrant, funnel-shaped flowers.

L. pomponium (*above*)
This very dramatic Turk's cap lily from southern France is best grown in a warm position on alkaline soils. Its 2–3ft (60–90cm) high stems carry many narrow leaves and brilliant waxy red, Turk's cap flowers.

L. pumilum (**syn. L. tenuifolium**) (*below*)
This lily is a red-flowered Turk's cap from eastern Asia. It is a small, slender plant, only 1½–2ft (45–60cm) high, with very narrow, grassy leaves, and up to 15 small, red, fragrant flowers. It is easily raised from seed.

L. pyrenaicum (*below*)
Yellow Turk's cap lily
Although not showy, this European Turk's cap is very hardy and easily cultivated. The stout, 2–4ft (60cm–1.2m) high stems are densely clothed with many leaves, and have up to 10 small, greenish-yellow Turk's cap flowers. These have black spots and lines in the centre; the more unusual variety *rubrum* has reddish-orange flowers.

L. regale
Regal lily
Undoubtedly one of the best of all the white trumpet lilies, *L. regale* is hardy and tolerates a wide range of conditions in the garden. It is quick to raise from seed, usually taking only two to three years. The wiry, 3–6ft (90cm–1.8m) high stems carry many narrow leaves, and 1–20 outward-facing trumpets. Each one is approximately 6in (15cm) long, deliciously scented, and white on the inside with a purple staining outside. 'Album' (*below*) is a white version without the purple stain.

L. rubellum (*next column*)
This dwarf Japanese lily is quite hardy and worth trying in a peat garden, or in partial shade with other low-growing perennials. It only reaches 1–2ft (30–60cm) high and has a

few lance-shaped leaves. The one to six fragrant, funnel-shaped flowers, about 3–4in (7.5–10cm) long, are a lovely soft shade of rose pink.

L. sargentiae (*below*)
Very similar to *L. regale*, *L. sargentiae* has rather wider leaves and flowers slightly later. It is, however, less hardy and is more susceptible to virus diseases.

L. speciosum
A beautifully fragrant Japanese lily, *L. speciosum* flowers rather later than most other species, often continuing into the early autumn, and it can be caught by early frosts in cold areas. It is a stem-rooting lily, and prefers cool, humid but well-drained growing conditions with plenty of humus incorporated into the soil. It usually grows up to 6ft (1.8m) high, and has rather thick, leathery leaves and up to 10 large, pendent flowers. The petals are rolled back like a Turk's cap, displaying long, protruding stamens and prominent hair-like projections on the inside. Several colour variants exist, but typical flowers are white suffused with pink, with crimson projections. 'Album' is a lovely white and 'Rubrum' a deeper carmine-pink, with pale margins to the petals.

L. superbum (*below*)
Swamp lily
This striking North American swamp lily grows up to 7ft (2.1m) high. It has whorled leaves and a large head of many pendent, Turk's cap flowers. These are orange, spotted maroon inside, with reddish tips to the petals. It needs a moisture-retentive rather than waterlogged soil, and enjoys neutral to acid conditions.

L. × testaceum (*below*)
Nankeen lily
Probably the oldest hybrid lily, this cross between *L. candidum* and *L. chalcedonicum* has soft apricot-coloured flowers with a few red spots in the centre. They are wide, open flowers with the petals rolled back from the mid-point; up to 12 are carried on 6ft (1.8m) high stems, which are densely packed with leaves. Like its parents, it prefers alkaline soil and a sunny position.

L. tsingtauense
This distinctive eastern Asiatic lily grows to a height of about 3ft (90cm). It has whorls of lance-shaped leaves and upward-facing flat flowers that range from red through to orange-red in colour, and are spotted darker maroon in the centre.

L. wardii
This Turk's cap from China has tough, slender, 4-5ft (1.2-1.5m) high stems, clothed with many deep green leaves. It bears up to 15 or more fragrant, pinkish-purple flowers which have dark spots in the centre. They are smallish and pendent, with their petals rolled right back.

Hybrid groups
There are thousands of lily hybrids which, for ease of reference and show purposes, have been grouped together into an internationally agreed classification. This is largely based on the parentage of the hybrids, the flower shape and the way in which the flowers are held on their stems, for example: trumpet; Turk's cap; or flattish; held in a pendent; upright; or horizontal ("outward-facing") position. A few select groups are given below in the order recommended by the Horticultural Classification of Lilies.

Asiatic hybrids
These hybrids are derived from a group of mainly eastern Asiatic lilies, and have given rise to a very popular range of hardy lilies, including the Mid-century hybrids, which are much used as cut flowers as well as in the garden. They subdivide into three groups: upright-flowered; outward-facing; and pendent.

Upright-flowered lilies
'Connecticut King' (*above*) has plain, bright yellow, upright, almost flat flowers; 'Sterling Star' (*next column*) is a similar shape, but is white with brown spots inside; 'Chinook' is upright and pale apricot; 'Enchantment', one of the oldest in this group and still popular, has a bunch of bright orange, upward-facing flowers spotted black inside. 'Destiny' is upright and yellow in colour, spotted brownish-red; 'Firecracker' is deep red; and 'Pirate' has orange-red, upright flowers.

Outward-facing lilies
'Corsage' has creamy white flowers shaded to a pinkish tinge at the tips of the petals, and spotted maroon inside; 'Fireking' (*below*) is an intense orange-red, also conspicuously spotted; and 'Brandywine' is apricot-orange-yellow, spotted dark red.

Pendent lilies
These tend to have Turk's cap-shaped flowers with reflexed petals. 'Lady Bowes Lyon' is a rich red, spotted black inside; 'Discovery' has rose pink flowers with darker tips to the petals and spots inside; and 'Yellow Star' (*below*) is very elegant, with lemon yellow, spotted-black flowers.

Martagon hybrids

These hybrids of the true Turk's caps involve either *L. martagon* or *L. hansonii*. Their flowers are generally small and their leaves are borne in whorls. Few are generally available, but 'Marhan' (*below*) is sometimes found in catalogues, and has orange flowers with brown spots. 'Mrs R.O. Backhouse' is also orange-yellow in colour, with a few spots inside, flushed pink on the outside. 'Jacques S. Dijt' is a pale, creamy yellow colour, spotted purple.

American hybrids

This group includes some of the most attractive lilies which make excellent long-lasting cut flowers. They have tall stems bearing whorled leaves and large, pendent flowers, which often have elegantly reflexed, pointed petals. The Bellingham hybrids are a vigorous, mixed group, in colours ranging through yellow to deep orange, with a strong spotting of darker orange-red. 'Shuksan' is an individual selection from the Bellingham hybrids, with orange flowers flushed red, spotted darker red inside. One of the best-known forms, it increases rapidly under ideal conditions. 'Lake Tahoe' (*below*), a lovely variety, has pinkish-red flowers with yellow and white centres, spotted deep red.

Asiatic trumpet hybrids

This is one of the more important groups. It contains all the large, fragrant, trumpet lily hybrids which are spectacular and easily grown subjects for the garden and containers. They are 4-6ft (1.2-1.8m) high, with large, funnel-shaped flowers, each approximately 6in (15cm) long. 'Green Magic' is white on the inside, with a lemon yellow centre and a green flush on the outside; 'Pink Perfection' has large trumpets in varying shades of pinkish-purple; 'African Queen' (*above*) is a soft orange, flushed pinkish-bronze on the outside; and 'Golden Splendour' (*below*) is a good, deep golden yellow, flushed purple outside. 'Bright Star' differs from the majority of the trumpet group because the flowers open out wide and the tips of the petals are recurved. The flowers are white, with orange-yellow bands radiating from the centre along the middle of each of the six petals, forming a star-shape.

Oriental hybrids

These are mostly derived from the gorgeous Japanese species *L. auratum* and *L. speciosum*, but some may involve *L. henryi* and other eastern Asiatic species. Their flowers, almost flat or with recurved petals, usually have prominent projections on the inside. They are deliciously fragrant. 'Black Beauty' has deep red, reflexed petals edged with white; 'Casa Blanca' has enormous, almost flat, white flowers which have contrasting brown stamens; 'Star Gazer' is rather unusual with its upward-facing flowers which are a rich crimson, spotted darker maroon; and 'Journey's End' (*below*) has deep crimson flowers, with the white-edged petals reflexed. The white flowers of 'Imperial Gold' are like those of *L. auratum* and are large and almost flat, with a yellow band along the centre of each petal.

LITTONIA

This interesting and attractive bulb from southern Africa is rarely seen although it is very easy to cultivate. It is tender, requiring greenhouse or conservatory cultivation in cold areas but, being winter-dormant, it can be grown outdoors in a container for the summer. The elongated tubers should be planted in spring at a depth of approximately 4in (10cm), in a medium strength, loam-based compost, and started into growth by slight watering. They require a minimum temperature of 55°F (13°C). Sticks or trellis should be provided since this climber can reach up to 6ft (1.8m) in height during summer growth. After flowering, it is kept growing until the leaves begin to die back in autumn, when the tubers can be dried and stored in a frost-free place for winter. In areas with mild winters, it can be grown outdoors as a permanent planting, at the edge of a supporting shrub. Propagation is by division at repotting time, the tubers naturally producing offsets. Hardiness zone: 9.

L. modesta

This slender-stemmed plant has lance-shaped leaves with tendrils at their tips, and bell-shaped, orange flowers in the axils of the upper ones. These are pendent and about 1-1½in (2.5-4cm) long.

MONTBRETIA (see CROCOSMIA)

MORAEA

Mostly from the tropics of Africa and South Africa, these bulbs are the African equivalent of irises. The flowers have three large, outer petals ("falls") and three smaller, inner ones the equivalent of the "standards" of an iris. They have a corm rather than a rhizome or bulb, and the leaves are usually narrow and flat, or channelled on the upper surface. They are much less hardy than irises, and most require a frost-free climate or cultivation in a greenhouse or conservatory. However, there are a few species from the eastern Cape region that are winter-dormant and fairly hardy. They should be planted in spring at a depth of 3in (7.5cm); the soil should not be waterlogged or be allowed to dry out too much during the summer growing season. In very cold areas where the ground freezes to a considerable depth (zones 5-6), the corms are best lifted over winter and stored in a frost-free place. Propagation is by seed sown in spring, which takes about two years to produce flowering-size corms. Hardiness zones: 7-8.

M. huttonii (*above*)
Growing to a height of 3ft (90cm), the tough stems of this species carry several flowers. These are initially encased within tight bracts and afterwards produced in succession over a period. They are yellow, marked with brown in the centre of the three larger, outer petals, and grow 2-3in (5-7.5cm) across.

M. moggi and *M. spathulata*
These types are very similar to *M. huttonii*.

NECTAROSCORDUM

This small group of bulbous plants from southern Europe and Turkey are related to the onion family (*Allium*) and release a similar but much more pungent smell if crushed. The bulbs are happy growing in ordinary garden soil; plant in autumn, in a sunny or partially-shaded position where they can be left to self-seed, although the seed heads can be cut off before the seed ripens. After flowering in early summer, the plants die down, but they may be left in the ground since they do not require particularly warm or dry conditions during the dormant season. The dried seed heads make attractive cut flowers for winter decorations. Propagation is by division of clumps or seed in autumn. Hardiness zones: 6-7.

N. bulgaricum
This grows to a height of 3-4ft (90cm-1.2m), and has long, channelled basal leaves and a bare stem. It is crowned by an umbel of bell-shaped flowers that are held on long, drooping stalks; each flower is white with a green tinge, and reaches $^3/_4$-1in (2-2.5cm) in length. After flowering, the stalks turn upwards so that, in the fruiting stage, the umbel resembles a shuttlecock.

N. siculum (syn. N. dioscoridis; Allium siculum) (below)
Similar in overall shape and size to *N. bulgaricum*, *N. siculum* has bell-shaped, green flowers that are strongly flushed with purple, although some are almost entirely reddish-purple in colour.

NOMOCHARIS

These very beautiful Himalayan and Chinese relatives of the lily are not as easy to grow, except in cool temperate gardens, where the atmosphere is damper and cooler during the summer growing period. The scaly bulbs and leafy stems are similar to the lily, but the flowers tend to be almost flat, with fringed margins to the petals, often with a darker eye or prominent blotches on a paler background. Plant the bulbs in partial shade in autumn at a depth of 4-5in (10-13cm); they require humus-rich soil. Propagation is best from seed, but it will take three to four years to produce flowering-size bulbs. Hardiness zones: 5-6.

N. aperta (*above*)
This nomocharis grows 2-3ft (60-90cm) high, with scattered or paired leaves and up to six, nodding, saucer-shaped flowers. Each flower is about 3-4in (7.5-10cm) in diameter, with a pale pink background and a dark purple eye in the centre, surrounded by reddish-purple-coloured blotches.

N. farreri
Similar in habit to *N. aperta*, *N. farreri* has whorls rather than pairs of leaves and up to 10 whitish flowers, which have slightly fringed edges to the petals.

N. mairei (below)
This very showy species grows to a height of 2-2$^1/_2$ft (60-76cm). It has whorls of leaves and almost flat, nodding flowers that are heavily blotched and spotted reddish-purple on a white background. The three inner petals are strongly fringed at the margins.

N. pardanthina (*above*)

The whorled leaves of this nomocharis grow on 2-3ft (60-90cm) tall stems. It produces up to 10 almost flat flowers; these are pink with a slight purple spot and a dark purple eye in the centre. The inner petals are fringed.

N. saluenensis (*above*)

The leaves of this nomocharis are held in pairs and it has from one to six saucer-shaped flowers which grow 3-4in (7.5-10cm) in diameter. These are mostly pink or reddish, although off-white forms are occasionally found, with a dark eye in the centre and a sprinkling of dark spots; the petals are not fringed.

NOTHOLIRION

A small group of bulbous plants from the Himalayas and China, notholirions are related to the lilies, but most have bulbs enclosed within brown, papery coats, smaller flowers and long, narrow basal leaves. After flowering, the bulb dies down having produced offsets, which carry the plant on to the next generation. They are best planted in autumn, in a sheltered position, near shrubs that provide winter protection for the developing leaves. The soil needs to be well-drained but moisture-retentive in summer, with a good humus content. Propagation is by growing on the offsets. Hardiness zone: 7.

N. bulbuliferum (**syn.** *N. hyacinthinum*)

This plant has long basal foliage and scattered leaves growing on the 2-3ft (60-90cm) tall stems. The raceme is made up of 10-30 funnel-shaped, pale lilac flowers that flare out at the mouth. They are 1½in (4cm) long, with green tips to the petals.

N. campanulatum

Similar in habit to *N. bulbuliferum*, this notholirion has drooping, 2in (5cm) long bells that are deep crimson, tipped green.

N. macrophyllum (*above*)

A shorter species reaching only 2ft (60cm) high, this has only a few wide, funnel-shaped flowers that are pale lavender spotted with purple on the inside. They are about 1-1½in (2.5-4cm) long, opening out to 2in (5cm) across at the mouth.

N. thomsonianum

This species produces its leaves in early autumn and requires a sunny, well-drained position that will dry out slightly in late summer. It has long, basal leaves and leafy stems up to 3ft (90cm) high, which carry up to 25 flowers, each about 2-2½in (5-6.5cm) long. These are funnel-shaped and pale lilac in colour; the petals have recurving tips.

ORNITHOGALUM
Star-of-Bethlehem

This is a very large group of bulbous plants from Europe, western Asia and South Africa, many of which are spring flowering. Being dormant in summer, they are mostly winter-growing plants but a few, such as the popular *O. thyrsoides* (chincherinchee), can be treated as summer-growers. The majority of the northern hemisphere species are much hardier than the South African ones, and can be planted out in autumn at a depth of 2-3in (5-7.5cm), in any reasonably well-drained

garden soil. They grow in sun or slight shade, but need a certain amount of sun at flowering time or the flowers will not open. The more tender species can be kept dry and frost-free over winter, and planted out in spring for summer flowering. In most cases, propagation is easy since they produce offsets quite readily; alternatively, seed takes up to three years to make flowering-size bulbs. Hardiness zones: 6-8.

O. arabicum

A striking and unusual species, *O. arabicum* has broad basal leaves and 2-3ft (60-90cm) high stems crowned with a dense head of almost flat, upward-facing, cream-coloured flowers. Each of these is about 1½-2in (4-5cm) in diameter, with a dark eye in the form of a blackish ovary. It needs a warm, sheltered position.

O. narbonense (*above*)

Producing a cluster of long, narrow, greyish basal leaves and tough, 12in-2ft (30-60cm) high stems, this star-of-Bethlehem bears a raceme of many star-shaped, white flowers, ½-1in (1.5-2.5cm) in diameter. Each petal has a pale green stripe along its centre on the outside. For the best results, plant the bulb in full sun.

O. pyrenaicum
Bath asparagus

Of similar habit to *O. narbonense*, Bath asparagus has smaller, pale greenish-yellow flowers; when in bud, the racemes look like thin asparagus shoots. The plant grows up to 3ft (90cm) high, and requires sunny or partially shaded conditions.

O. thyrsoides (*next column*)
Chincherinchee

A South African species, chincherinchee is naturally winter-growing but, in cold-winter areas, planting can be delayed until spring to provide flowers in summer. In winter, it can be grown in a frost-free greenhouse or conservatory. It grows 1-2ft (30-60cm) high, with dense, conical racemes of many white flowers, each one cup-shaped and approximately 1in (2.5cm) in diameter. They are a popular cut flower and last a long time in water.

OXALIS

An extremely large group of plants, oxalis are quite unlike the rest of the bulbs described in this book, but many have swollen rootstocks and can be bought from bulb nurseries. The majority have attractively divided leaves and buds which unfurl in the sun like an umbrella into rounded, showy flowers with five petals. Plant them in autumn or, if purchased as pot plants, in spring, at a depth of about 2in (5cm) unless otherwise stated. They require a well-drained site that receives sunshine for the greater part of the day. Propagation is by division once clumps have formed. Hardiness zones: 7-8.

O. adenophylla (*above*)
A native of Chile and Argentina, this oxalis has a curious bulb resembling a ball of felt, which should be planted just below the

surface of the ground in gritty soil. The plant is only 2-3in (5-7.5cm) high, and forms a clump of attractive greyish-coloured leaves, each one consisting of several small leaflets. In early summer, it produces many short-stemmed, pale pinkish-lilac flowers that are almost flat, each one growing about 2-2½in (5-6.5cm) in diameter.

O. enneaphylla
From the Falklands, this is similar to *O. adenophylla*, but has a more elongated, rhizome-like rootstock. It is an attractive plant for the rock garden.

O. tetraphylla (**syn.** *O. deppei*) (*above*)
This can grow up to 4in (10cm) high, with tufts of clover-like leaves consisting of four leaflets, which are green with a reddish-brown zone near the base. The light carmine-red flowers are carried in small umbels in early summer. It will grow in the front of a border or in the rock garden.

PANCRATIUM

A small genus of the amaryllis family, pancratium has beautiful, fragrant flowers resembling large, white daffodils, consisting of a cup surrounded by narrow petals. The Mediterranean species begin to grow in autumn after a summer dormancy, and should be kept in growth until the leaves die away in mid-summer, after which the bulbs should be kept as warm and dry as possible. Although not very hardy, it is worth trying them outdoors in mild areas, planted at the foot of a sunny wall or in containers that can be moved under cover during cold periods. They are best left undisturbed to build up into clumps. Propagation is by seed sown in autumn, which takes up to five years to produce flowering-size bulbs, or else by offsets detached in early autumn. Hardiness zone: 8.

P. illyricum
A beautiful plant from Corsica, this is the hardiest species of pancratium and will flower reliably if given a warm rest period. It has grey-green, strap-shaped basal leaves and 12in-1½ft (30-45cm) high stems. In early summer, these carry an umbel made up of 10-15 fragrant, white flowers; each is about 3-4in (7.5-10cm) in diameter, with a fairly small central cup.

P. maritimum (*below*)
Sea lily or sea daffodil
P. maritimum is much less hardy than *P. illyricum*. In late summer, it produces up to six flimsy flowers per umbel, each with a large cup. It seldom flowers in cultivation and is often found growing on the beach at sea level in the Mediterranean.

PARADISEA

Although related to many of the bulbous members of the lily family, this is a herbaceous plant with fleshy roots that cannot be dried off in the same way as bulbs. Since it is usually obtained as a pot-grown plant, it can be planted out at any time, preferring a sunny, well-drained position. The single cultivated species is a clump-forming perennial which can be lifted and divided in early autumn or spring before new growth commences; young plants can be raised from seed. An established clump may reach 6-12in (15-30cm) in diameter. After division it may not flower for a season. Hardiness zones: 4-5.

P. liliastrum
St Bruno's lily
A hardy plant, *P. liliastrum* grows 12in-2ft (30-60cm) high, with long, narrow, grassy leaves and, in early summer, racemes of up to 10 white, funnel-shaped flowers, each 1½-2in (4-5cm) long.

POLIANTHES

Although from a small genus of Mexican plants, *P. tuberosa* is a centuries-old, well-known garden species that is cultivated in many parts of the world, mainly for its sweetly scented, white flowers. The large, bulb-like rootstocks are planted in spring, in a warm, sunny situation in rich soil but, in cold areas, they are best started off in pots ready for planting out when the soil has warmed up. Alternatively, grow them under glass in larger containers and move them outdoors during summer. They die down over winter and should be kept warm and relatively dry until spring, after which they are repotted. Except in very mild areas, those planted outdoors should be lifted for winter storage. Propagation is by division of the bulbs at repotting or replanting time. Hardiness zone: 9.

P. tuberosa (*above*)
Tuberose
The tuberose has long, greyish-green leaves and a 2–2½ft (60–76cm) high stem which bears a raceme of fragrant, white, waxy flowers. These have a narrow, funnel-shaped tube a minimum of 1in (2.5cm) long, which opens out into six flattish lobes at the mouth. 'The Pearl' is a double form which has many more lobes to the flowers.

RANUNCULUS
Buttercup

Since most ranunculus do not have swollen rootstocks and cannot be dried off during their dormant season, they are not sold by bulb nurseries. However, one species, *R. asiaticus*, is traditionally found in bulb catalogues and has been much developed from its original wild forms.

R. asiaticus comes from the eastern Mediterranean and has claw-like, fleshy roots that naturally lie dry and dormant over summer, before starting into growth

during autumn and winter. They should be planted in autumn, in a well-drained, sunny situation which is sheltered from very severe weather, at the foot of a sunny wall or near a group of evergreen shrubs, for example. The tubers are planted at a depth of 2in (5cm), spaced 4in (10cm) apart, with the "claws" pointing downwards. In cold-winter areas, they should be kept dry over winter and then planted in spring for flowering in summer; they are sometimes found in spring catalogues. Propagation is by division of the tubers into separate crowns at replanting time. Hardiness zone: 8.

R. asiaticus (*above*)
The wild form has a basal cluster of long-stalked, lobed leaves, and 12in–2ft (30–60cm) high stems that carry erect, saucer-shaped flowers in a range of colours, from red and pink to yellow, orange and white. Each flower has a single row of petals and a large central mass of stamens, but some of the highly developed cultivated forms, such as the Turban- and Peony-flowered types, have tight, double blossoms.

RHODOHYPOXIS

These delightful dwarf bulbs come from the eastern Cape region of South Africa. They are dormant in winter and produce a long succession of flowers from early to late summer, which range in colour from white to various shades of pink and red. They are dormant in winter and will survive freezing conditions of –5°C (23°F) but, in very cold areas, they are best lifted over winter and stored in peat in a frost-free place. Planting takes place in spring in a light soil with a good sand and peat content, the small tubers being planted at a depth of 1in (2.5cm), spaced 1in (2.5cm) apart. They need sunny or partially shaded positions in hot, dry climates, but do not

like to be too sun-baked in the growing season. They are also suitable subjects for shallow pots or pans in an alpine house or conservatory. Propagation is by offsets and stolons in spring. Hardiness zone: 7.

R. baurii
Growing 2–4in (5–10cm) high, *R. baurii* has narrow, hairy leaves and slender stems. Each bears a solitary, flat flower with six petals meeting in the centre, completely closing off the eye of the flower. The flowers are about 1in (2.5cm) in diameter and come in a range of colours: 'Ruth' has rather large, white flowers; 'Fred Broome' is a large-flowering, strong pink; 'Pictus' has white flowers with pink tips to the petals; and 'Albrighton' is a deep pink version. The popular 'Susan' (*above*) is a deep reddish-pink colour.

SANDERSONIA

A genus of just one species, this is a climbing plant from southern Africa that may be grown outdoors in mild-winter areas, but elsewhere is best treated as a greenhouse or conservatory plant. The finger-like tubers are planted in spring at a depth of 4in (10cm), in a well-drained, sandy potting soil in a sunny spot; they will need watering to start into growth. Feed them every two weeks with a liquid feed of proprietary flower fertilizer, and provide them with a trellis or pea sticks to climb up. They should be lifted and stored in a frost-free place during winter dormancy. The tubers increase naturally and propagation involves division at repotting time. Hardiness zone: 9.

S. aurantiaca
This bulb grows up to 3ft (90cm) high, and has scattered, lance-shaped leaves, with solitary, orange, pendent flowers in the axils of the upper ones. The urn-shaped flowers are about 1in (2.5cm) long.

SAUROMATUM

Like most other aroids, these curious, tuberous-rooted members of the arum family carry their tiny flowers on a pencil-like spadix surrounded by a large spathe which is tubular at its lower part. In the case of sauromatum, the spathes are produced before the leaves, and the bulbs will flower unplanted if placed on a windowsill. However, they must be potted or planted out if they are to be kept. In cold areas, grow them under glass in large pots of humus-rich potting medium. Feed them with a liquid fertilizer during the growing season and dry them off in winter. If planted outdoors, plant the tubers about 4in (10cm) deep, in well-drained, rich soil in a sheltered, partially shaded position; in areas where the ground freezes, they will need lifting over winter. Propagate by offsets at replanting or repotting time. Hardiness zone: 10.

S. venosum (syn. *S. guttatum*) (*above*)
Voodoo lily or monarch of the east
This is a Himalayan plant whose tubers produce a 12in-2ft (30-60cm) long spathe, with a tubular, bottle-like lower part that widens out into a coiled blade in the upper half. It is yellowish-orange, greenish or purplish in colour, with large, purple blotches. The flower is followed by a single leaf with several finger-like lobes, which may reach a height of 1½ft (45cm).

SCADOXUS (see HAEMANTHUS)

SPARAXIS
Harlequin flower
Although these colourful South African bulbs normally begin to grow in the autumn and flower in early spring, the corms are often kept dry through winter and sold for spring planting to flower in summer. It is necessary to lift the corms in

late summer and dry and store them in a frost-free place over winter, otherwise they will revert to their normal habit of starting into growth in the autumn. While not a problem in very mild-winter areas, in frosty-winter regions they will not survive. Sparaxis do well in sandy soil but require plenty of moisture while growing. The corms should be planted about 2-3in (5-7.5cm) deep. Propagate by division or seed in autumn. Hardiness zone: 9.

S. elegans (syn. *Streptanthera elegans*) (*below*)
This sparaxis has fans of upright, lance-shaped leaves and 12in (30cm) tall stems. These carry loose spikes of up to five, almost flat flowers, each about 1-1½in (2.5-4cm) in diameter. The blooms are orange or white, with a purplish-black zone surrounding a central yellow eye.

S. grandiflora
Similar in general appearance to *S. elegans*, *S. grandiflora* has deep purple flowers.

S. tricolor (*below*)
This has large flowers 2-2½in (5-6.5cm) in diameter, available in a range of bright colours, from red and orange to purple and pink, and with a blackish or red eye.

SPREKELIA
Jacobean lily
A lovely Mexican bulb of the amaryllis family, the Jacobean lily is best treated as a pot plant for a greenhouse or conservatory. In mild areas, however, it can be grown outdoors in a sheltered position. The bulbs should be planted in a well-drained, loam-based potting compost in spring, one per 5in (13cm) pot, with the tip of the bulb just protruding. Start into growth by gentle watering and keep the bulb at a minimum temperature of 60°F (16°C). During the growing period, apply a liquid tomato feed. When the plant dies back in autumn, withhold water and keep dry and frost-free over winter, repotting in spring before starting into growth again. Propagate by removing offsets at repotting time. Hardiness zone: 9.

S. formosissima (*below*)
With narrow, strap-shaped leaves held in a basal cluster, the stems of this plant reach a height of 6-12in (15-30cm) in early summer. Each stalk bears one large, deep red flower made up of six petals; the upper three are wide-spreading and the lower ones are pendent, held close together to form a lip.

TIGRIDIA
These very striking, late summer bulbs from Mexico can be grown outside in areas that have only slight winter frosts; where the ground freezes, they are best lifted in autumn and stored in dry peat in warmer conditions. The bulbs are planted in spring, requiring a sheltered, sunny position and well-drained soil. In areas with a cold, late spring, it is better to start them off in pots and plant them out when the soil has warmed up. Propagation by seed sown in spring will produce flowering plants in the first or second flowering season.

Named varieties should be propagated by division of clumps since they will not necessarily breed true from seed. Hardiness zone: 8.

T. pavonia (*above*)
Tiger flower
This has erect, sword-shaped leaves with prominent veins, and 12in-2ft (30-60cm) high stems bearing green spathes that enclose several buds. They emerge in succession to give a long flowering period, but each flower is very short-lived, lasting only one morning. The blooms are 4-6in (10-15cm) in diameter and are somewhat iris-like in appearance, with three large, outer petals. The most frequently seen form is a deep flame red, with a heavily red-blotched centre on a whitish background. There are, however, many forms: 'Alba' has pure white flowers; 'Aurea' is a yellow-flowered type; 'Liliacea' has reddish-purple flowers which are variegated white in the centre; and 'Canariensis' is a deep yellow colour, although there is also a pinkish form sometimes offered under the same name.

TRITONIA
A small genus of southern African, cormous plants, some tritonias are winter-growing, while others flower in summer. The former are normally planted in autumn, in frost-free conditions, for spring-flowering, but are sometimes kept dry over winter and sold in spring. These must be lifted in late summer and dried off again or they will revert to their normal behaviour and try and grow through winter. The summer-growing species are hardier since they die down over winter and are protected underground. They need ordinary, reasonably fertile garden soil and a sunny situation. Propagation of both types is by division at replanting time. Hardiness zones: 7-8.

T. crocata (*below*)
A winter-growing species, *T. crocata* can be kept dry for a spring planting and summer flowering. It grows from 12in-1½ft (30-45cm) high, with sword-shaped leaves and a loose spike of up to 10 flowers, each one 1-2in (2.5-5cm) across. The rounded flowers narrow to a short tube and are usually orange.

T. rubrolucens (**syn.** *Crocosmia rosea*)
This summer-growing species flowers late in the same season. It grows up to 2ft (60cm) high, with narrow leaves and loose spikes of five to eight flowers. They are pink and funnel-shaped, and open out to 1-1½in (2.5-4cm) across in the sun.

VALLOTA
Vallota is now botanically regarded as a *Cyrtanthus*. It is a tender, bulbous plant from South Africa which, after flowering in summer, has a period of winter rest although, being evergreen, it does not die down and should never be dried out completely. The bulbs are potted in early spring, one per 5in (13cm) diameter container filled with a loam-based potting medium. Start it into growth by lightly watering it, and keep it at a temperature of 60-65°F (16-18.5°C). It is best left undisturbed for several years, with monthly feeds of liquid fertilizer during the growing season. In areas with very mild winters, it can be grown outdoors in a sheltered, sunny situation, provided the bulbs are planted at a depth of about 4-6in (10-15cm). Propagation is by offsets, which can usually be detached without disturbing the larger bulbs. Hardiness zone: 10.

V. speciosa (**syn.** *Cyrtanthus purpureus*)
Scarborough or George lily (*top right*)
This grows to a height of 12in-2ft (30-60cm), and has strap-like, bright green leaves and

large, wide, funnel-shaped, scarlet-red flowers. These reach 3-4in (7.5-10cm) across, and are held several to an umbel at the top of a stout stem.

WATSONIA
A large genus of gladiolus-like plants from South Africa, watsonias are very striking, with their dense, symmetrical spikes of brightly coloured, funnel-shaped flowers. They are mostly rather tender, but are very easy to grow in sunny situations that experience only slight winter frosts. Elsewhere, they can be grown in large containers and moved under glass over winter. On the whole, they perform best if left undisturbed, although they can be lifted and dried over winter. The large corms should be planted 6in (15cm) deep in a light soil; in areas of heavy, badly drained soil, add sand. Propagation is by division of clumps or by seed, which may take three to five years to produce flowering-size corms. Hardiness zone: 8.

W. angusta (*above*)
Growing 3-6ft (90cm-1.8m) high, this watsonia has tough, narrow leaves and branched flower spikes, that bear several narrow, tubular, red flowers; each one reaches 2-2.5in (5-6.5cm) across the mouth.

W. densiflora (*below*)

This is an aptly named species because its unbranched flower spikes bear up to 40 funnel-shaped, pink flowers that are packed tightly together. Each one measures about 2in (5cm) long and 1½in (4cm) across at the mouth. The stiff, tough, sword-like leaves are erect, and the whole plant may reach 4ft (1.2m) or more in height.

W. meriana

This watsonia measures 2-6ft (60cm-1.8m) high, and has broad, tough, sword-shaped leaves. The stems are mostly unbranched, although some have one or two branches. The loose flower spike is made of tubular orange, red or pink flowers that open out 1½-2in (4-5cm) wide at the mouth. There is also a form in cultivation that produces bulbils on the flower spike, known as var. *bulbillifera*.

W. pillansii (**syn.** W. beatricis) (*below*)

This plant reaches 1½-3ft (45-90cm) in height, and has tough, narrow, erect leaves. The densely flowered spikes of up to 30 bright orange or pinkish flowers are usually unbranched; each narrow bloom is funnel-shaped and about 3in (7.5cm) long, opening out 1½in (4cm) wide at the mouth.

ZANTEDESCHIA
Arum lily

These showy members of the arum family are well-known for their large, upright, funnel-shaped spathes, which are often used by florists throughout the year as cut flowers. In a warm greenhouse, they can be brought into flower at almost any time, but they can also be grown outdoors in mild climates for summer flowering, in which case they are usually evergreen. In colder areas, they make good container plants: start them into growth in spring and move them outside in early summer; they should be returned to a frost-free place and dried off over winter. The tubers should be planted at least 6in (15cm) below soil level in deep containers, in a well-drained, rich potting medium, and given liquid feeds at two-week intervals during the growing season. For the majority of the species and varieties, a minimum winter temperature of 50°F (10°C) is necessary, but *Z. aethiopica* is hardier and may be grown outdoors in areas where the ground does not freeze, if planted at a minimum depth of 2in (5cm). It can also be grown as a water plant, either in the boggy soil at the edge of a pool or actually in a pool with up to 12in (30cm) of water covering the tubers. Propagation is by removal of offsets at repotting or replanting time. Hardiness zones: 8-9.

Z. aethiopica

This South African species has dark green, arrow-shaped leaves and 2-3ft (60-90cm) high stems, each carrying a large, white spathe up to 8in (20cm) long that encloses a yellow, club-shaped spadix. The variety 'Crowborough' (*above*) is considered to be a hardier version, and the particularly attractive green and white 'Green Goddess' (*next column*) has greenish spathes; these are splashed green on a white background in the centre.

Z. rehmannii (*below*)
Pink arum

This is a much shorter plant, about 12in-1½ft (30-45cm) high, with a yellow sparix surrounded by pink to reddish-purple spathes about 3in (7.5cm) in length.

Z. 'Black Eye Beauty' (*below*)

This cultivar has striking, creamy-coloured spathes with a blackish central eye, hence its cultivar name.

Z. 'Solfatare'

One of the yellow-spathed varieties, 'Solfatare' is a paler sulphur yellow, with a contrasting blackish centre.

AUTUMN BULBS

Garden highlights

Autumn-flowering bulbs make outstanding features in the garden, whether planted individually or mixed with other plants. Their prize quality lies in the fact that they flower towards the end of the season, just when the garden is about to die down, creating an exquisite burst of colour. All are fairly amenable characters and, with careful placement, most areas of the garden can benefit hugely from their presence.

Colchicum is a very valuable autumn highlight; even a small group tucked into a gap between two shrubs can make a startling difference on a dull autumn morning. As well as the white-flowered forms like *C. autumnale* var. *album* and *C. speciosum* 'Album' there are those with pink flowers, all of which look good planted in a straight, narrow strip in front of a conifer hedge or a row of evergreen such as *Viburnum davidii*, or with a few small-leaved hollies like *Ilex crenata*

(Japanese holly). Pink colchicums also look good clustered around the base of a white-berried shrub like *Gaultheria cuneata* or the snowberry, *Symphoricarpos albus* 'White Hedge', or planted beneath the lovely *Sorbus cashmiriana*. White-variegated hollies can also be used, with white-variegated ivies as ground cover. When growing large-flowering *Colchicum* hybrids, do not forget that in the spring their leaves are quite substantial, and the plants can swamp their smaller neighbours, particularly squills or anemones.

One of the most important and impressive autumn bulbs is the exotic *Amaryllis belladonna*, which requires a sunny spot, ideally at the base of a wall. It can either be planted on its own for a bold display, or grown among climbers and wall shrubs that are nearing the end of their season and are beginning to lose their colour. With its heads of beautiful pink

PREVIOUS PAGE Naturalized clumps of Colchicum speciosum *'Album' show up well among the carpet of golden-brown autumn leaves.*

BELOW The brilliant colour of this Colchicum speciosum *hybrid when used in a bold grouping makes an unforgettable impact.*

RIGHT During flowering, the goblet-shaped colchicums open wide to reveal their orange stamens, as shown here.

or white, trumpet-shaped blossoms, it looks quite stunning when pushing up through the steadily fading, tangled mass of *Clematis orientalis* with its feathery seed heads, or mixed with the almond-scented, creamy white, late-flowering *Clematis flammula*. For a bold combination of strong colours, mix *A. belladonna* with *Ceratostigma willmottianum*, a shrub with bright blue flowers produced in late summer and continuing well into autumn. Wall-trained espalier apple and pear trees also provide an unusual, interesting association. However, for a simple but effective show, plant the bulbs in gravel-topped soil at the base of a wall which will act as a uniform background against which the elegant beauty of the leafless flowers will stand out. To reap the full benefit of their architectural shape, space the bulbs in a line a small distance apart rather than in a loose, random clump.

Nerine bowdenii is infinitely more delicate-looking than the amaryllis, with slender, bright pink blossoms. It can be treated in the same way but needs to be planted much closer to the wall. Unlike most bulbs, it only prospers when crowded; plant the bulbs cheek by cheek and leave them to grow. The choice of companion plants for *N. bowdenii* is limited, but

the flowers look good against a wall covered with *Trachelospermum jasminoides* 'Variegatum' which, in some weather conditions, develops pinkish margins on its leaves. The *Agapanthus* Headbourne hybrids can also be recommended as companion plants, especially for narrow borders in enclosed, walled areas, against a backdrop of large-leaved ivy. They are hardy, vigorous, exotic-looking plants with umbels of bright blue flowers that start to open before the nerines but fade around the same time. The autumn-flowering *Liriope muscari* (lily turf), with its spikes of rounded, lavender or purple-blue flowers and narrow, glossy, dark green leaves, creates a bold, colourful display when mixed with *N. bowdenii*, but more formal companions include *Yucca* and *Phormium*, the coppery leaved *Phormium* making a truly outstanding statement, standing proud among the nerines.

While there is no doubt that *Nerine bowdenii* can be utilized to the full to create exotic-looking gardens, it also makes a good subject for a cottage garden theme. Plant the bulbs beneath the upright spring growth of *Rosa moyesii* or its variety 'Geranium', both popular shrub roses with butter-yellow autumn foliage and masses of crimson red hips the colour of sealing-wax in autumn. Alternatively, *Rosa glauca* (syn. *R. rubrifolia*) provides a misty blue background punctuated with bright red hips. In a more confined space, insert *N. bowdenii*

LEFT The soft pink of Nerine bowdenii *planted in a leafy spot creates a subtle, airy effect.*

BELOW Vibrant crimson and purple asters frame these pink nerines in a bold and vibrant border planting.

between the spreading branches of the herringbone *Cotoneaster horizontalis*, so the blossoms just peep up among the partially defoliated branches of the shrub, which are also heavily laden with colourful fruit.

Crinums are among the most attractive of the autumn-flowering bulbs. They are large, showy plants with umbels of funnel-shaped flowers. Some are tender and need a warm, sunny spot, ideally against a wall. *Crinum × powellii*, the hardiest of the group, can be grown in a border. With its drooping flowers in white or shades of pink, it is ideal for providing early-autumn colour. Crinums are best planted in clumps on their own as they swamp nearby plants with their leaves.

LEFT Crinum × powelli *is ideal for a large-scale planting. Here, the bulbs are used boldly and generously, massed together in parallel borders beneath a walk of apple trees. The foliage of the crinums overhang the edge of the path, softening the effect and inviting the visitor to walk slowly along the path to admire the plants. A largely frost-free site with plenty of sun is essential for crinums, otherwise they will not perform well. For a good show of flowers as seen in this example, they must have a plentiful supply of water in summer during the growing season and during flowering. Crinums do not mix well with other plants.*

RIGHT Eucomis comosa, *commonly known as the pineapple flower, requires a sheltered site in order to produce a good display of flower spikes such as these. A position against a sunny wall is ideal.*

Another good plant for autumn is the eucomis. However, this is not a showy bulb, and its tall spikes of star-shaped white or pink flowers and rosettes of strap-shaped basal leaves are best appreciated when silhouetted against a wall or background of dark foliage.

Schizostylis coccinea 'Grandiflora' can be used as a colourful, red border highlight when mixed with late-flowering red dahlias and *Sedum spectabile* (ice plant), which has fleshy, grey-green leaves and vibrant pink flowers. If the border is big enough, plant a large drift of *Anaphalis triplinervis* (pearly everlasting) at the back. This forms a good robust clump of neat, grey foliage, topped by masses of star-shaped, white flowers which hide the otherwise straggly foliage of the schizostylis.

ABOVE LEFT Although it may be a year or two before Sternbergia lutea *flowers, if it is left undisturbed it will grow into clumps.*

ABOVE RIGHT Despite its fragile appearance, Colchicum speciosum *'Album' will naturalize readily under trees and shrubs, and even in rough grass.*

RIGHT Both the pink and white forms of Cyclamen hederifolium *are happy growing in a cool, semi-shaded spot like this one.*

Bulbs for naturalizing

There are many superb opportunities for naturalizing some of the smaller autumn bulbs, but great care must be taken with their positioning. The two small autumn crocuses, *Crocus speciosus* and *C. sativus*, can certainly be naturalized in grass, but they cannot be raised in a regularly mown area or the flowers might be decapitated before they have had a chance to open. The sparse, grassy patches under the edge of a tree canopy are the perfect spot for naturalizing crocuses, as are areas of turf around shrubs, where the grass can be left to grow without being mown until the bulbs have died down. Instead of grouping an individual species, mix a number of different varieties together at planting time. All will flower during autumn, over a period of several weeks rather than all at once. In more open ground, autumn-flowering crocuses are quite sensational when mixed with the steely-blue, short-growing grass *Festuca glauca* (blue fescue). This is a hummock-forming plant rather than a spreading grass, so the crocus corms can easily be planted around it. A different but equally appealing combination involves the golden-leaved grass *Milium effusum* 'Aureum' (wood millet).

Crocus sativus (saffron crocus) is probably the most popular crocus for naturalizing. It has purple, lilac or deep purplish-mauve blossoms which are a delight when irregularly sprinkled in a grassy sward. *C. sativus* can also be grown through a clump of the violet *Viola labradorica* 'Purpurea', which has dark purple-green, kidney-shaped foliage. *Crocus kotschyanus* is another good choice, although it does not spread as

quickly in open grass as when planted beneath trees and shrubs or in the bare earth. It is a gorgeous, delicate-looking yet quite robust crocus, the masses of pale lilac, chalice-like blossoms contrasting superbly with the foliage of brightly coloured autumnal plants. For the best effect, select a shrub that lies reasonably close to the ground and scatter a ring of crocus in the dark, damp soil underneath it.

Fothergilla major (syn. *F. monticola*) is an especially fine companion shrub, with clusters of fragrant, white flowers in spring, and fiery orange-red leaves which coincide with the appearance of the autumn crocus. *Crocus kotschyanus* can also be planted among the rugged stems of *Rhus typhina* (stag's-horn sumach), which has fiery autumn foliage.

Crocuses mix well with ground-cover plants, particularly *Ajuga*, many of which have strikingly colourful leaves. *Ajuga reptans* 'Multicolor' is a first-class choice, with its rose, cream and purple foliage, as is the dark purple-copper *A. r.* 'Atropupurea'. Even the ordinary plain green *Ajuga pyramidalis* makes an appealing feature when interspersed with *Crocus speciosus*. The almost evergreen, rounded foliage of *Lysimachia nummularia* (creeping Jenny) can be enlivened with a sprinkling of autumn crocuses for a fine display, and its golden-leaved cultivar *L. n.* 'Aurea', despite fading as autumn moves into winter, remains sufficiently colourful to make a first-rate companion. The golden yellow *Thymus × citriodorus* 'Aureus' (lemon-scented thyme) and *Trifolium repens* 'Purpurascens', a purple-leaved clover, also provide suitable ground cover for naturalized crocuses.

Colchicum can also be naturalized successfully. However, they produce large leaves in spring which can be a handicap unless the bulbs are in soil beneath shrubs, in which case the foliage is useful for covering the otherwise bare earth.

The best shrub for mixing with *Colchicum* is the rhododendron. This combination is particularly useful since few plants grow well in close proximity to the rhododendron because of the dense shade and its extensive surface roots. However, colchicums can be grown under the edge of the foliage canopy so the rhododendron is fringed with streaks of colour. Rhododendron hybrids grown in a formal garden combine well with hybrid *Colchicum* like 'Lilac Wonder' and 'The Giant'. If the rhododendrons are species or primary hybrids underplant them with lilac-pink *Colchicum autumnale* var. *album*.

Other mixtures involve *Colchicum* and plants like *Hosta glauca* (plantain lily), *Bergenia purpurascens* and peonies. These companions are particularly useful because their new growth hides the fading summer foliage of the bulbs.

Sternbergia lutea is an attractive autumn highlight, requiring free-draining soil in a sunny position at the base of a wall. A waxy, crocus-like plant of quite startling appearance, it is one of the few bright yellow autumn flowers and will spread into patches if left undisturbed. Possible companion plants include *Thymus vulgaris* (common thyme), *T.* × *citriodorus* (lemon-scented thyme) and *T.* × *c.* 'Aureus', a golden-leaved relation.

The colourful autumn-flowering *Cyclamen* deserves a place in any garden. The best choice of hardy cyclamen is the pink or white-flowered *C. hederifolium*, which has contrasting dark green and silver-marbled foliage. Since it enjoys partial shade, it can be naturalized beneath a fine specimen tree like one of the Japanese maples or a birch like *Betula utilis* var. *jacquemontii* (Himalayan birch). This tree has a white trunk against which the rose-pink cyclamen look particularly striking. As autumn progresses, the birch loses its bright yellow leaves, which fall in a light sprinkling around the cyclamen.

Cyclamen can also be planted under any of the mountain ash group of *Sorbus*. For a truly vibrant display, underplant *Sorbus* 'Joseph Rock' with *C. hederifolium* 'Album'; the mahogany-red leaves and brilliant yellow fruit of the tree look quite marvellous with the show of cool, icy-white flowers beneath. The bright red-fruiting *S. commixta* 'Embley' is equally beautiful, best mixed with the deep rose-pink hues of ordinary *C. hederifolium* rather than its clear white cousin.

BELOW Autumn-flowering colchicums need careful siting as they produce large foliage in spring. They are ideal for naturalizing in the light shade of tree canopies and the more vigorous types grow well in grass.

ABOVE The unusual-looking Gladiolus papilio *is very hardy and will spread into sizeable patches in free-draining conditions.*

ABOVE Sternbergias enjoy free-draining conditions as provided by this sunny gravel bed, and the flowers show up well against the pale chips.

ABOVE Colchicum bivonae *thrives in well-drained soil. For the greatest impact, group the plants together in large clumps.*

Bulbs for the rock garden

A selection of autumn-flowering bulbs add colour and interest to the rock garden at a time when few other alpine or dwarf plants are producing attractive displays. Crocuses are especially valuable because they can be planted among established alpines without interfering with their lifestyles. Unlike many other bulbs, crocuses present few problems when dying back as they discreetly fade into the associated plant cover without smothering nearby growth.

The hardiest of the autumn crocus, *Crocus speciosus* and *C. kotschyanus*, thrive among most of the popular hummock-forming rock plants such as aubrieta and arabis. *C. speciosus* has also yielded some particularly fine cultivars which can be tucked into tiny niches in the rocks where hummock-forming plants cannot establish themselves; plant two or three corms together in a group and top-dress with a layer of fine grit to form a pleasing background. The bluish-lavender 'Cassiope' and pale violet-blue 'Pollux' are both attractive, although the blue 'Oxonian' is the finest, but it is rather difficult to establish. *C. speciosus* shows up well against soft grey-green plants like *Artemisia schmidtiana* 'Nana', but they also mix well with brightly coloured plants such as *Polygonum vacciniifolium*, which have deep pink flowers held on red stems.

The purplish-lilac *Crocus longiflorus* is another good choice for the rock garden, along with the deep purple *C. nudiflorus* and creamy white *C. ochroleucus*. Each is best grown alone in a pocket without competition from permanent plants, but there is no reason why small-growing annuals such as *Limnanthes douglasii* (poached-egg plant) and night-scented or Virginian stocks should not be sown over the top to provide summer colour. Care must be taken when removing these plants at the end of the season not to disturb the crocus corms.

Equally valuable as crocuses in the rock garden, cyclamen thrive when planted in pockets of free-draining compost that is rich in organic matter. *Cyclamen hederifolium* is the most decorative species; it has attractive, patterned, ivy-like foliage with a velvety feel to it, and pale pink flowers which are stained darker around the mouth. *C. graecum* is also handsome, with pale to deep pink flowers which are stained purple around the mouth, and the silver-marked, dark green leaves have reddish undersides. The pink- or white-flowering *C. cilicium* is not quite so attractive, with dark green, silver-blotched, heart-shaped leaves, but the smaller, more delicate, fragrant flowers are charming, particularly appropriate for a small rock garden where it is easier to cultivate the more refined alpines.

The interesting but much neglected autumn-flowering snowdrop *Galanthus reginae-olgae* grows well in a sheltered corner of the rock garden, in free-draining, leafy compost. Closely allied to the common snowdrop *G. nivalis*, it requires drier summer conditions than its more familiar cousin. Plant it towards the summit of the rockery to ensure good drainage.

Containers and window boxes

The majority of autumn-flowering bulbs are too transient for use in containers and window boxes, where a constant and colourful display is vital. However, autumn crocuses are well-suited to this type of cultivation because they provide an excellent show the first year round. Tuck them in among established plants like winter pansies, polyanthus or *Bellis* (cushion daisies) for some late autumn colour. After flowering, the crocus corms can be pulled out of the compost and returned to the garden; they will continue to grow provided they are planted out immediately.

Colchicums are also useful for container and window box displays, despite their brief flowering period. The double, lilac-pink 'Waterlily', the magnificent 'Lilac Wonder' and the lilac-mauve 'The Giant' are all to be recommended. All flower for about three weeks, after which they can be planted outdoors and replaced with winter-flowering pansies and spring bulbs. 'Waterlily' can also be grown in containers, planted among the purple-black leaves of *Ophiopogon planiscapus* 'Nigrescens'. To achieve the greatest impact, position

ABOVE An unusual container such as this one demands a dramatic planting, as provided by these hardy cyclamen and tendrils of trailing ivy.

the container against a stone wall.

Even some of the taller bulbs are suitable for containers. Some, such as *Eucomis comosa* (pineapple flower), can be grown alone for a really dramatic feature. Plant a handful in an antique-looking container positioned in a corner of a courtyard, set against a brick or stone wall draped in ivy. Lead, real or imitation, looks particularly good with the purple-spotted stems and greenish white flowers.

Nerine grows happily in containers, looking best in terracotta pots. Planted alone, they produce a fabulous show for approximately four weeks, after which they should be hidden away in a frost-free place; if the compost in the container freezes solid, the bulbs will quickly perish. They can also be mixed with other plants for a more varied show. Generally speaking, *Nerine bowdenii* is the best choice for mixing because it is the hardiest and most reliable of them all. Choose companions with plenty of verdant foliage, as the flowering spikes of the bulbs look most attractive when seen pushing up through a mass of greenery. In a large tub or trough, *N. bowdenii* associates

well with ferns like *Athyrium filix-femina* (lady fern) or *Polypodium vulgare*.

The moisture-loving *Schizostylis coccinea* and its various cultivars, usually seen in large patches near ponds or streams, can also be grown in large, deep containers, provided they are given a rich, organic compost. Mix them with hostas and evergreen ferns

*ABOVE Pink nerines (*Nerine bowdenii*) and bright green ferns complement one another, and the fern fronds help mask the bare stems of the nerines.*

like *Polystichum acrostichoides* (Christmas fern) or interplant them with *Vinca minor* (lesser periwinkle). The last combination works particularly well in a large, stone trough; by the time the bulbs flower, the periwinkle will be over, leaving only a carpet of lovely dark green foliage around the base of the tall *Schizostylis* stems.

Large urns or vase-like containers are good for displaying *Crinum* × *powellii* and *C.* × *p.* 'Album'. These giant bulbs, with their long, strap-like leaves and bold heads of pink or white, trumpet-like flowers, create a luxuriant, tropical impact. However, they must be given winter protection because, while they are hardy enough to cope with life in

the open ground, in a container they are more vulnerable as their roots are very near the freezing air. Plant them on their own rather than mixing them with other plants so the full splendour of the bulb is displayed.

BELOW A simple terracotta window box is ideal for this combination of lilies, cyclamen, skimmia and ornamental cabbage.

Indoor bulbs

Indoor bulbs can be planted in pots and bowls and forced into early growth for indoor autumn-flowering displays. *Colchicum* is the easiest to grow; it can flower as an unplanted bulb because it has a substantial food store, together with embryo flowers, within its large, fleshy bulb. Prop up the bulbs or place them in a square glass vase or goldfish bowl on a windowsill. In a light position, they will flower without any assistance. Immediately after flowering, the bulbs should be planted out in the garden so that they can produce a root system and subsequent foliage in order to build up their food reserves for next year. The smaller-flowering *Colchicum autumnale* var. *album* is suitable, as are the large double-flowered 'The Giant', 'Waterlily' and the beautiful 'Lilac Wonder'.

ABOVE The purple-green cotinus leaves used to cover this container tone in beautifully with the pink flowers of this autumn-flowering cyclamen.

Some of the tender nerines also make lovely autumn-flowering pot plants, the bright pink *Nerine sarniensis* being the most attractive. Although all naturally flower at this time of the year, the main benefit of a year-long indoor cultural regime is that plants blossom in perfect condition, and a little protection can advance the display. Pack several bulbs into a pot or bowl filled with soil-based compost for the very best results. *Nerine masonorum* is a much shorter

species, ideal for small pots, rarely growing more than 8in (20cm) high. It sports beautiful, small, undulating, crimped blossoms of the softest pink. The closely allied *N. filifolia* is also short, its loose umbels of rose-pink blossoms being held on stems no more than 12in (30cm) high. It has narrow, rush-like leaves that, unlike most other nerines, are evergreen when grown indoors. If regularly watered, *N. filifolia* can become a permanent, colourful, indoor feature, even after flowering.

Of all the autumn-flowering indoor bulbs, *Eucharis amazonica* is the most difficult to grow, demanding a consistently high temperature if it is to perform well. It can rarely be cultivated to perfection without a heated greenhouse, although it is well worth considering for

a conservatory or sun lounge. A magnificent plant with a stout stem up to 2ft (60cm) high, it is studded with spikes of large, icy white flowers of the richest fragrance. The Amazon lily is such a magnificent plant that it deserves a special container, such as a polished brass or copper vessel, or an Italian-style terracotta pot, so as to create a really eyecatching centre-piece.

RIGHT These soft apricot-coloured begonias are particularly appropriate for a mellow autumnal indoor display.

BELOW Autumn-flowering cyclamen make excellent indoor plants provided they can be kept at a constant cool temperature and are not exposed to direct sunlight. They will also grow well in cool conservatories. Interest is added here with spiky, lichen-encrusted twigs, which provide a contrasting shape to the plant yet pick up the silvery green of the cyclamen leaves.

Cut flowers

There are comparatively few autumn-flowering bulbs suitable for cutting, but those there are tend to be colourful, stately characters which are best displayed on their own or mixed with a few branches of autumn foliage to bring out their colour. More ambitious arrangements suitable for celebrating harvest time, however, might include a variety of ornamental berries, as well as grain, fruit and vegetables.

Autumn-flowering nerines, especially the hardy pink *Nerine bowdenii*, make excellent, long-lasting cut flowers, as do *Amaryllis belladonna*. Neither bulbs require special cultural treatment in order to be suitable for cutting but, if they become congested, the stems are sometimes shorter than they would otherwise be. Careful lifting of the clumps, splitting them sparingly, and then replanting the smaller clumps will reduce overcrowding and produce longer flower stems. However, if the plants are divided too much, flowering will be impaired for several seasons.

Nerines come in a wide variety of colours, from white through pink to scarlet-red. Being such intricate flowers, they look good in plain vases, especially glass ones. For added colour, include the orange-red-leaved *Prunus*, small branches of copper beech, or stems of pink, autumn-flowering sedums. The belladonna lily, however, looks best on its own; either bunch them together in a colourful mass or, for a more simple

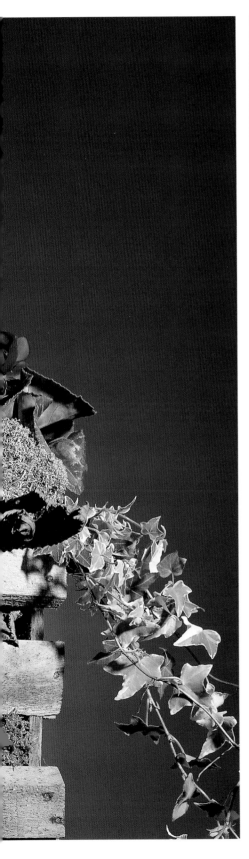

buffeting winds, and must be grown in a sheltered spot. In order to ensure high quality flowers and long stems, the bulbs need lifting and dividing every three or four years; congested plants growing in a border will make a better overall display but will not produce good individual blooms that are suitable for cutting.

Gladiolus papilio can also be cut for indoor use. The delicate-looking, yellowish-green flowers are suffused violet, with hooded upper petals and darker yellow patches on the lower petals. Plant a handful of bulbs approximately 3in (7.5cm) apart and, once the flower spike appears, feed the plants with tomato feed to strengthen the spike. When cutting the stems, remove as little foliage as possible so the corm will be replenished for the following year.

ABOVE A jar of shiny conkers provides a solid foundation for these exotic-looking amaryllis blooms.

RIGHT The elegance of Lilium longiflorum *demands simple arrangements in which their form can be admired without distraction.*

LEFT For a harvest-time display, mix Gloriosa *'Rothschildiana',* Anemone *'Mona Lisa' and* Crocosmia *'Emily McKenzie' with fruit and foliage.*

arrangement, place a few stems in a glass container.

All the popular varieties of the kaffir lily, *Schizostylis*, are good for flower arrangements. The flower spikes look very effective on their own or mixed with glossy, dark green trailing ivy stems. For an especially vibrant display, however, include a few brightly coloured flowers like dahlias.

Because they flower so late in the autumn season, kaffir lillies are vulnerable to weather damage, particularly

ALLIUM
Ornamental onion

Most alliums are dealt with in the Spring and Summer Directories (see pages 87 and 150), but there is one small species, *A. callimischon*, which is well worth growing in autumn. Although not a showy plant, it is nonetheless delightful when viewed closely. This allium grows best in a sunny spot in sharply drained soil; it is perhaps best treated as an alpine house plant or placed in a trough beside small alpines. If planting outdoors, choose a sheltered spot where the soil is unlikely to freeze deeply for any appreciable time. Propagation is by offsets which, in some species, are produced quite freely, or by seed, which may take up to three years to produce flowering bulbs. Hardiness zone: 8.

A. callimischon (*below*)
The best form of this allium is the Cretan subspecies *haemostictum*, which is only 2-6in (5-15cm) high and has umbels of small, papery, whitish flowers with red spots on the petals. When growing well, it may form clumps up to 4in (10cm) across.

AMARYLLIS
Cape belladonna or Jersey lily

The hardy amaryllis from South Africa should not be confused with the tender South American hippeastrums (see page 228), which are often sold for indoor pot cultivation during winter under the erroneous name "amaryllis". The true amaryllis flowers in autumn before the leaves appear, having lain dormant during summer. To succeed, it requires a hot, sunny, well-drained position where the warmth of the summer sun promotes bud formation. It also needs protection from severe winter frosts which can damage the leaves and lead to a loss of vigour. Given these conditions, the Cape belladonna is capable of developing into clumps 12in-1½ft (30-45cm) across in three to five years. Large clumps can be divided in late spring; replant as soon as possible and water in the bulbs to encourage new root development. Established clumps benefit from a light dressing of a potash-rich fertilizer in autumn or spring. Hardiness zone: 8.

A. belladonna (*above*)
The very large bulbs of this plant produce stout, leafless flower stems 1¾-3ft (53-90cm) high in autumn and bear up to six or more large, fragrant, bright pink, funnel-shaped flowers with petals that curl out gracefully at the tips. Once the flowers are finished, the bright, glossy, strap-shaped leaves appear and remain green until the following summer. There are several named cultivars in slightly different shades of pink or carmine, with varying amounts of white or pale yellow in the throat. There is also a lovely but uncommon pure white cultivar called 'Hathor'. The hybrid × *Amarcrinum* looks similar to *A. belladonna* but bears leaves throughout the year; it is a hybrid with the seldom cultivated *Crinum moorei* and is an attractive plant for a sheltered, sunny spot.

COLCHICUM
Meadow saffron

These outstanding autumn corms are incorrectly referred to as autumn crocuses; they are more closely related to lilies than true crocuses. The two can easily be distinguished because colchicums have six stamens and crocuses only three. The leaves also differ: those of most colchicums are much larger than those of crocuses, which are narrow with a whitish stripe along the centre. The common name meadow saffron is also confusing since saffron is obtained from *Crocus sativus*, whereas all colchicums are poisonous.

Most of the autumn colchicums produce large, showy flowers before the leaves emerge in winter and spring and they last until early summer. Although not requiring a hot, sunny position to thrive, they look their best when the flowers receive as much autumn sun as possible to encourage them to open out into a graceful goblet shape. A well-drained soil, acid or alkaline, is suitable and the robust ones will also do well in heavy clay if it is not too sticky and wet. Because the colchicums are leafless at flowering time, they look best planted close together in clumps or between other plants like purple- and grey-leaved sages. However, the leaves of colchicums are large when fully developed and will swamp nearby small plants. Although the flowers may be only 4-6in (10-15cm) high, the foliage can grow up to 12in-1½ft (30-45cm) tall, and in favourable conditions even a small clump of corms may have a spread of 1½ft (45cm) when fully developed.

Colchicums look particularly good when planted in rough grass; this compensates for the naked appearance of the flowers and provides some support in inclement weather. The grass can be mown from early summer when the leaves die away until early autumn when the flowers appear.

Seed propagation is possible but very slow, and it is more practical to lift and divide established clumps in late summer. The corms must be planted at a minimum depth of 4in (10cm). Hardiness zones: 5-8.

C. × agrippinum (*above*)
This excellent early-flowering colchicum has wide, funnel-shaped flowers that are strongly chequered purple on a pale background. It is best planted in a sunny position and will tolerate drought in summer. The foliage is much smaller than other types of colchicum.

C. autumnale

This is the common European meadow saffron which produces a succession of small, long-tubed, pink, goblet-shaped flowers in early autumn. They are weak and do not stand up well to wind and rain, so plant the bulbs in grass or among a ground cover of other plants for support. Large, glossy green leaves are produced in spring. There is a lovely white form known as *C. a.* var. *album* (*below*) and a double version with many-petalled, pinkish-lilac-coloured flowers called var. *pleniflorum*; the white double form is called *C. a.* var. *alboplenum*.

C. bivonae (syn. C. bowlesianum) (below)

One of the chequered-flower species, *C. bivonae* has elegant, goblet-shaped flowers with a squarish, purple, tessellated pattern on a pale pink background. The flowers are much larger than those of *C. autumnale*. It grows best in a sheltered, sunny position.

C. byzantinum

Similar to *C. autumnale*, *C. byzantinum* has slightly larger, pinkish-purple flowers, many of which are produced by each corm to provide a good show in early autumn. The leaves, which appear in spring, are very large when fully expanded.

C. cilicicum (above)

An excellent species for a sunny, well-drained spot, *C. cilicicum* produces many rosy-purple, wide, funnel-shaped flowers with fairly short, stocky tubes. A very hardy bulb, it will withstand bad weather.

C. speciosum (above)

This is the showiest species, having large, goblet-shaped flowers held well above the ground on strong tubes. It comes in variable shades of purple and usually has a large, white zone in the throat; the bold leaves are shiny green. It is extremely hardy and does well in sun or partial shade, in reasonably well-drained soil. If left undisturbed, it will increase into sizeable patches, creating a striking display. The pure white form 'Album' is one of the best of all autumn bulbs.

C. variegatum

This is a rare species in cultivation that requires a sheltered, sunny situation. It has a short tube and almost flat, wide, funnel-shaped flowers conspicuously marked with a purple tessellated pattern on a pale background. This coloration has been passed on to the hybrid *C. × agrippinum* which is much easier to obtain and cultivate. The small, basal leaves of *C. variegatum* are greyish-green in colour, usually with wavy-edged margins.

Cultivars and hybrids

In addition to the species, a large number of cultivars and hybrids are available. 'Lilac Wonder' is a vigorous hybrid with lilac-pink flowers; 'The Giant' has large, well-formed, goblet-shaped flowers in lilac-mauve; 'Waterlily' (*below*) is a double-flowering colchicum with many rich pinkish-lilac flowers produced together in a bunch; and the hybrid 'Conquest' has attractive chequered flowers which are a deep purple-pink, strongly tessellated darker purple.

CRINUM

Although mostly tropical, a few South African crinums are hardy enough to be cultivated in cooler, temperate regions. They are large, showy plants with umbels of funnel-shaped flowers similar to those of an amaryllis. In warm, sheltered gardens, it is possible to grow them in a border with other perennials to provide a display in late summer or early autumn, but in colder areas, a warm, sunny position against a wall is necessary. Crinums also make attractive subjects for large containers which can be moved into a frost-free greenhouse or shed over winter when the bulbs are dormant. The very large bulbs are normally planted with the neck just protruding from the soil but, in containers, it may be necessary to leave the upper half exposed because of the limited soil depth. Propagation of these bulbs is best by division of established clumps in spring. Hardiness zones: 6-8.

C. bulbispermum

This is a striking species with 2-3½ft (60cm-1m) high stems, each with up to 12 long-tubed, funnel-shaped flowers that are white with a pinkish-red streak along the centre of each petal. It bears long, strap-shaped, spreading leaves on a short stalk.

C. moorei

This crinum reaches about 3½-5ft (1-1.5m) high at flowering time. Each of its leafless, stout stems carries several fragrant, white or pale pink, funnel-shaped flowers that have long, arching, slender tubes.

C. × powellii

The hardiest of the group, the hybrid *C. × powellii* makes a good herbaceous border subject; it is also the most readily obtainable. Up to 10 large, funnel-shaped flowers are produced in an umbel on 3½ft (1m) high stems; the blooms are a soft shade of pink or white, as in the variety 'Album' (*above*).

CROCUS

These are the true autumn crocuses, not to be confused with the colchicums (see page 203). They are ideal for providing a splash of autumn colour but need to be sited where they will receive as much available sun as possible to open up the flowers. With a few exceptions, most of those mentioned require an open, sunny spot in well-drained soil.

Since these crocuses are fairly short at flowering time, they are best planted in a rock garden, at the front of a border or in grass, grouped close together to provide a vivid show. The corms should be planted at a depth of about 1-2in (2.5-5cm). When clumps have built up, they can be lifted and divided in late summer or new stocks can be raised from seed, although it takes about three or four years to produce flowering corms. Most of those mentioned have no leaves when in flower. Hardiness zones: 4-6.

C. banaticus (*next column*)

This crocus is an exception to the general rule because it requires damp soil that does not become hot and sun-baked in summer, although it still needs autumn sun to open up

the flowers. These are pale to mid-violet-blue and long-tubed, with three large outer petals and three small inner ones, resembling an iris flower when fully open.

C. cancellatus

This Turkish species has pale lilac or whitish flowers striped with violet on the outside. It needs a sunny spot in a rock garden but can also be cultivated in an alpine house.

C. cartwrightianus

A beautiful Greek plant, this crocus is worth growing in an alpine house where the large, wide, open, fragrant flowers can be appreciated. It will also grow outside in a sharply drained, sunny position. The blooms are either purple with a darker centre or white; both colour forms have showy, brilliant red stigmas like the saffron crocus.

C. goulimyi (*above*)

This crocus has very long-tubed, goblet-shaped, lilac flowers which appear with the leaves. It needs a sheltered, sunny spot.

C. hadriaticus

Another of the saffron crocuses with bright red stigmas, this has creamy white flowers with a yellow zone in the throat; the flowers appear with the leaves in mid-autumn.

C. kotschyanus (**syn.** *C. zonatus*) (*below*)

An excellent Turkish species, it rapidly increases into clumps and is one of the first to flower in early autumn. The pale lilac flowers have a yellow zone or blotches in the throat, but the variation known as *C. k. leucopharynx* has a white throat.

C. longiflorus

One of the most fragrant of the autumn crocuses, *C. longiflorus* has deep lilac flowers, with darker veins on the outside and a yellow throat; the flowers appear with the leaves.

C. niveus

Needing a sheltered sunny position, *C. niveus* is one of the largest-flowered of all crocuses. The goblet-shaped flowers appear with the leaves and are white or very pale, soft lilac with a deep yellow zone in the throat. In cold areas, it is better grown in an alpine house or frame.

C. nudiflorus (*below*)

Because it grows in moist meadows in the wild, this crocus is best planted in grass or partial shade where it will not get too hot and dry in summer. The elegant, long-tubed flowers are rich purple with an orange stigma. This is one of the few species of crocus that is stoloniferous. It naturalizes well in grass.

C. ochroleucus (*above*)

A seldom seen but attractive small-flowering species for a sunny position, the flowers are white with a yellow throat.

C. pulchellus (*above*)

This excellent autumn crocus increases by seed and division into patches. The small, goblet-shaped flowers are palest blue with a deep yellow throat and darker veins.

C. sativus (*above*)
Saffron crocus

The very large, wide, open, purple flowers of *C. sativus* appear with the leaves in mid- to late autumn. Each bloom has three long, deep red stigmas, the source of saffron, for which it is mainly cultivated in Mediterranean countries. In cold areas, it does not flower freely and the

best chance of success is to plant the corms deeply, about 4-6in (10-15cm) below ground, in a well-drained, alkaline soil where they will dry out in summer.

C. serotinus

This Spanish crocus has sizeable lilac-blue flowers appearing with the leaves. The best and most readily obtainable variant is *C. s. salzmannii* which is easily cultivated and increases well into clumps.

C. speciosus (*above*)

This is the most well-known of all autumnal species. Cheap to buy, it is suitable for naturalizing among deciduous shrubs or in grass where the long-tubed flowers receive some support in bad weather. Its large blooms come in shades of lilac or bluish-violet with a network of darker veins. 'Albus' is a most attractive white form, and 'Oxonian' one of the darkest blues.

C. tournefortii (*above*)

This beautiful late autumn crocus comes from the Greek Islands. It will grow outside in a warm, sunny spot but is best when protected in an alpine house or cold frame. The blooms, which accompany the leaves, open out almost flat and are soft lilac-blue with a large, frilly, orange stigma. They remain open all the time, even at night.

CYCLAMEN

The florists' cyclamen, sold annually in huge quantities as winter house plants, are developed from the frost-tender scented species *C. persicum*. Much less well-known are the small-flowered hardier species from the Mediterranean and Near East which make an excellent addition to the garden and give an interesting autumn display. Most require sheltered positions in partial shade and well-drained soil that has a good humus content, preferably in the form of leaf mould rather than acid peat. They are dwarf plants, not more than about $3\frac{1}{4}$in (8cm) high, and are ideal for a rock garden or for pot cultivation in an alpine house. The tubers should be planted just below the surface in autumn, or at almost any time of year if they are purchased as growing pot plants. The only practical method of propagation is by seed which can produce flowering-size tubers in two to three years. Apart from the small, graceful flowers with their swept-back petals, cyclamen often have attractive, silvery mottled and zoned foliage. Each tuber produces many leaves, giving the plant a total spread of 4-6in (10-15cm). Hardiness zones: 6-8.

C. cilicium

A small Turkish species, *C. cilicium* has rounded or heart-shaped leaves with pale green and silvery zones. The white or pink flowers have a dark purplish-red stain around the mouth.

C. cyprium (*above*)

This is best pot grown in the protection of an alpine house or conservatory where the small, very fragrant flowers can be appreciated. The blooms are white with a ring of carmine markings around the mouth, and are accompanied by dark green, triangular leaves zoned with silvery green.

C. graecum (*above*)

A Greek species, this cyclamen has pale to deep pink flowers with a darker stain around the mouth, produced just before or with the heart-shaped leaves. The leaves have a satiny appearance with green and silvery patterns. Provide a hot, sun-baked position in a rock garden or against a sunny wall; in cold areas, grow in pots in the alpine house.

C. hederifolium (**syn.** *C. neapolitanum*)

This Mediterranean species is the best and hardiest garden plant among the autumn cyclamen; it is also very free-flowering. The ivy-shaped leaves have attractive patterns and form ground cover from flowering time in early autumn through to late spring; it is well worth planting a patch in the dappled shade of deciduous shrubs. It will also do quite well under pines provided it receives some winter moisture. Seed is produced very freely and, if growing conditions are suitable, the plant will naturalize. The flowers are either pale pink with a darker mouth (*above*) or pure white, as in the variety 'Album'.

C. mirabile

This is an unusual species similar to *C. cilicium* but with distinctly tooth-edged petals and heart-shaped leaves which are scalloped at the margins. The foliage is stained deep red on the underside.

C. purpurascens (**syn.** *C. europaeum*)

A deliciously fragrant species, this cyclamen produces a succession of flowers over a long period, from summer into autumn. They are pale to deep pinkish- or reddish-purple and accompany rounded leaves which vary from plain, deep green to silvery patterned.

EUCHARIS

This group of South American bulbs, mainly tropical, may be grown in containers outdoors in summer if they are returned to a heated greenhouse or conservatory for the winter. However, in cool areas, it is best to treat them as greenhouse plants throughout the year. The potting medium should be a well-drained, loamy, sandy, leaf mould mixture, and the bulbs require a minimum winter temperature of 50°F (10°C). On the whole, they are best left undisturbed for as long as possible but, if repotting becomes necessary due to overcrowding, this should be done in spring when the bulb clumps can be divided. Flowering is in mid-summer to early autumn. Hardiness zone: 10.

E. amazonica (*above*)
Amazon lily

This plant produces tufts of broad, oval, deep green leaves and 1½–2ft (45-60cm) high stems. These carry several fragrant, white flowers like large daffodils, each about 3¼–4in (8-10cm) in diameter, with a cup-shaped corona in the centre.

EUCOMIS
Pineapple flower

These South African plants are mostly from the eastern Cape region where they remain dormant and dry in winter and grow during the rainy summer season. In cultivation, they behave the same way, flowering in late summer or early autumn. They all have a basal tuft of broad leaves

with a spread of 12in (30cm) or more in the larger species. From the centre, a stout flower spike appears with densely packed, almost flat flowers, topped by a further tuft of small, leaf-like bracts, hence the allusion to the pineapple. The large bulbs should be planted in spring, about 4in (10cm) deep, in well-drained soil that will not become too dry and sun-baked in summer since they require plenty of moisture in the growing season. Eucomis also grow well in containers but should be moved to a frost-free shed in winter because they are more likely to succumb to frost. Propagation is best by clump division, but seed is produced and will take about three years to produce flowering bulbs. Hardiness zones: 4-5.

E. bicolor (*above*)

This is the most readily available eucomis. It has 12in (30cm) tall spikes of green flowers with purple-edged petals. The flower stem is also heavily blotched purple.

E. comosa (*below*)

An attractive species up to 1½ft (45cm) high, *E. comosa* has long spikes of pinkish flowers, made more colourful by a purple ovary forming a dark eye in the centre of each individual flower.

E. pallidiflora

This very large plant has leaves up to 2-2¹/₄ft (60-68.5cm) long. These are sword-shaped, crinkly edged and semi-erect. It has 1³/₄-2ft (53-60cm) tall spikes of greenish-white flowers, and requires a sheltered position.

E. undulata (**syn.** *E. autumnalis*)

A robust species, *E. undulata* reaches 1¹/₂ft (45cm) in height and has long, wavy-margined leaves and a spike of greenish-white-coloured flowers.

E. zambesiaca (*above*)

The dwarf of the genus, this garden form is a delightful little plant with 8in (20cm) tall spikes of white flowers and a compact rosette of wavy-edged leaves.

GALANTHUS
Snowdrop

Autumn-flowering snowdrops may come as a surprise, but the Greek *G. reginae-olgae* produces autumnal blooms almost before the leaves appear above ground. It is uncommon in cultivation and therefore expensive but quite easy to grow. This snowdrop prefers a sunnier spot than the spring snowdrops (see page 97), and a position where the bulbs will dry out more during summer but some shade is also necessary. As with other snowdrops, the bulbs can be successfully moved while in growth or, in late summer to early autumn, while still dormant. Propagation by division is the best way to increase stocks. Hardiness zone: 7.

G. reginae-olgae

The flowers appear before the foliage and are very similar to those of the common spring species, *G. nivalis*. The leaves are different, however, having a silvery grey stripe along the centre. It requires more sun than its spring-flowering relatives.

GLADIOLUS

Most of the gladioli cultivated in gardens are the spectacular summer-flowering hybrids developed from several South African species (see page 162). However, a much hardier species from the eastern Cape in South Africa flowers in the autumn. *G. papilio* can be grown in sun or partial shade in a position where it will not dry out too much during its summer growing season. It does well in shrub borders, where it may spread into sizeable patches. While not very showy, it provides good interest when the summer bulb display is nearing an end. It increases by stolons and forms extensive patches 3¹/₂ft (1m) or more across; propagation is by division in spring. Hardiness zones: 5-6.

G. papilio (**syn.** *G. purpureo-auratus*) (*above*)

This gladiolus grows to about 3¹/₂ft (1m) high and carries up to 10 flowers in a curious mixture of smoky, dull purple, yellow and green. These are cowl-like, with hooded upper petals and darker, blotched lower ones.

LEUCOJUM
Snowflake

The stronger-growing spring and summer snowflakes (see page 103) are much better known than the tiny autumnal ones, but the latter have a delicate charm and are ideal for growing in an alpine house where they can be viewed more easily. The potting is carried out in late summer because flowering occurs early in autumn; the planting medium should be quick-draining with plenty of gritty sand. Watering continues through until late spring when it can be withheld until the following autumn. For propagation, remove offsets when repotting or alternatively collect seed; if sown in the autumn, it may produce flowering-size bulbs in just two to three years. Hardiness zones: 6-7.

L. autumnale (*below*)

Thread-like, 4-6in (10-15cm) high flower stems carry up to four tiny, white, pendent, bell-shaped flowers that are followed by equally slender leaves. Grow outside in a warm, sunny spot in the rock garden.

L. roseum

This is a shorter version of the above but with soft pink flowers. It is best grown in an alpine house or frame because it is tender.

MERENDERA

A relative of the colchicum, the merendera is an attractive plant, although it is smaller and less showy. Grow it in an alpine house or in a sunny, sharply drained position in a raised bed or in a rock garden where the corms will dry out during the summer rest period. Propagation is by seed sown in autumn or by division of clumps in early autumn. Hardiness zone: 6.

M. montana (**syn.** *M. pyrenaica* or *M. bulbocodium*) (*above*)

This plant has wide, funnel-shaped, pinkish-purple flowers with a large, white eye in the centre. They are about 1¹/₂-2¹/₄in (4-6cm) in diameter and almost rest on the ground. The narrow leaves appear shortly after the blooms, forming a rosette.

NERINE

The South African nerines are delightful autumn-flowering members of the popular amaryllis family. They have long-lasting, pink to bright red flowers whose narrow, crinkled petals have a sparkling crystalline appearance. The leaves are narrow and strap-shaped. The bulbs range from the frost-hardy to the rather tender, but even the hardy ones are best grown against a warm wall where they will receive some protection in severe winters. Plant the large bulbs with the neck just protruding from the soil either in early spring, as in the case of the hardy *N. bowdenii*, or in late summer or early autumn for the greenhouse varieties.

Nerines will tolerate acid or alkaline conditions but the soil or potting medium must be well-drained and not too rich in fertilizers since it encourages strong leaves at the expense of flowers; additions of sharp sand are ideal for quick drainage. Greenhouse pot bulbs should be dried off in summer after the leaves have died down; they flower best if left undisturbed, but if they become too crowded they should be repotted in late summer with as little disturbance as possible. Propagate by offsets or seed; seed may take at least three years to produce flowering-size bulbs. Hardiness zones: 7-8 for *N. bowdenii* and its forms; 9 for other species and hybrids.

N. bowdenii (*above*)
This is the hardiest species, flowering in mid-autumn with stout, 1½-2ft (45-60cm) tall stems, each carrying an umbel with up to 12 bright pink, glistening flowers which have elegant, undulating petals. The variety 'Mark Fenwick' is a taller, more vigorous version, growing as much as 3ft (90cm) tall with larger heads and deeper pink flowers. There is also a white form, known as 'Alba', which is rather rare in cultivation.

N. filifolia (*above*)
A graceful, smallish species, *N. filifolia* is only 10-12in (25-30cm) high and has very narrow leaves and umbels of small, pink, wavy-petalled flowers. Keep the plant frost-free in cold areas.

N. flexuosa (*above*)
This nerine is usually about 12in (30cm) high, with an umbel of pink flowers that have narrow petals reflexed and crinkled near the tips. There is a pure white form called 'Alba'.

N. masonorum (*above*)
One of the smallest nerines, this is only 6-8in (15-20cm) tall, with thread-like leaves and slender stems bearing up to 10 small, pink flowers held in an umbel. It is best pot-grown in a frost-free greenhouse or conservatory.

N. sarniensis
Although called the Guernsey lily, *N. sarniensis* is South African in origin. It has 1½-2ft (45-60cm) high stems, strap-like leaves and scarlet flowers. Because of its intense colour, it has been used in hybridization.

Hybrid cultivars

Many exciting hybrid cultivars are available for greenhouse and conservatory cultivation. They require frost protection because they are in leaf in winter, but it is not necessary and is actually harmful to keep them in too warm conditions. In summer, give a warm rest period but avoid baking the bulbs under glass in full sun or they may roast. 'Corusca Major' is an old favourite; the bright scarlet flowers held on 1½-2ft (45-60cm) tall stems are grown for the cut flower trade. 'Baghdad' bears umbels of soft carmine red flowers later on in autumn than most, and 'Blanchfleur' is an excellent pure white nerine which has beautifully crinkled and waved petals.

SCHIZOSTYLIS
Kaffir lily

This most valuable autumn-flowering member of the iris family can be grown in sun or partial shade in soil that does not dry out excessively in summer. Because the small rhizomes produce stolons, the plants can grow into relatively large patches, perhaps 3ft (90cm) across in ideal conditions, and they never go dormant. For propagation purposes, clumps can be lifted and divided in spring when the worst of the frost is past, the rhizomes being replanted with a 1in (2.5cm) covering of soil. Hardiness zone: 6.

S. coccinea
The 1-2ft (30-60cm) high stems of *S. coccinea* carry racemes of funnel-shaped, red flowers, each about 2in (5cm) in diameter. They open out almost flat in the autumn sun. 'Major'

(page 209 *bottom right*) has even larger red flowers; 'Sunrise' is a bright pink selection; 'Mrs Hegarty' (*below*) paler pink; and 'Alba' is a good clear white.

STERNBERGIA

Although these showy autumn bulbs with their goblet-shaped flowers are similar to large yellow crocuses, sternbergias are, in fact, members of the amaryllis family. They are occasionally referred to as autumn daffodils but their only similarity is the colour and daffodil-like bulb. Being mainly Mediterranean plants, they require hot, sunny positions in well-drained, neutral or alkaline soil. In colder climates, they are best placed at the foot of a sunny wall where the bulbs will ripen to form flower buds during their summer dormancy. They are planted in autumn, at a depth of about 2in (5cm), but may take a year or two before flowering. Once established, they are best left undisturbed to grow into clumps for the most effective display. Propagation is by division of clumps in early autumn. Hardiness zone: 6-7.

S. clusiana (*above*)
This is one of the largest-flowering species, producing greenish-yellow, goblet-shaped flowers in mid-autumn before the appearance

of the strap-shaped, greyish-green leaves. Unfortunately, it does not perform well in most gardens and is best planted in a bulb frame for added winter protection and extra soil-warmth in summer.

S. lutea (*above*)
The best known species, *S. lutea* has large, bright yellow, funnel-shaped flowers amid glossy green, strap-like leaves in early autumn. It usually reaches about 6-8in (15-20cm) in height at flowering time.

S. sicula (*above*)
Like a smaller version of *S. lutea*, the flower stems of *S. sicula* are only 2-3in (5-7.5cm) high and the narrow, dark green leaves have a pale stripe running along the centre.

ZEPHYRANTHES
Rain lily or windflower

Another autumn member of the amaryllis family, the rain lily has funnel- or wineglass-shaped flowers not unlike large crocuses. As with the sternbergias, they require a hot, sunny spot where the bulbs will dry out in summer and form flower buds for the coming season. They are best planted in spring and left undisturbed for as long as possible; they thrive in light, sandy soils. Propagation is by division of clumps in early autumn. Hardiness zones: 9-10.

Z. candida (*above*)
This plant is the hardiest species, with rush-like leaves and 6in (15cm) tall stems, each bearing a solitary, upright flower about 2in (5cm) long. These are pure white with a greenish centre.

Z. grandiflora (*above*)
One of the showiest species, *Z. grandiflora* is less hardy and requires a frost-free greenhouse or conservatory in cold areas. It has rosy pink flowers about 3in (7.5cm) long.

Z. rosea (*below*)
Also for a cool greenhouse in cold districts, this zephyranthes is hardy in mild areas and may be grown in a sunny border. Its 2in (5cm) long, funnel-like flowers are pale pink.

WINTER BULBS

Garden highlights

In winter, there is little of interest in the garden apart from a few winter-flowering shrubs and one or two ornamental trees with coloured bark. However, there is a small collection of bulbs including crocuses and cyclamen which can be grown outside at this time of the year, and these are invaluable for providing cheerful highlights in an otherwise drab setting. In mild areas, snowdrops, winter aconites and daffodils may also burst into early flower although, in colder climates, they will not appear until spring. To make the most of any colour, plant the bulbs close to the house so they can be seen from indoors as well as outside.

One of the best winter-flowering bulbs is *Crocus laevigatus* 'Fontenayi'. A colourful subject with purple flowers striped a dark purple on the outside, it benefits from a sheltered, sunny spot which will protect it from inclement weather. The best companion plants are shrubby Mediterranean natives like lavender and rosemary which require similar gritty, free-draining soil conditions. These plants have attractive grey-green leaves which complement the slender chalices of the crocuses. Other herbs like winter savory, hyssop, sage and wild thyme can also be used; push a few of the nut-like crocus corms through a fine, leafy carpet of creeping *Thymus serpyllum* and wait for the spear-like buds to pierce the foliage and erupt into splashes of eye-catching lilac-mauve.

A good winter display can also be achieved using *Cyclamen coum*, a very hardy bulb that starts to flower in mid- to late winter. There are many colour forms to choose from including bright magenta-purple, carmine-pink and white, each one accompanied by either plain dark green or silver-zoned foliage. These bulbs associate well with winter heathers but look equally good massed on their own, where the beauty of the individual flowers can be appreciated.

PREVIOUS PAGE This combination of Cyclamen coum, *winter aconites and snowdrops naturalized under trees forms a bold swathe of glowing colour.*

BELOW Narcissus cyclamineus, *with its dainty back-swept petals and soft golden colour, is perfect massed round the base of this shrub.*

RIGHT Woodland is ideal for growing drifts of naturalized snowdrops which thrive in the winter sun as it slants through the leafless trees.

For handsome winter foliage, nothing beats *Arum italicum* 'Pictum'. This tuber has rich green leaves marbled with white veins and is ideal for a border near the house, especially when mixed with crocuses or cyclamen. It is also highly successful in association with hellebores (Christmas or Lenten roses); the pale green-flowered *Helleborus argutifolius* looks particularly fine growing among a group of arums. A shady corner is the perfect place for a planting of *H. niger* and *A. i.* 'Pictum', with the white flowers of the Christmas rose silhouetted against the marbled foliage of the arums.

An equally exciting combination involves the arum and the shrubby *Rubus cockburnianus* (white-washed bramble), a bizarre relative of the blackberry with pure white, thorny winter stems. While looking very effective against the dark soil, this shrub looks even more impressive rising out of a clump of fresh green arum foliage. The same effect can be created using the contorted golden stems of *Salix matsudana* 'Tortuosa' (corkscrew willow). For some colour, interplant the arum with *Cyclamen coum*.

LEFT Snowdrops and winter aconites combine to good effect here to provide a colourful display, especially welcome in dull weather.

BELOW The delicate Crocus tommasinianus *is one of the hardiest late-winter bulbs, at its most rewarding when used boldly, as shown here.*

ABOVE Borders near a house need year-round appeal, as provided here by Arum italicum 'Pictum' *and* Helleborus orientalis.

Bulbs for naturalizing

Crocuses, cyclamen and arums can be used for naturalizing in winter to provide a welcome, colourful show. However, they are not suitable for naturalizing in grass and must be colonized in bare soil and left undisturbed to reproduce freely over the years.

The very fine, purple-flowering *Crocus laevigatus* 'Fontenayi' will naturalize quickly, forming a sparkling sheet of colour in the depths of winter. It is happiest when allowed to spread alone but it will tolerate shrubs which have deep root systems, such as *Prunus triloba*, *Cornus mas* (Cornelian cherry) and *Hamamelis mollis* (Chinese witch hazel).

Cyclamen coum, with its magenta-purple blossoms, will often naturalize if left alone in a leafy, free-draining soil. The plants stand out best against a background of stone or earth, or silhouetted against tree trunks. Birch provides a suitable backdrop; *Betula pendula* (silver birch), with its somewhat rugged, silvery bark, and the pendulous *B. pendula* 'Youngii', with its weeping, twiggy branches, provide perfect settings for clusters of naturalized cyclamen.

The snowy white form of *Cyclamen coum*, known as 'Album', will also naturalize quite freely. For the most startling effect, plant a group in front of the glossy, mahogany-like trunk of *Prunus serrula*; few winter scenes surpass the skeletal beauty of the prunus etched against a bright blue sky, surrounded by a colony of *C. c.* 'Album'.

For difficult, shady situations with richly organic soil, *Arum italicum* 'Pictum' can be colonized. Not only does this easy-going, hardy member of the arum family have attractive green- and silver-marbled foliage but, in autumn, it also produces striking orange-red fruits held just above the leaves on neat, tight spikes. The leaves appear from autumn onwards and intensify in colour during the increasingly short winter days, persisting through until the end of the season.

These showy arums are best planted around deciduous shrubs, particularly those that flower over winter. One of the best combinations involves the arum and the pink-flowering *Viburnum* × *bodnantense* 'Dawn', a popular scented shrub which starts flowering in late autumn and continues into spring, when the leaf buds break into growth. The bright, eye-catching, trailing stems of *Jasminum nudiflorum* wreathed in waxy, primrose-yellow blossoms also provide a fine contrast to the foliage of the arum. The arum is also useful as ground cover beneath a shrub like *Euonymus fortuneii* 'Silver

Queen', either on its own or mixed with some winter-flowering cyclamen, and a peripheral scattering of *Arum italicum* 'Pictum' will greatly enhance the mounds of foliage produced by dwarf rhododendrons. Alternatively, try a naturalized patch of the bulb in front of a large drift of *Lunaria* (honesty).

Bulbs for the rock garden

Again, it is the winter-flowering crocuses and cyclamen that provide most interest in the rock garden at this time of the year. These bulbs are very useful, bringing colour and form to the rockery and, after flowering, will die down to make way for spring and summer alpines.

A free-draining, sunny position provides a natural home for *Crocus laevigatus* 'Fontenayi'. For the greatest impact, plant a small patch of bulbs on their own so that the purple flowers stand out against a stark background of rock. Their beauty is further brought out by a top-dressing of chippings.

For a good visual mix, grow *Crocus laevigatus* 'Fontenayi' alongside *Arenaria caespitosa* 'Aurea' (sandwort). This golden-leaved rock plant contrasts pleasingly with the crocuses, as does *A. balearica*, with its bright green leaves.

BELOW There is nothing more cheering in the winter frost and snow than the sight of tiny winter aconites and snowdrops breaking through a crust of ice to open their exquisite petals in the sun.

The rock garden is an ideal setting for *Cyclamen coum*. This corm can be planted on its own against a rocky backdrop, or it can be mixed with other plants for a more varied display. Since it tolerates light shade, it is particularly useful for planting beneath an established prostrate yew or dwarf pine, which will also offer protection from any bad weather.

Narcissus bulbocodium romieuxii can be grown in a well-drained, sheltered spot in the rock garden. This relative of the hoop-petticoat daffodil has flared, sulphur-yellow blossoms and narrow, grassy foliage. Unlike most other miniature narcissi, *Narcissus bulbocodium romieuxii* should be lifted and dried off once the foliage has died back.

ABOVE LEFT **Cyclamen persicum,** *with its exotic-looking flowers and heart-shaped, silver-marbled leaves, is perfect for lighting up a dark corner.*

ABOVE RIGHT **Arum italicum 'Pictum'** *is invaluable during winter, both as a foil for shrubs and as a ground-cover feature in its own right.*

BELOW This later-flowering **Narcissus bulbocodium** *has an early-flowering relative with creamy-yellow flowers, known as N. b. romieuxii.*

Containers and window boxes

Plants grown in containers and window boxes will not always survive cold winters but, in more temperate regions, it is possible to enjoy container subjects throughout the year. If uncommonly cold weather does threaten, small containers can be moved inside until the danger of frost has passed.

A visit to the local garden centre will yield some brightly coloured bulbs suitable for containers and window boxes, such as narcissi, cyclamen and hyacinth. Hyacinth are particularly popular, and few winter displays are worth considering without the bright colours and sweet fragrance of these bulbs, although they are very vulnerable to the cold. However, a foundation planting of evergreens such as ivies like 'Parsley Crested' and 'Anne Marie' will provide some protection.

The same ivies are suitable for mixing with crocuses and cyclamen and, for some added colour and height, a few clumps of the paperwhite narcissi can be added. On the borderline of hardiness, these narcissi make a lovely scented display. For a large container, they can be used to underplant dwarf conifers and, in window boxes, they can be planted with variegated ivies and a few brightly coloured primulas.

ABOVE This delightful, fresh-looking window-box planting combining white cyclamen and small-leaved ivies is ideal for a shady position.

RIGHT For a cheerful window-box composition, mix together Narcissus *'Tête-à-Tête', dwarf conifers, primroses and variegated ivy.*

Bulbs for forcing

While there is relatively little happening in the garden during winter, inside there is a wealth of colour. Winter is the time for forcing bulbs for early indoor flowering which would otherwise flower later on in the season outside. After flowering, they can be planted out in the garden where they will eventually multiply and form patches of naturalized bulbs.

Hyacinths are commonly forced for attractive winter displays. Popular commercial cultivars are best because the bulbs are available in large sizes, having first been prepared for early forced flowering. Among the most widely available are 'Delft Blue' and 'Ostara', both blue-flowering, the crimson-red 'Jan Bos', 'L'Innocence', a pure white hyacinth, and the primrose-yellow 'City of Haarlem'.

Grow the forced hyacinths as single plantings, with several of each bulb combined if you wish, but do not mix the cultivars because they will flower at different times. The best companion plants are ferns like *Pteris* and similar plants like *Selaginella*. The glossy rich green *Selaginella martensii* is one of the easiest to grow tucked in among a few

BELOW Nothing matches the fragrant perfection of hyacinths when they are forced in containers for an indoor display as early as mid-winter.

of the bulbs. Provided that the foliage receives a daily misting of water, it should thrive. Once the hyacinths have faded, the ferns can be repotted and left to grow for the following season in a conservatory.

The fragrant, multiflowering hyacinths known as Roman hyacinths resemble elegant, refined bluebells. They are usually sold by colour and have the advantage of naturally flowering quite early on in the season. Although they do not mix readily with other plants, they will happily grow through fresh green sphagnum moss, provided both are regularly misted.

Hippeastrums, with their large, colourful trumpets, can also be forced for indoor winter-flowering. For the full benefit of their wonderful sculptured flower, a single specimen should be placed on

ABOVE The glowing colours of hyacinths and winter-flowering pansies combine to make a fine feature in this window box.

its own in a prominent place, such as on a windowsill or table. For more of a show, however, a number of different-coloured hippeastrums can be planted together in a trough with a few green-leaved ivies like 'Parsley Crested' and 'Sagittifolia' or some creeping fig (*Ficus pumila*) as an underplanting.

The delicate and deliciously scented paperwhite narcissi are another popular choice of forced bulb. With their upright clusters of succulent, bright green leaves and tight heads of small, white blossoms, they look most attractive when they are surrounded by fresh, damp, green moss or tumbling green or silver-variegated ivies like 'Anne Marie' and 'Variegata'.

Many small-flowered hardy bulbs can also be forced into early blossom; plant them in their individual pots rather than crowding different kinds into the same container. Some of the most successful are the pale blue *Scilla mischtschenkoana*, the dark blue *S. siberica* 'Spring Beauty' and the striped squill *Puschkinia scilloides*. Among the iris family, the dwarf *Iris histrioides* 'Major', the cultivars of *I. reticulata*, including 'Harmony', 'Joyce' and 'J.S. Dijt' and *I. danfordiae* can all be grown.

Outdoor bulbs indoors

Another splendid way of enlivening dull, dark, winter days is to grow spring-flowering outdoor bulbs inside where the warmth will encourage early flowering. Crocuses are best for this; they look good planted in colourful containers, including terracotta crocus bowls, which have many small planting holes in them for each corm. The best Dutch crocuses to choose for growing indoors include the pure white, violet-flushed 'Joan of Arc', the violet-purple 'Remembrance' and 'Dutch Yellow', along with the bunch-flowering *Crocus chrysanthus* hybrids. Some of the best dwarf beauties include 'Blue Bird', 'Cream Beauty', 'Snowbunting' and the orange and bronze 'Zwanenburg Bronze'.

ABOVE All the dwarf irises lend themselves to container growing because the dainty flowers may otherwise be overlooked.

Indoor bulbs

Indoor cultivation provides the ideal opportunity to grow tender bulbs that will not survive outdoor conditions. The choice varies from the fragrant to the exotic-looking, but all provide a great deal of colour.

The scented *Cyclamen persicum* is a popular indoor tuber. An elegant plant with slender, upright stems, it has beautiful back-swept blossoms in blush-pink or white, held above boldly marked, ivy-shaped or rounded leaves. It will last much longer if placed in a cool porch or conservatory rather than a warm living room or kitchen, and the bulbs can be kept from one year to the next, either indoors or, during the summer months, outside.

Lachenalias (Cape cowslips) are some of the easiest subjects to grow and they will thrive in the house. Enjoyable for their interesting foliage as well as their unusual flowers, they are ideal for the windowsill. The free-flowering *Lachenalia aloides* is the most colourful, with its pendulous yellow, red-tipped blooms and handsome purple-mottled leaves. It is a clump-forming plant and a good potful will be quickly covered with flowers which, if kept cool, will last for most of the winter. *L. bulbifera* is also very striking, with dark-spotted foliage and spikes of pendent, deep orange or red flowers, and the bluish-purple *L. glaucina*, although much less colourful, is equally

attractive. To reap the full benefit of their majestic appearance, lachenalias are best displayed alone as specimen plants but, for a truly vibrant display, they can be teamed up with one or two containers of bright blue forced squills.

Veltheimia bracteata is another reliable choice of indoor bulb. An unusual-looking plant, it has tall stems crowned with a cluster of drooping, tubular, pinkish-red flowers and strap-shaped basal leaves. For the best effect, combine it with a few pots of bright red poinsettias or *Solanum capsicastrum* (winter cherry).

ABOVE These neat clusters of small, white Narcissus papyraceus *flowerheads are bound tightly together in a witty, fragrant arrangement.*

A limited number of freesias can also be grown indoors over winter in a cool, bright room. With their brightly coloured, perfumed flowers, they are a welcome sight but, because of their somewhat untidy foliage, they should be grouped with other pot plants like Ivies.

ABOVE The glowing crimson of these cyclamen is set off perfectly by the colour of the marbled basket-style container.

Cut flowers

Apart from *Arum italicum*, which is used a great deal in flower arrangements, there are very few winter-flowering bulbs suitable for cutting. A handful of cyclamen can be plucked from a clump and placed in a small glass or teacup, but crocuses dislike being picked and will not last for more than a day or two in water.

For this reason, most indoor displays are supplemented with shop-bought flowers. Narcissi, tulips and gladioli are among the most popular bulbs, although lilies are also available, together with anemones and ranunculus.

For a seasonal flavour, however, the flowers can be mixed with the foliage of *Arum italicum* 'Pictum' and winter berries like cotoneaster. *Cotoneaster cornubia* has lovely carmine-red berries held in big bunches on naked branches, and the yellow-berried *C. salicifolius* 'Fructuluteo' is equally attractive. *Hippophae rhamnoides* is also good for indoor decorations; although rather thorny, it has vibrant orange fruit that mix readily with the simplicity of white tulips.

LEFT A traditional-looking winter arrangement, the warm reds of amaryllis, cyclamen, gladioli and tulips are set off by evergreen foliage.

RIGHT A few stems of waxy white amaryllis blooms with willow branches and simple foliage make a sparse yet dramatic arrangement.

ARUM
Lords and ladies or cuckoo pint

Although not winter-flowering, some of the hardy arums are worth growing for their ornamental foliage which lasts through the dullest months of the year, continuing well into spring (see page 88) before dying down for summer. The cut leaves also last well in water and are very useful for winter flower arrangements. The tubers should be planted in autumn unless bought in pots, in which case they can be planted at any time. Plant them at a depth of about 6in (15cm) in a semi-shaded position, in any reasonably fertile, acid or alkaline soil. When settled, the tubers will produce off-sets and form clumps 8-12in (20-30cm) wide in about three years, after which they can be lifted and divided in autumn. Hardiness zone: 6.

A. italicum
This is an extremely valuable winter plant producing arrow-shaped, rich green leaves with a striking marbled pattern of cream-coloured veins. *A. italicum* 'Pictum' (syn. 'Marmoratum') (*above*) is a particularly attractive arum.

CROCUS

Autumn- and spring-flowering crocuses are well-known for providing a fine display during both seasons, but there are few to bridge the winter gap in between. For this reason, *Crocus laevigatus* is especially welcome since it flowers at any time from early to late winter, pushing up a few blooms whenever there is a mild spell. The corms are planted in autumn in an open, sunny, preferably sheltered position in well-drained soil; if the ground is heavy and damp, mix in sharp sand. In time, the crocuses will increase into clumps and can be lifted and divided in late summer. Hardiness zone: 6.

C. laevigatus (*below*)
This Greek species is variable in colour and flowering time. 'Fontenayi' is one of the best variants, with lilac-blue flowers strongly striped and veined dark purple on the outside and yellow throats. It is also pleasantly scented. Although quite hardy, it makes an excellent alpine house plant.

CYCLAMEN

While most small species of cyclamen flower either in autumn or spring (see pages 206 and 92), *C. coum* and *C. persicum* flower during the winter months.

C. coum is very hardy and will start to flower in mid- to late winter in mild areas, slightly later elsewhere. It can be planted in autumn in a partially shaded spot where it is sheltered from cold winds, in a light, open soil enriched with organic matter; use leaf mould rather than acid peat. Alternatively, purchase them as pot plants any time and cover the tubers with $^3/_4$in (2cm) of soil. Since each plant may cover 4-6in (10-15cm) when in leaf, a planting distance of the same is sufficient.

C. persicum is a tender species, available in a great range of colours and sizes. It is one of the most popular pot plants, usually sold in full flower in winter. These cyclamens do not last long indoors since they dislike the heat and are much better if given a light, cool position at a maximum temperature of about 50°F (10°C) in a frost-free porch or conservatory. From seed to flowering they take just over one year and, if sown in mid-summer, they will flower in early winter the following year. The seedlings should be potted individually, the larger types requiring a pot size of 5in (13cm) in diameter and the small ones 4in (10cm). In winter, the young plants should be grown in a greenhouse at approximately 55-60°F (13-16°C) and, in summer, kept in growth by watering and weak liquid feeds until they flower. Older tubers that have finished flowering can be kept for the next year, but they are best given a rest period; dry them off and repot them in early autumn and renew watering. Propagation of both types is by seed sown in autumn; *C. coum* takes about two to three years to produce flowering-size tubers. Hardiness zones: 6 for *C. coum*; 9 for *C. persicum*.

C. coum (*above*)
This cyclamen reaches only $1^1/_2$in (4cm) high and has rounded leaves about 1in (2.5cm) in diameter, either plain dark green or patterned silver. The flowers are small, about $^1/_2$in (1.3cm) long, and are bright carmine pink with a dark stain around the mouth. 'Album' has white flowers with a purple-stained mouth, and 'Pewter' has silvery leaves.

C. persicum (*above*)
This wild species has silver-zoned, heart-shaped leaves topped by white or pale pink, deliciously fragrant flowers that have long, elegantly reflexed petals. Very large-flowered forms have been selected, but these are often unscented and have since been crossed with the wild species to produce smaller-flowered plants in a greater colour range, some of which are fragrant.

C. persicum **cultivars** (*above* and *below*)
The 'Kaori' types of cyclamen have compact rosettes of foliage and many small, red, pink or white flowers standing well above the leaves. 'Firmament' is a hybrid with medium-size flowers in a wide range of colours, from white to deep red, some of the paler ones having a darker pink mouth. Many of the compact, stronger-scented forms are offered as 'Dwarf Fragrant', 'Dwarf Scented' or 'Sweet Scented'. 'Decora' is notable for its wonderful silver-zoned foliage and its wide range of flower colours.

FREESIA

The many wild species of freesia are South African plants little-known in cultivation, but some have been hybridized to produce a range of large-flowered cultivars in many colours. They are naturally winter-growing plants that flower in early spring and, with slight forcing, can be brought into flower in mid-winter. Their colourful, fragrant, funnel-shaped blossoms make popular cut flowers.

The corms can be bought in early autumn and are best planted with six per 5in (13cm) diameter pot filled with a sandy potting medium. It is useful to insert support sticks at this stage. After potting, sink the pots up to their rims in sand and

water the bulbs in. By late autumn, when the shoots appear, the pots can then be moved into a cool greenhouse or conservatory and kept in a bright, airy place at a maximum temperature of 50°F (10°C). When the buds show colour, bring them indoors, although the flowers will not last as long in the heat as in the cool greenhouse. After flowering, keep them in growth until the leaves die back and dry them off over summer.

Freesias can be propagated by offsets detached at repotting time in autumn, or by seed sown in early spring at about 65°F (18.5°C). If they are kept growing through the summer with watering and liquid fertilizer they will often flower the following winter. They all have narrow, erect leaves and are mostly 1³/₄in-2¹/₂ft (53-76cm) high at flowering time, with the flower stem characteristically bent near the apex. Hardiness zone: 9.

F. alba

This freesia has spikes of fragrant, white, funnel-shaped flowers, sometimes flushed purple on the outside, with yellow marks on the lower petals.

F. armstrongii

Sometimes included with *F. corymbosa*, this is one of the parents of the hybrid cultivars and, although an attractive shade of rose pink with yellow markings near the base, the flowers are not scented.

F. refracta (*above*)
The flower colour of this freesia ranges from pale yellow to a greenish or purple colour, with deeper yellow-orange marks on the lower petals. Although not the showiest of freesias, the flowers have a good scent and it has been hybridized with the above two species to produce some of the excellent large, fragrant freesias available today.

F. **'Elegance'** (*above*)
An appropriately named freesia, *F.* 'Elegance' has white flowers suffused with chartreuse-green on the outside.

F. 'Romany'

One of the many double freesias with large, pale purple, fragrant flowers.

F. 'Yellow River' (below)

This freesia has spikes of large, bright yellow, sweetly scented flowers.

HIPPEASTRUM

These dramatic, tender, bulbous plants from South America are usually, but incorrectly, sold as amaryllis; the true amaryllis, the autumn-flowering Cape Belladonna lily, is a much hardier South African species (see page 203). There are many wild species of hippeastrum, the most commonly found being the larger-flowered hybrids available in a wide range of colours. Propagation is by division of offsets in autumn. Hardiness zone: 9.

H. reginae

A large-flowered species with stout stems 1¹/₂-2ft (45-60cm) high, *H. reginae* carries two to four slightly drooping, red flowers that are marked with a green star in the centre.

H. reticulatum (*above*)
This daintier species, about 12in (30cm) high, has up to six, reddish-purple flowers which have a darker, net-veined pattern.

H. rutilum
Approximately 12in (30cm) high, this hippeastrum has two to four flowers in colours ranging from crimson to orange, often with a green stripe on each petal.

Hybrids
The hybrids are about 2ft (60cm) high when in flower, with two to four flowers per stem and sometimes two stems per bulb.

H. 'Appleblossom' (*above*)
H. 'Appleblossom' has very large, soft pink flowers that have a pale band along the centre of each petal and a pale throat.

H. 'Belinda'
The rich, deep red, velvety flowers of *H.* 'Belinda' shade to darker red at the throat.

H. 'Star of Holland'
The large, bright red flowers have a white band along the centre of each petal, producing a white, star-like effect.

H. 'White Dazzler'
This is a very good, pure white variety.

HYACINTHUS
Hyacinth
The hyacinths are fully described in the Spring Directory (see page 100) because they naturally flower at this time. However, they are perhaps best appreciated as forced bulbs for mid-winter indoor flowering, where their fragrance can be enjoyed to the full. For early winter-flowering, it is necessary to buy prepared bulbs that have been subject to special treatment the previous summer; these must be planted in early autumn. If the flowering time is not so important, ordinary bulbs are less expensive and can be planted a little later.

The bulbs are planted almost touching in any open potting mixture or fibre, with the tops just peeping above soil level. The pots are then placed in a cool room, shed or garage and kept slightly damp while the roots develop. After a minimum of eight weeks, when the young leaves and flower buds start pushing up, the pots can be moved to a light indoor place; this must be fairly cool otherwise they will rapidly elongate. Unprepared bulbs are grown in exactly the same way, but they will flower later on in the year.

A great range of large-flowered varieties is now available in shades of blue, pink, red, white, peach, yellow and purple, in single and double forms as well as the smaller 'Roman', 'Cynthella' and 'Multiflora' types, which are often even more fragrant, like the original wild type. Propagation is by division in early autumn. Hardiness zone: 5; for winter-flowering, grow under glass or indoors.

LACHENALIA
Cape cowslip
These small, neat, bulbous plants from South Africa produce dense spikes of tubular or bell-shaped flowers over strap-shaped leaves. The foliage is often ornamental with dark blotches on a paler green background. The bulbs are dormant during summer, growing in autumn and winter and, although not hardy, they require only minimal heat in cold districts to keep them frost-free; a cool, bright greenhouse, conservatory or windowsill are ideal places.

The small bulbs are planted in autumn in a sandy, well-drained medium; they will need watering straight away. At least three bulbs spaced about 1in (2.5cm) apart are needed for a good display. Half pots or pans give an adequate depth of soil since the bulbs do not need to be more than $\frac{1}{2}$in (1.5cm) deep. After flowering when the leaves die back in spring, they can be dried off until autumn but not sun-baked, after which they can be repotted. Propagation is by offsets which are usually produced freely. Hardiness zone: 10; frost-free under glass.

L. aloides (**syn.** *L. tricolor*) (*above*)
L. aloides has glaucous leaves marked with green or purple blotches and 4–6in (10–15cm) tall spikes of pendent, tubular flowers. These may be yellow with red tips, plain golden yellow (as in var. *aurea*) or multicoloured (as in var. *quadricolor*), with zones of orange, green, yellow and purplish-red.

L. bulbifera (*above*)
This very striking plant has dark-spotted leaves that are topped by 4–6in (10–15cm) tall spikes of tubular, pendent flowers in shades of deep orange to red, tipped even darker. It produces bulblets at the base of the leaves.

L. contaminata
This plant looks different from the others since it has dense, 2–6in (5–15cm) tall spikes of much shorter, bell-shaped flowers that stand out horizontally. They are white with maroon tips on the outer petals.

L. glaucina (**syn.** *L. orchioides* **var.**
glaucina) (*above*)
The dense, 4–8in (10–20cm) tall spikes of
L. glaucina have many small, blue to purple
flowers tipped dark purple, all facing
obliquely upwards.

L. mutabilis
A colourful species, *L. mutabilis* has 4–8in
(10–20cm) tall spikes of small, bell-shaped
flowers, with dark-tipped, pale blue outer
petals and brown-tipped, yellow inner ones.
The entire upper part of the spike consists of
bright blue, sterile flowers.

L. rubida
A most attractive plant, it has spotted leaves
topped by 4–7in (10–18cm) tall spikes of long,
tubular, pendent flowers. These blossoms
range from coral red to deeper ruby red in
colour, and they are sometimes tipped with a
darker colour.

NARCISSUS
Narcissi are the mainstay of the spring
bulb garden display and are fully
described under that section (see page
104), but a few flower so early, especially
in mild areas, that they can be classed as
winter-flowering subjects. There are two to
recommend, both differing widely in their
cultural requirements. Propagation is by
division of clumps in autumn. Hardiness
zones: 6-8.

N. papyraceus
Paperwhite
This narcissus has clustered heads of small,
fragrant, white flowers, and is about 12in
(30cm) high. Although it can be grown
outdoors in sheltered spots or mild areas, it is
more often treated as a subject for forcing for
an early flower display in a conservatory or
on a windowsill. The bulbs will produce
flowers in about six weeks after planting

without the need for a cool, damp preparation
period as required by hyacinths. However, do
not keep them in a warm living room because
they will become weak-stemmed.

Almost any open potting medium or bulb
fibre will suffice since the buds are already
formed inside the bulb when purchased in
autumn; they only need water to make them
grow. After flowering, if being saved for the
following year, they are best kept in a cool,
bright, frost-free place and given a potash-
rich liquid fertilizer to strengthen the bulbs.
After the leaves die down in late spring, dry
off the bulbs and keep them in a warm but
not sun-baked place until autumn, when they
can be repotted or planted in a sheltered spot
in the garden. However, results are not
always reliable and for indoor forcing
purposes it is better to buy and plant new
bulbs each autumn.

N. bulbocodium romieuxii (**syn.** *N.*
romieuxii) (*above*)
One of the hoop-petticoat types, this is a small
species only 4–6in (10–15cm) high. The
unusual-looking pale sulphur-yellow flowers
produced in early to mid-winter have narrow
petals surrounding a wide, funnel-shaped
trumpet. In cold areas, grow them in pots in an
alpine house or frost-free conservatory where
the delicate blooms can receive some protection.
A well-drained sandy soil mix is best. The bulbs
should be dried out in summer during the
dormant period, although they should not be
sun-baked, and repotted in autumn.

VELTHEIMIA
Unfortunately, these unusual but delightful
winter-flowering bulbs from South Africa
are not frost-hardy, but they make excellent pot plants for a slightly heated greenhouse, conservatory or cool windowsill. The
large bulbs should be potted with the tips
just showing; plant them in well-drained
potting soil in early autumn, and start them

into growth by slight watering, increasing
as growth commences. As much light as
possible should be given to keep the
leaves and developing flower spikes compact. After flowering, they should be kept
in growth until late spring, when watering
can be reduced. *V. capensis* will die down
completely and must be kept warm and
dry for the summer, but *V. bracteata*
remains in leaf, only requiring a little water
from time to time. The bulbs occasionally
produce offsets that can be detached at
repotting time. Seed is also produced but
will take several years to produce flowering-size bulbs. Hardiness zone: 10.

V. bracteata (*above*)
This is a vigorous plant with broad, shiny,
bright green leaves and 12–15in (30–38cm)
tall dense "red-hot-poker" type spikes of
pinkish-red, tubular flowers.

V. capensis (*above*)
The pink, tubular flowers of *V. capensis* are
carried in dense spikes about 12in (30cm)
high; it has narrower, grey leaves that are
very wavy at the edges.

V. 'Rosalba'
This attractive cultivar has tubular, cream-
coloured flowers which are suffused with
pink in the lower part.

GLOSSARY

Acid Soil or water with a pH value of below 7; often peaty or richly organic; opposite to alkaline.

Alkaline Soil or water with a pH value of above 7; often derived from limestone or chalk; opposite to acid.

Alpine In nature, a plant growing above the tree line in mountainous areas; in cultivation, the term applied to a rock garden plant.

Alpine house An unheated, well-ventilated greenhouse used for alpine or bulb cultivation.

Alternate leaves The term applied to leaves that progress up the plant's stem at different levels on opposite sides.

Annual A plant that completes its life cycle in one growing season.

Apex The pointed end or tip of a leaf or petal.

Axil The junction at which a leaf and stem join.

Baking To plant certain bulbs in hot, sunny sites so that they will "bake" or ripen in order to produce next year's flowers.

Basal leaves The term applied to leaves that grow directly from a bulb or rootstock without any intervening stem.

Basal plate The hard, central core at the base of a bulb which holds the scales together and from which the roots are produced.

Bedding plant Annual or biennial "bedded out" in temporary, formal display.

Bent Any perennial grass that has spreading panicles of tiny flowers; ideal for lawns.

Bone meal A material used to fertilize plants made from ground animal bones.

Bract A modified, usually reduced, leaf that grows just below the flowerhead.

Bulb A storage organ consisting of fleshy scales attached to a basal plate; for example, narcissi and tulips. The general term used to collectively describe true bulbs, corms, tubers and rhizomes.

Bulb fibre A soilless mixture used to grow bulbs in pots consisting of peat, oyster shell and charcoal.

Bulbil A small bulb produced in the leaf and inflorescence axils, and occasionally on the stem, of mature bulbs.

Bulblet A small bulb produced around the parent bulb.

Channelled leaf The term applied to a leaf that has a "V"-shaped cross-section.

Cluster Leaves, buds or flowers growing closely together.

Coir A soilless planting medium made from coconut fibre.

Cold frame A structure made of brick, metal or wood with a hinged or removable glass cover; used to protect plants from adverse weather conditions, and to harden off young plants.

Compost A mixture of materials consisting of loam, peat, sand and fertilizer; used as a medium for seeds and potting plants.

Compound A leaf or flower divided into two or more parts.

Corm A short, usually erect, swollen underground organ that resembles a true bulb but does not have scales; for example, crocuses and gladioli.

Cormlet A small corm growing on the base of the parent corm.

Corolla A collective term for petals; most commonly used to describe the six petals surrounding the corona of a daffodil.

Corona The cup or trumpet of a flower; most commonly used to describe the central projection of a daffodil.

Cultivar A cultivated as distinct from a botanical variety; for example, *Narcissus cyclamineus* 'February Gold'; 'February Gold' is the cultivar.

Cutting A piece of stem, root or leaf cut from the plant in order to propagate a new plant.

Dead-head To remove spent flowers or unripe seed pods from a plant.

Deciduous A plant that loses all its leaves annually at the end of the growing season.

Division A method of propagating a plant by dividing it into small clumps, each with a piece of root attached to it.

Dormancy The resting period of a bulb. This state can be affected by length of daylight, temperature and supply of water.

Dot plant A plant used in bedding displays to add height, colour and interest.

Double flowers The term applied to a flower with a double row or multiple rows of petals.

Dry off The process of withholding water to induce dormancy.

Elliptic leaf The term given to a broad leaf which has narrow, tapering ends.

Evergreen A plant that retains its leaves throughout the year.

Eye The term given to a growth bud; for example, as produced by tubers.

Falls The three, usually larger, outer, reflexed petals; most commonly used to describe the outer petals of an iris.

Family A collection of related genera; for example, the family *Iridaceae* includes the genera *Iris*, *Crocus* and *Crocosmia*.

Fescue Any grass of the genus *Festuca*; ideal for garden lawns.

Flowers of sulphur A chemical powder used as a fungicide.

Force To induce plant growth and early flowering.

Frond The leaf of a fern.

Fungicide A substance used to control diseases caused by fungi.

Genus A group of related species sharing certain characteristics and forming a family; for example, *Crocus sativus*, *Crocus chrysanthus* and *Crocus aureus*; *Crocus* is the genus.

Germination The development of seed into seedlings.

Glaucous Waxy, bluish-white, bluish-green or bluish-grey leaves or flowers.

Ground cover A low-growing plant that covers the surface of the soil.

Growing medium Soil or compost in which plants are grown.

Growing season The period during which a plant is actively producing leaves and flowers.

Half-hardy A plant that is unable to survive severe winters outside but does not require protection all the year round.

Harden off To acclimatize a plant that has been raised under cover for outside growth.

Hardy A plant able to survive freezing winter condition outdoors without any protection.

Heavy soil The term applied to soil with a high proportion of clay and little sand.

Herbaceous A non-woody, fleshy plant grown in borders; usually a perennial.

Humus Well-rotted organic matter in soil.

Hybrid A plant produced by the cross-fertilization of two species or variants of species; for example, *Anemone* x *fulgens* is a product of *A. pavonina* x *A. hortensis*.

Incurved petal The term applied to a petal that curves inwards at the top.

Inflorescence The part of a plant that bears the flower or flowers.

Internode The section of stem between two nodes.

Interplant To plant two or more plants together.

Leaf mould Rich, fibrous, decomposed leaves that are used to improve soil.

Light soil The term applied to soil with a high proportion of sand and little clay.

Lime A substance containing calcium used to reduce acidity in soil.

Liquid feed A liquid fertilizer; the one recommended for bulbs is that given to tomatoes.

Loam Soil of a medium texture containing equal parts of sand, silt and clay; the best type of soil for a wide range of plants.

Microclimate A miniature, localized environment within a larger one; for example, that created by a protective wall.

Mulch A material applied in a layer around the base of a plant to enrich the ground, conserve moisture or protect the plant.

Native plant The term applied to a plant cultivated in the area from which it grows naturally.

Naturalize To establish and grow plants as if in the wild; to colonize.

Node The point on a stem from which a leaf, shoot or flower bud grows.

Offset A young plant produced at the base of the parent; a natural form of propagation.

Opposite leaves The term applied to leaves that progress up the stem at the same level on opposite sides.

Peat Decaying, humus-rich material; often added to light, sandy soils to increase moisture retention.

Pendent A flower or leaf that hangs down.

Perennial A plant that lives for more than two years.

Perlite Small granules of a volcanic mineral; often added to growing mediums to increase moisture retention.

Pesticide A chemical used to control pests and diseases.

pH The degree of acidity or alkalinity; below 7 on the pH scale is acid, above is alkaline.

Photosynthesis The synthesis of organic compounds from carbon dioxide and water using light absorbed by chlorophyll.

Plunge To sink a pot up to its rim in soil, peat or sand.

Prepared bulbs Bulbs that have been specially treated and are used for forcing into early flowering indoors.

Prick out To plant out young seedlings in beds or pots so that they have enough room to grow on.

Propagation The production of a new plant from an existing one.

Raceme An inflorescence in which the flowers are borne along the main stem, usually with the oldest at the base.

Reflexed petal The term applied to a petal that bends back at an acute angle.

Rhizome A creeping, usually horizontal, stem that acts as a storage system; for example, certain iris rootstocks.

Rooting hormone A chemical powder or liquid used to encourage root development when propagating cuttings.

Rootstock The underground part of a plant from which roots and shoots are produced.

Rose The spray attachment of a watering can used to disperse and regulate a fine spray of water, especially used for newly sown seeds.

Rosette A circular cluster of leaves growing from the base of a shoot.

Scale The separate, fleshy, leafy parts that make up a true bulb.

Scaling A means of propagating lily bulbs.

Scooping and scouring Means of propagating hyacinth bulbs.

Seed head A faded flower head containing seed.

Seedling A young plant raised from seed.

Selection A plant possessing a desirable new trait created by natural cross-pollination, mutations or hybridizing.

Sepal The outermost, leaf-like part of a flower.

Shrub A woody-stemmed plant.

Single flower The term applied to a flower which has a single layer of petals.

Slow-release fertilizer A fertilizer that gradually releases nutrients into the soil over a long period of time.

Spadix The term given to an inflorescence with small flowers borne on a fleshy stem, the whole being enclosed within a spathe.

Spathe A large bract which encloses an inflorescence.

Spawn The term given to the mass of cormlets produced around some types of parent corm during dormancy; they are often detached and grown on for propagation purposes.

Sphagnum moss Moss common to bogs; valued for its moisture-retentive quality and used to top-dress indoor plants.

Species A naturally occurring individual within a genus; for example, *Narcissus cyclamineus*; *Naricissus* is the genus, and *cyclamineus* is the species.

Specimen A special tree, shrub or plant grown for its striking or unusual appearance.

Spike An inflorescence consisting of a raceme of flowers.

Spur A hollow projection of a flower; for example, as seen in the flowers of *Corydalis*.

Stake To support tall-growing bulbs with metal plant supports, sticks or canes.

Stamen The male reproductive organ of a flower, consisting of a stalk bearing an anther.

Standard The term applied to the three inner, often erect, petals of a flower; most commonly used to describe an iris.

Stem propagation A way of increasing a variety of tubers by rooting detached stems.

Stolon A horizontal spreading or arching stem with intermittent roots which produce new plants at their extremities.

Strap-like A tongue-shaped leaf.

Sun-bake see **Baking**

Tender A plant that is vulnerable to frost damage.

Tessellated Flowers or leaves that are chequered or patterned.

Tilth A fine, crumbly layer of cultivated soil.

Top-dress A layer of fertilizer or compost applied to the surface of the soil that is not dug in; an ornamental dressing scattered around a plant; for example, moss or, in rock gardens, small stone chippings.

Trumpet The cup (corona) in the centre of a flower; most commonly used to describe a daffodil.

Tube A flower in which the petals join together at the base to form a hollow stalk.

Tuber A swollen, usually underground, organ used for storage; for example, begonias.

Tunic The outer often fibrous membrane of bulbs and corms; hence tunicated.

Umbel A flat-topped or domed flowerhead in which the flowers are borne on stalks rising from the top of the main stem.

Underplant To plant low-growing plants around larger plants.

Variegated A leaf that is marked with an irregular pattern, usually cream, white or yellow on green.

Variety Botanically: a natural variation of a species; for example, *Narcissus triandrus* var. *albus*. Commonly: used to describe a distinct variant of a species, either a cultivated form (a cultivar) or a naturally occurring form; for example, *Narcissus* 'Spellbinder'; 'Spellbinder' is the variety.

Vegetative propagation Any method of propagating a plant that does not involve seed.

Water in To water around the stem of a newly planted plant to settle the soil around the roots.

Whorl Three or more flowers, buds, leaves or shoots growing out of the same place.

DIRECTORY OF BULB SUPPLIERS

Jacques Amand Ltd
The Nurseries, Clamp Hill
Stanmore, Middlesex
HA7 3JS
Tel: 081 954 8138
(Wide range)

Avon Bulbs
Burnt House Farm, mid-Lambrook
South Petherton, Somerset
TA13 5HE
Tel: 0460 42177
(Species and dwarf bulbs)

Bakker Holland
P O Box 111, Spalding
Lincolnshire, PE12 6EL
Tel: 0775 711411

Ballydorn Bulb Farm
Killinchy, Newtownards
Co. Down, N. Ireland
BT23 6QB
Tel: 0238 541250
(Species daffodils)

Walter Blom & Son Ltd
Coombelands Nurseries
Thurleigh Road, Milton Ernest
Bedfordshire, MK44 1RQ
Tel: 0234 782424
(Tulips, lilies, narcissi, hyacinths)

Rupert Bowlby
Gatton, Reigate
Surrey, RH2 0TA
Tel: 0737 642221
(Unusual bulbs and corms)

Bridgemere Garden World
Bridgemere, Cheshire, CW5 7QB
Tel: 09365 381
(Wide range)

Broadleigh Gardens
Barr House, Bishops Hull
Taunton, Somerset
TA14 1AE
Tel: 0823 286231
(Wide range)

P. J. Brown Irises
Westlees Farm, Logmore Lane
Westcott, Dorking
Surrey, RH4 3JN
Tel: 0306 889827
(All types of irises)

Cambridge Bulbs
40 Whittlesford Road
Newton
Cambridge, CB2 5PH
Tel: 0223 871760
(Wild species and specialist bulbs
for alpine and bulb frames)

Carncairn Daffodils
Major and Mrs Reade
Broughshane, Ballymena
Co. Antrim, N. Ireland
BT43 7HF
Tel: 0266 861216
(All types of daffodil show
varieties, breeder of 'Foundling',
and wide general list)

Paul Christian Rare Plants
P O Box 468, Wrexham
Clwyd, LL13 9XR
Tel: 0978 366399
(Wide range of rare bulbs and a
comprehensive selection of
greenhouse bulbs)

Copford Bulbs
Dorsetts, Birch Road
Copford, Colchester
Essex CO6 1DR
Tel: 0206 330008
(Species daffodils and cyclamen
tubers)

Brian S. Duncan
Knowehead,
15 Ballynahatty Road
Omagh
Co. Tyrone, N. Ireland
BT78 1PN
Tel: 0662 242931
(Daffodils for exhibitors)

Groom Bros. Ltd
Pecks Drove Nurseries
Claylake, Spalding
Lincolnshire, PE12 6BJ
Tel: 0775 722421
(Daffodils)

Highland Liliums
Kiltarlity-by-Beauly
Invernesshire
Scotland, IV4 7JQ
Tel: 046 374 365
(Lilies, deliveries only in Scotland
and Northern England)

**P. de Jager & Sons Ltd and
Wallace & Barr Ltd**
Staplehurst Road, Marden
Kent, TN12 9BP
Tel: 0622 831235
(Wide range)

Kelways Nurseries
Langport, Somerset
TA10 9EZ
Tel: 0458 250521
(Irises)

Knightshayes Plant Shop
The Stables, Knightshayes
Bolham, Tiverton
Devon, EX16 7RQ
Tel: 0884 259010
(Wide range)

Little Creek Nursery
39 Moor Road, Banwell
Weston-super-Mare
Avon, BS24 6EF
Tel: 0934 823739
(Hardy cyclamen species)

Lochside Alpine Nursery
Ulbster, Nr Wick
Caithness, Highland
KW2 6AA
Tel: 095 585 320
(Hardy cyclamen)

John Morley
North Green Only, Stoven
Beccles, Suffolk
NR34 8DG
(Galanthus, species and hybrid)

Paradise Centre
Twinstead Road, Lamarsh
Nr. Bures, Suffolk
CO8 5EX
Tel: 0787 269 449
(Unusual bulbs and tubers with
emphasis on shade and bog)

Potterton & Martin
The Cottage Nursery
Moortown Road, Nettleton
Caistor, Lincolnshire
LN7 6HX
Tel: 0472 851792
(Wide range including dwarf
bulbs, cyclamen, *Anenome
nemerosa* and *Corydalis*)

John Shipton (Bulbs)
Felin, Henllan Amgoed
Whitland, Dyfed
FA34 0FL
Tel: 0994 240125
(Native bulbs)

Tile Barn Nurser
Standen Street, Iden Green
Benenden
Kent, TN17 4LB
Tel: 0580 240221
(Cyclamen species)

Mr K. J. Townsend
17 Valerie Close, St Albans
Herts, AL1 5JD

White House Nurseries
Stokesley Road, Hutton
Rudby, North Yorkshire
TS15 0JL
Tel: 0642 701069
(Wide range)

Van Tubergen UK Ltd
Thetford Road, Bressingham
Diss, Norfolk
IP22 2AB
Tel: 0379 888282
(360 varieties of bulbs, some rare
and unusual)

Zephyrwude Irises
48 Blacker Lane, Crigglestone
Wakefield, West Yorkshire
WF4 3EW
Tel: 0924 252101
(Wide range of irises including
bearded, dwarf, intermediate
and tall)

INDEX

Page numbers in *italic* refer to the illustrations

ACKNOWLEDGEMENTS

The publisher would like to thank the many individuals and organizations who allowed them to reproduce their photographs in this book. The publisher and Clive Nichols would also like to thank the many individuals and organizations who allowed them to photograph their gardens. Page numbers are followed by codes denoting left (l), right (r), centre (c), top (t) and bottom (b); location and garden owners are given in brackets where relevant.

Jacques Amand/John Amand 95 bl, 165 br; **A-Z Botanical Collection** 115 tr, 153 tc, 156 bc, 165 tr, 166 l & c, 169 bl, 209 bc, 228 tr, 231 c; **Gillian Beckett** 159 r, 177 c, 211 bl; **Eric Crichton** 31 t, 128-9 b, 131 r, 178 r, 190-1, 195 r, 207 c & br, 215, 229 tr, 231 tr; **John Fielding** 87 r, 88 tl, tr & c, 89 l & r, 90 tr & b, 91 tr & br, 92 tc, tr & b, 95 tr & br, 97 tl & tr, 99 bl, 100 bc, 101 tl, r & bc, 102 tl, tr, c & bl, 103 tc, 106 tl, tc, tr, bl, bc & br, 107 tr & c, 108 tl & tr, 110 bc, 113 tr, 114 t, cl, c & bl, 115 cl & br, 117 cr, bc & br, 118 cl & bl, 137, 150 tl, 152 tr, l, cr, 153 tl, tr & br, 158 tl, c, bl & bc, 160 tc & br, 161 tr & bl, 162 c, 165 tc & bl, 166 bc, 167 l, 169 bc, 171 bl, 174 t, 175 l & c, 176 tl, 178 c, 180 l, 182 c, 195 l & c, 206 cl, bl & br, 207 tl, 209 br, 228 bc; **Fleurmerc bv**, 154 b, 182 br; **Garden Picture Library/Linda Burgess** 21, /Menk Dijkman 120-1, /John Glover 30 b, 76, /Jerry Pavia 180 c; **John Glover** 6 t, 107 bl, 130 l, 133; **Derek Gould** 126 b, 191 r; **Jerry Harpur** 35 br, 60, 61, 70 b, 123, 132 bc, 139 tr, 186, 188, 189, /Beth Chatto 29, 187; **Marijke Heuff** 20, 30 c, 31 b, 68 bl, 122, 124-5, 127, 128-9 t, 194, 214, 220; **International Flower Bulb Centre** 91 tl, 96 tl, 100 cr, 104 bl, 115 tc, 118 c & br, 119 t, c & cr, 150 l, 155 r & b, 161 tc, 162 tc, tr, l, cr & br, 163 tl, tc & bl, 211 br; **Andrew Lawson** 87 tc, 88 br, 89 t, 90 tr & c, 92 tl, 94 tl, tr, c & br, 95 tl, 96 tr, bc & br, 97 bl, 99 tc & c, 100 tr & bl, 103 cl & br, 104 tl, c & br, 107 tl, 108 bl, bc & br, 109 tr, cl, c & bl, 110 tl, tc, r & bl, 112 l, tr & br, 113 l, c & br, 114 c l & br, 115 tl & c, 117 c, 118 tr, 119 l & br, 124 tc, 132 bl, 135, 150 br, 152 c, 153 c, 154 c, 155 l, 158 tr & br, 159 l & c, 160 l & bc, 161 br, 163 tr, 166 tr, 167 r, 168 l, tc, tr, bc & br, 169 tc, tr, cl, cr & br, 170 tl, tc, c, c r, bl & br, 171 tl, tc, cl, 171 tr & cr, 173 tl, tr, c & bl, 174 cl, r, bl & bc, 177 tl & r, 178 l, 180 r, 181 l & tr, 182 tr, cr & bl, 203 c & r, 204 t, cl, c & r, 205 tc & br, 206 c, 207 cr, 208 tr & br, 209 t, 211 tl & tr, 226 tr & br, 229 tl, bl & br, 231 tl; **Brian Mathew** 94 cr, 107 bc, 161 tl, 173 br, 205 tr, 208 l, 211 tc, 226 l; **Ian McKinnell** 1, 2, 8, 26-7, 36-7, 38, 80-6, 93, 99, 105, 111, 116, 138 bc, 140-9, 151, 157, 164, 172, 179, 183, 196 tr, 196-7, 198-201, 202, 207, 210, 222 tr, 222-3, 223 br, 224-5, 226, 230; **Clive Nichols** 30 t (Abbotswood Garden, Gloucestershire), 68 tl (Mr and Mrs Baker, Old Rectory Cottage, Berkshire), 184-5, 192 tr, 73 br (John Bond, The Saville Garden, Surrey), 58-9, 62 t, 70 tl, 71, 217 t (Sarah Butt, Bennington Lordship, Hertfordshire), 135 (Capel Manor Horticultural and Environmental C, Middlesex), 66 tl, 66-7, 72, 73 b (Darlington Hall, Devon), 96 t (Eggleston Hall Gardens, Co. Durham), 23 t, 22, 126 t (Wendy Lauderdale, Ashtree Cottage, Wiltshire), 130 (Wendy Francis, The Anchorage, Kent), 192 tl (The Sir Harold Hillier Gardens and Arboretum, Hampshire), 64, 65 l, 78 t, 78-9 b, 76 bl, 79 tr (The Keukenhoff Gardens, Holland), 126 c (Pam Lewis, Sticky Wicket, Dorset), 138 l, 223 tr (The Lygon Arms Hotel, Broadway, Worcestershire), 23 t, 34 t, 103 l (Elizabeth Macleod Matthews, Chenies Manor, Buckinghamshire), 73 tr (Mrs Merton, The Old Rectory, Burghfield, Berkshire), 68-9, 70 tr (Mr and Mrs Norton, East Lambrook Manor Garden, Somerset), 33, 63 t, 75 c (Ripley Castle, North Yorkshire), 62 b (Mrs H. H. Robinson and Mrs J. Brookes, Denmans, West Sussex), 16, 23 b, 65 r, 75 t, 125 bc (Royal Horticultural Society's Garden, Wisley, Surrey), 34 br (Mr and Mrs Terry, 28 Hillgrove Crescent, Hereford and Worcestershire), 193 (Mrs Thorp, Coates Manor, West Sussex), 138 tr (Caroline Todhunter, The Old Rectory, Farnborough, Oxfordshire), 212-3 216, 218 bl, tl, 218-9 (Colonel Watson, The Door House, Gloucestershire), 67 b (Wolfson College, Oxford), 6, 23 b, 65 r, 75 t (Rosemary Verey, Barnsley House, Gloucestershire), 77 (Mrs Voges, Holland); **Hugh Palmer** 132 br; **Jerry Pavia** 32, 74, 251, /Joanna Pavia 25 r, 217 b; **Photos Horticultural/Michael Warren** 91 ac, 97 tc & bc, 99 r, 104 bc, 107 br, 107 br, 108 tc, 112 c, 117 l, 173 cr, 176 cl, 180 bc, 181 br, 203 l, 208 c, 211 cr, 228 tl & bl, 231; **Reed International Books Limited** 89 c, /Jerry Harpur 87 bl, 100 cl, /George Wright 32; **Christine Skelmesdale** 152 tc, 153 cl, 154 r, 156 r, 167 c, 176 r, 177 bl, 204 bl, 205 bc, 206 tl, 211 c; **Harry Smith Collection** 87 bc, 88 bl, 90 cl & bl, 91 cl & c, 94 bl, 95 tc & bc, 96 bl, 99 tl, 101 c, 102 br, 109 bc, 112 bc, 150 bc, 156 tc & l, 160 cr, 166 br, 175 tr & br, 176 c, 182 tr, 206 bc, 209 c, 226 c, 228 br; **Curtice Taylor** 24, 69 r; **Elizabeth Whiting Associates** 6 b, 134; **Timothy Woodcock** 222.

List of plates in Plant Directories